CLASSICAL MODERN PHILOSOPHERS

CLASSICAL MODERN PHILOSOPHERS

Descartes to Kant

RICHARD SCHACHT

London and New York

First published in 1984 by
Routledge & Kegan Paul Ltd
11 New Fetter Lane, London EC4P 4EE
Reprinted 1987

Reprinted by Routledge 1991, 1993, 1995
Simultaneously published in the USA and Canada
by Routledge
29 West 35th Street, New York, NY 10001

Set in Sabon by Intype, London
and printed in Great Britain by
T. J. Press (Padstow) Ltd, Padstow, Cornwall

British Library Cataloguing in Publication Data
A catalogue record for this book is available from the British
Library

Library of Congress Cataloguing in Publication Data
A catalogue record for this book is available from the Library
of Congress

ISBN 0–415–06577–1 (pbk)

To Marsha

CONTENTS

Contents

ACKNOWLEDGMENTS

Acknowledgment is gratefully made to the following: to Cambridge University Press, for permission to cite from René Descartes, *Philosophical Works of Descartes*, Volume One, translated by Elizabeth S. Haldane and G. R. T. Ross, first edition published 1911, and reprinted with corrections in 1931 and subsequently; to The Bobbs-Merrill Company, for permission to cite from Gottfried Wilhelm von Leibniz, *Monadology and Other Philosophical Essays*, translated by Paul Schrecker and Anne Martin Schrecker, Copyright © 1965; from David Hume, *An Inquiry Concerning Human Understanding*, edited by Charles W. Hendel, Copyright © 1955; and from David Hume, *Dialogues Concerning Natural Religion*, edited by Norman Kemp Smith, Copyright © 1947; to Dover Publications, for permission to cite from Benedict de Spinoza, *Works of Spinoza*, Volume II, translated by R. H. M. Elwes, first published by Dover in 1951, and originally published by G. Bell & Son in 1883; to Charles Scribner's Sons, for permission to cite from George Berkeley, *Berkeley: Selections*, edited by Mary Whiton Calkins. Copyright © 1929 Charles Scribner's Sons, copyright renewed 1957; to St Martin's Press and to Macmillan & Co., Ltd, for permission to reprint cited passages from Immanuel Kant, *Critique of Pure Reason*, edited by Norman Kemp Smith, Copyright © Macmillan & Co., Ltd, 1929, and first published by St Martin's Press in 1965.

I also wish to thank Ms. Glenna Wilson, for typing the final manuscript of this book; the Research Board of the University of Illinois, for an award in support of its preparation for publication; and Mr. John Cantú, for his assistance in the preparation of the Index.

REFERENCES

Unless otherwise indicated, the page or section references given in the various chapters are to be understood as follows:

Chapter I   Descartes
References are to page numbers in René Descartes, *Philosophical Works of Descartes*, vol. One, transl. Elizabeth S. Haldane and G. R. T. Ross (Cambridge: Cambridge University Press, 1967).

Chapter II   Leibniz
References are to page numbers in Gottfried Wilhelm von Leibniz, *Monadology and Other Philosophical Essays*, transl. Paul Schrecker and Anne Martin Schrecker (Indianapolis: Bobbs-Merrill, 1965).

Chapter III   Spinoza
References are either to designated passages from Spinoza's *Ethics* or to page numbers in Benedict de Spinoza, *Works of Spinoza*, vol. II, transl. R. H. M. Elwes (New York: Dover Publications, 1951).

Chapter IV   Locke
References are to book and section numbers in John Locke, *An Essay Concerning Human Understanding*, ed. A. D. Woozley (Cleveland and New York: World Publishing Co., 1964).

Chapter V   Berkeley
References prefaced by a 'P' are to section numbers of George Berkeley's *Principles of Human Knowledge*, and those prefaced by a 'D' (indicating that the passages cited are from his *Three Dialogues Between Hylas and Philonous*) are to page numbers in *Berkeley: Selections*, ed. Mary W. Calkins (New York: Charles Scribner's Sons, 1957).

Chapter VI   Hume
References in the first three parts of this chapter are to page numbers in David Hume, *An Inquiry Concerning Human Under-*

standing, ed. Charles W. Hendel (Indianapolis: Bobbs-Merrill, 1955). References in the fourth part of the chapter are to page numbers in David Hume, *Dialogues Concerning Natural Religion*, ed. Norman Kemp Smith (Indianapolis: Bobbs-Merrill, 1947).

Chapter VII   Kant

References are to page numbers in Immanuel Kant, *Critique of Pure Reason*, transl. Norman Kemp Smith (New York: St Martin's Press, 1965).

INTRODUCTION

Seven men have come to stand out from all of their counterparts in what has come to be known as the 'modern' period in the history of philosophy (i.e., the seventeenth and eighteenth centuries): Descartes, Spinoza, Leibniz, Locke, Berkeley, Hume and Kant. Their thought constitutes the core and defines the mainstream of classical modern philosophy; and however interesting, important and different the efforts of subsequent philosophers on both sides of the English Channel may be, no one can be considered 'educated' philosophically who is familiar only with the latter, and has not undertaken a close and careful study of these great predecessors of theirs. Thus a survey of their work constitutes one of the cornerstones of concentration in philosophy at practically every Western institution of higher learning, even though the traditional characterization of them as 'modern' philosophers becomes more anachronistic with each succeeding generation, and new contributions continue to modify the direction and substance of philosophical thinking in many different areas. And this undoubtedly will remain true, for as long as philosophy as we know it remains a part of intellectual life. Philosophy had a two-thousand-year history prior to Descartes, and has had a career of nearly two centuries since Kant; but these seven men had so profound an impact upon its course that it is almost impossible to conceive of the very existence of the various forms of inquiry which collectively constitute the enterprise of philosophy today – as well as the diverse issues debated and positions taken by contemporary philosophers of all persuasions – had they not made their different contributions to it.

Still, given the widespread assumption (which in many instances is by no means unsound) that the latest word in a cognitive discipline is likely to be the best and that most deserving of attention, it would not be at all unreasonable of someone to wonder, in this context: Why read these philosophers, from Descartes to Kant, who are 'modern' largely owing simply to terminological conven-

1

tion? After all, the issues they discuss have been dealt with by a great many more recent philosophers; and these more recent philosophers at least like to think that their discussions of these issues are significantly *better* than those of our so-called 'modern' philosophers. In fact, many philosophers have argued that these classical discussions often contain fundamental errors, and even that many of the problems with which these earlier philosophers deal are either meaningless or mere pseudo-problems, which *seem* to be real problems only owing to linguistic or conceptual confusion. If this is so, then to spend time on these earlier discussions would be pointless, except perhaps to someone interested in intellectual history. So why bother with Descartes, Spinoza, Kant and the rest?

My answer is as follows. First, one ought not simply take someone's word that these philosophers are mistaken or wrongheaded, even if that someone is an influential contemporary philosopher. That would be a kind of acquiescence to authority which is out of place in philosophy, in which only experience and cogent reasoning are supposed to carry weight.

Second, those contemporary philosophers who belittle these classical discussions in this way seldom make anything like a compelling case for their point. In fact, it often turns out that their conclusions concerning the meaninglessness or muddle-headed character of these classical discussions are themselves based upon some quite problematical philosophical or methodological assumptions. (This is now recognized to be so with regard to the positivists; and it is coming to be recognized with regard to ordinary language philosophers as well.) At the very least, one must learn something about the classical discussions before one can even begin to consider the issue of whether they are meaningful and important.

Third, a great deal of current philosophical discussion continues to be devoted to many of the problems – or at least to related ones – with which the philosophers to be considered were concerned. Moreover, these classical discussions constitute the general context and frame of reference within which much of the current discussion takes place. It would be very difficult to understand what many contemporary philosophers are talking about, and why they think what they are saying is important, if one knew nothing of the background of their deliberations and debate. And this background, or at least an important part of it, is to be found in the literature to be considered here.

Next, a more general point. There can be progress in philosophy, and later discussions can be improvements upon earlier ones. It is by no means the case in philosophy, however, as is generally the case in the social and natural sciences, that early discussions are quickly rendered inadequate by more extensive accumulations of data and the refinement of experimental and mathematical techniques, and that the last word on a given subject is likely to be the best that has been said about it. Most if not all of the relevant data bearing upon philosophical problems that is available to us was available to Descartes, Spinoza and Locke; and we must make do with the same basic tool in analysing this data that they had: our power of reflection. Great progress has been made in the last century in the field of formal logic; but there are few truly philosophical problems which are soluble simply by the application of our sophisticated logical apparatus to them. Philosophical inquiry may not be entirely timeless and ahistorical, and philosophers may certainly make mistakes; but a philosophical discussion written 200 years ago is not thereby rendered outdated, irrelevant to the world today, and unworthy of serious consideration.

Finally, the philosophers to be dealt with are worth reading because they are making important claims about some of the most fundamental and important matters it is possible to think of. The problems they discuss are generally not problems of the sort which are continually arising in our everyday lives. They also are not the kinds of problems we must solve if we are to be able to get to Mars, or end war in the world, or eliminate racism, or save the environment. And, in the works to be considered, those philosophers are not for the most part concerned with moral and ethical problems either; though many of them wrote on ethics elsewhere. The problems they deal with in these works perhaps *become* problems for people only to the extent that they are able temporarily to set aside pressing particular practical and moral concerns. They are problems which arise only when one is able to step back out of immediate involvement with the world and reflect about what it is one is involved with, what one's knowledge of it amounts to, and what one is.

What *is* the world anyway? What is its fundamental character? And what am I – I who ask about the nature of the world, and who exist in the world? And what is there, if anything, in addition to me and others like me and the world? Is there any reason to think that there is also anything like the God so many people have believed in? These are the basic questions of *metaphysics*, which

3

thus may be divided into *cosmology, philosophical psychology* or *anthropology* (or the philosophy of mind), and *philosophical theology*. And there is a further question, perhaps less basic than those of metaphysics, but in a way preliminary to them: What account is to be given of the knowledge we have of these things, or at least, which we think we have and wish to have of these things – and of other matters as well, in science and in ordinary life? What, in short, is the nature of knowledge? This question, which in part is a question asked about the status of the metaphysical program of philosophy itself – the program, namely, of achieving knowledge of what there is – is the question of *epistemology*, or the theory of knowledge: a branch of philosophy inseparable from metaphysics, which has come increasingly to preoccupy philosophers in the history of modern (and recent) philosophy. If one cannot satisfy oneself that one can have *knowledge* of the objects of metaphysical inquiry, the program of metaphysics itself cannot be carried out. For to have *beliefs* about God, the nature of the world, and the nature of man, is not enough; since what distinguishes philosophy from religion or literature is that philosophers are supposed to affirm only what they can legitimately claim to *know* – that is, only what they can justify either by appeal to experience or by rational argument.

It is to these fundamental metaphysical and epistemological questions that the philosophers to be considered address themselves. And whatever one may ultimately come to think of the answers to these questions they give, one should profit from having to decide what to make of them. We all tend to have ideas about the issues they are discussing. We generally neither question nor really stop to think about them. But we should. For however remote from our everyday problems these issues may seem to be, the way we understand ourselves and the world is ultimately a matter of very great importance. And this is something we are better able to do through encountering and coming to terms with these philosophers.

CHAPTER I

DESCARTES

René Descartes is commonly considered to be the 'father of modern philosophy,' and for good reason; for both the program he set for himself, and the general sort of method he adopted in his attempt to carry it out, involved something of a break with medieval philosophical tradition, and greatly influenced the subsequent course of modern philosphy. This may not be immediately apparent, considering the full title of his *Meditations* (i.e., 'Meditations on the First Philosophy in which the Existence of God and the Distinction Between Mind and Body are Demonstrated'), and his dedication of the book to the Theological Faculty of the Sorbonne. But one should take what he says there with a grain of salt; for he was very worried that the radicalism of his method, in effect involving a declaration of independence from the Church on the part of philosophy, would result in the censorship of his book by the Church. In France in the first half of the 1600s that would have been a serious matter indeed, both in terms of the kind of hearing Descartes would be able to get in philosophical circles, and in personal terms.

The problem was not that Descartes's conclusions with regard to the nature and existence of God and with regard to the world and the soul were themselves heretical; on the contrary, they were not. What *was* rather heretical was his suggestion that assertions about them could not be said to have the status of *knowledge*, and could not be said to be *known* to be true, *unless* they were capable of rational demonstration – unless they could be *shown* to be true on the basis of clear and distinct perceptions and rational argument alone. And to say that revelation was not enough, and that the autonomous use of 'the natural reason' *and that alone* can give us knowledge of these things, was to suggest that philosophy is not simply the handmaiden of theology, but rather is in an important way superior to it, stands in no need of it, and indeed *must* proceed independently of divine revelation. So Descartes had good reasons for saying the kinds of things he does in his 'Dedication.'

Program and method

This was not the first occasion on which Descartes had exercised such caution. Some years earlier, upon learning of what had happened to Galileo, he had suppressed a book he had written on *The World*, in which he had come out in favor of the Copernican system. But there was more to this than prudence; for he seems to have been genuinely reluctant to depart from the teachings of the Church. Born in a small town in France in 1596, and educated in a Jesuit college, he remained persuaded of the basic soundness of the main tenets of the theology and faith in which he had been instructed, even while seeking to put them on what he regarded as a new and better footing, through the development of a comprehensive and rigorous philosophical system and method. (He believed himself to have been called to this task, as a result of some dreams he had one night at Ulm in Germany, while serving in a Dutch army.)

Frenchman though he was, Descartes spent the greater part of his later life in Holland; and it was there that he did most of his philosophical writing, which included an extensive correspondence with other thinkers of the day. In this way he kept his distance from the theologians in Paris (after a famous early encounter, in which he came off rather well); they were never far from his mind, but he may have felt more comfortable and better able to develop his own views in a different location. And his choice of French rather than Latin as his preferred language in his philosophical writing is also indicative of his desire to breathe (and think) rather more freely than was possible in an atmosphere dominated by theological orthodoxy.

It is one of the misfortunes in the history of philosophy that Descartes did not remain in Holland; for his departure led to his death at the relatively early age of 54, in 1650. Queen Christina of Sweden was his undoing. She persuaded him to come to Stockholm in 1649, to join the group of intellectuals she was assembling there; and after only a year of the combined rigors of Swedish winter and the regimen she established for them, he died of pneumonia. (This suggests that, however unusual and flattering it may be for philosophers to receive the attention of people in high places, they should perhaps think twice before accepting invitations from them.)

While the title of the *Meditations* suggests that Descartes is concerned simply with the two issues of the existence of God and the immortality of the soul, his actual program is a much broader one, and is to be conceived in quite different terms. He says in the *Discourse* that he very early in life came to long for 'a clear and certain knowledge . . . of all that is useful in life' (83). And as time passed, he dropped the concern with utility, and came to desire passionately to know whatever there is to be known about the world, and man, and God. He desired *knowledge* – and not just what commonly and customarily passes for knowledge, but 'clear and certain knowledge.' He wanted knowledge that was worthy of the name – and no knowledge was worthy of the name unless it was completely certain and conclusively demonstrable.

What one thinks one knows is not really knowledge, for Descartes, if it involves or depends upon any assumptions which are not free from the possibility of doubt; and he felt that the kind of so-called knowledge which was to be obtained in the universities of his time, as well as what passes for knowledge in ordinary life, simply did not measure up to the standard he had in mind. He felt that both the various sciences and the philosophy of his day rested upon foundations that were 'far from firm', and so it seemed to him that, while the acquisition of true knowledge about the natures of things 'is the most important [endeavor] in all the world,' people in point of fact had *no* such knowledge at all. He therefore set about to wipe the slate clean of former opinions based upon questionable assumptions and to start from scratch, beginning with nothing which was not absolutely certain, and upon this firm foundation building step by step – each step itself being entirely free from the possibility of doubt – until a reconstruction of the sciences had been achieved, and genuine knowledge of the world and the soul and God had been achieved. And he was highly optimistic about his chances of succeeding, saying, in the *Discourse*, 'there can be nothing so remote that we cannot reach it, nor so recondite that we cannot discover it' (92). This seems rather inconsistent with his contention, in the *Meditations* and the *Principles*, that our faculty of understanding is limited; but even there he maintains that we can come to know a great deal about the world and God and the soul without lowering our standards of what counts as knowledge in the least, whatever the ultimate limitations of our faculty of understanding may be.

One reason why Descartes was dissatisfied with what previously had passed for knowledge in the sciences and in philosophy was that he was very greatly impressed with mathematics, and in particular geometrical analysis and algebra, which were making great strides

7

in his day, and which were impressing everybody. Descartes was not just an outsider looking in on what was going on in mathematics; he was one of the outstanding mathematicians of the time, and so knew what he was talking about when he talked about mathematics. What impressed him so much about mathematics (and notably geometry) was, as he tells us in the *Discourse*, its methodological and conceptual rigor, 'the certainty of its demonstrations and the evidence of its reasoning'; and he goes on to say that he had been 'astonished that, seeing how firm and solid was its basis, no loftier edifice had been reared thereupon' (85). He desired that philosophy and the sciences should have foundations equally firm; and that we should settle for nothing less in them than 'the certainty of demonstration and the evidence of reasoning' of which geometry affords us an example. He explicitly says that in seeking a method by which to achieve true knowledge in philosophy, he sought a method which 'comprised the advantages' of logic, geometrical analysis and algebra. And he took as his model 'those long chains of reasoning . . . of which geometricians make use' (92).

Two points emerge from this, the first programmatic, and the second methodological. The programmatic point is that Descartes felt it was necessary to achieve the same degree of certainty in philosophy and the sciences as is required in mathematics, if the results achieved in philosophy and the sciences are to have the status of genuine knowledge. This was a new and very radical requirement, and it set a standard very difficult to live up to. And it implied – and Descartes explicitly accepted this implication – that were it to turn out that certainty comparable to that achievable in mathematics is not possible in relation to the world and God and the soul, we could have no knowledge of these things. We would be driven to the conclusion that where these matters are concerned – and this would include the sciences as well as metaphysics – we can have nothing but beliefs, no one of which can be shown to be any more valid than any other. In other words, we would have to adopt an extreme form of skepticism. So Descartes says, in the First Meditation, 'if by this means it is not in my power to arrive at the knowledge of any truth' – if, that is, I cannot be as certain of my results as the geometer can be of his – 'I may at least do what is in my power, i.e., suspend judgement' (148). In fact, I not only *may* do this; I *must* refrain from making judgments about the world and God and man's nature, or else expose myself to the likelihood of error.

A question which must be raised here is whether Descartes is right in imposing the same sort of requirement upon philosophy and the sciences as mathematicians impose upon themselves. For one might well ask whether it isn't important that geometries are self-contained formal systems, whereas what metaphysics and the sciences have to deal with is reality; and whether therefore there aren't important differences between the way in which geometrical theorems relate to geometrical axioms and definitions, and the way in which philosophical or scientific theories about the world relate to the world, or to our experience of the world. It would perhaps be very nice if we *could* have the same sort of certainty about the latter that geometers have; but if we can't, must we conclude that our only knowledge is really no more than unsubstantiated belief, and that we would do best simply to refrain from making judgments about the world? I do not mean to be giving an answer to this question; I only wish to raise it, and to suggest that one should keep it in mind in reading Descartes, and also when reading writers like Hume, who accept the Cartesian alternative of certainty or skepticism, but who feel the sort of certainty Descartes thinks *can* be achieved can*not* be achieved.

The second point to be made is methodological. Seeking a method for philosophy analogous to that employed in such mathematical disciplines as geometry, in order to achieve a comparable sort of certainty, Descartes arrives at the four 'precepts' which he states in the *Discourse*, and which he restates in one form or another in his other writings. The first is: 'to accept . . . nothing more than what was presented to my mind so clearly and distinctly that I could have no occasion to doubt it.' The second is: 'to divide up each of the difficulties which I examined into as many parts as seemed requisite in order that it might be resolved in the best manner possible.' The third is: 'to carry on my reflections commencing with objects that were the most simple and easy to understand, in order to give rise little by little . . . to knowledge of the most complex.' And the fourth is: at the end to enumerate and review the matter thoroughly so as to 'be certain of having omitted nothing' (92). This method is closely and self-consciously modeled upon the method employed in geometry; and it has the merit, in Descartes's eyes, that it 'contains everything which gives certainty to the rules of arithmetic' (94).

The crucial notion here is that of the 'clear and distinct.' For what this method amounts to is restricting oneself at the outset to that and that alone which one perceives clearly and distinctly, and making no subsequent step which does not clearly and distinctly follow from what has already been thus firmly established. The latter stricture in effect means that no subsequent step in the argument is permissible if it is not warranted by the rules of deductive logic. And the former amounts to saying that nothing is to be affirmed initially which admits of the slightest possibility of doubt.

This brings us to the matter of Descartes's famous systematic doubting, which is the principal subject of the First Meditation. If one wishes to arrive at conclusions which are completely certain, then they must not be based on assumptions which are not completely certain. As a methodological principle, therefore, Descartes says: 'We ought to consider as false all these things of which we may doubt' (219). His point is not that all those things of which one may possibly doubt *are* false. Rather, it is that we ought not to accept any of them as true unless and until we can *prove* they are true by an argument which begins solely with what *is* indubitable and which proceeds by steps each of which is indubitably valid. It is going to turn out, on his view, that we will in the end be able to affirm most of the things we are inclined to affirm in the first place. But he argues that we cannot be said to *know* these things until we have justified them by proceeding in the manner he is describing. His systematic doubt is not intended to *undermine* the claims of the sciences; rather, it is the first step in this attempt, as he says at the beginning of the First Meditation, 'to build anew from the foundation . . . , [and thereby] to establish [a] firm foundation and permanent structure in the sciences' (144).

What, then, is it which fails to survive this initial systematic doubt? What is it that must at least temporarily be placed in question, and set aside? Descartes has in mind, first of all, everything that we have 'learned either from the senses or through the senses'; in other words, all of our opinions about the existence and natures of those things with which we have become acquainted through our senses. This includes everything which we ordinarily take to make up the world, and also ourselves insofar as we are a part of the world – our bodily existence. The first reason he cites for setting aside our opinions based on the testimony of our senses is that we all know that our senses sometimes deceive us. We sometimes find that things are other than we originally took them to be, and we sometimes find that we are only hallucinating or imagining things or are under an illusion of some sort when we think we see something. And Descartes argues that 'it is wiser not to trust entirely to any thing by which we have once been deceived' (145). For if our senses have proven to be untrustworthy on some occasions, how can we be certain of them on others? It is rather like the case of someone whom you have discovered has lied to you; the next time he tells you something, you can't be sure that what he is telling you is the truth. And since all that is necessary is to cast the least bit of doubt on something to require that it be set aside if certainty is to be achieved, the testimony of our senses must thus for the time be set aside.

The second reason Descartes cites is a more general one, in case one has not been entirely persuaded by the first. Though there are cases in which it would seem to be virtually impossible to imagine that your senses might be deceiving you, you cannot be certain in any given instance that you are not *dreaming*; and that what you think is some actual state of affairs in the world that you are perceiving is only a part of some dream you are having, and hence is not real or true at all. Here Descartes makes reference to the common experience of feeling quite sure, while one is having some dream, that what one is dreaming is really going on; and he contends that 'there are no certain indications by which we may clearly distinguish wakefulness from sleep,' at least on any given occasion in our experience (146). So here again, there exists the possibility of a doubt about the veracity of the testimony of our senses; and the possibility of a doubt is all that is required to rule out their testimony as a part of the certain foundation Descartes is seeking.

Descartes then goes on to contend that the truths of arithmetic and geometry must be set aside as well, however clearly and distinctly we may think we perceive them. Even things like 'two plus three equals five' and 'a square has four sides' are not immune from doubt. For, he asks, 'How do I know that I am not deceived every time that I add two and three, or count the sides of a square . . . ?' (147). However implausible it may seem, it is nonetheless *possible* that not 'God who is supremely good . . . , but some evil genius not less powerful and deceitful, has employed his whole energies in deceiving me' (148). Such an all-powerful evil genius could make it seem to me that I perceive certain things clearly and distinctly, which however are not in fact the case. And if it is so much as possible for me to conceive of such a thing, then I cannot be *certain*, without proof to the contrary, that this is not so. In short, Descartes concludes, 'there is nothing at all that I formerly believed to be true, of which I cannot in some measure doubt . . . , for reasons which are very powerful and maturely considered' (147–8).

11

How is he ever going to get out of the skeptical corner into which he seems to have painted himself? How is any sort of knowledge to be possible at all? Descartes's answer, which comes out in the Fourth Meditation and the corresponding part of the *Principles*, is that true knowledge is possible if we confine ourselves to judgments based upon clear and distinct perceptions, because it can be demonstrated that the evil genius hypothesis is untenable, that there is a God, that God is good and therefore not a deceiver, and that since he is not a deceiver he would not have given us the faculty of forming clear and distinct ideas without it being the case that what we perceive clearly and distinctly is true.

Now the reason I have jumped ahead to the Fourth Meditation is that I wanted to bring out a problem, which should be apparent from his remarks about such truths as those of arithmetic in the First Meditation, even though I have not yet considered his proofs of God's existence and goodness. If it is held not only that the testimony of our senses, but also our knowledge of mathematics and the like (which rests not upon our senses but upon our clear and distinct ideas) is not to be trusted, and if the reason for the latter is that we cannot be certain that some evil genius or infirmity of our nature is not leading us to regard as clear and distinct what is not true, prior to our finding a proof that God exists and is good, then how are we ever to come up with such a proof, which itself would be immune from the possibility of doubt and deception? For any such proof must rest upon some clear and distinct ideas, as we will see; yet if we cannot know that our clear and distinct ideas are to be trusted *until we have* such a proof, then we cannot have such a proof which meets Descartes's criterion of indubitability in the first place. Otherwise the argument will be circular; something is being assumed which depends upon the validity of the conclusion of the argument.

This, I think, is an unavoidable difficulty for Descartes; or at least, he can avoid it only by restricting his original claim about what is to be doubted to the testimony of the senses, and by assuming that our clear and distinct ideas may be relied upon without first having to prove the existence and goodness of God. Yet as he saw, this is an assumption that we are not entitled to make, if our aim is complete and absolute certainty; for it certainly would seem possible that what we think we perceive clearly and distinctly might in fact not be the case. This is the first clear indication that, while we may not have to adopt a complete skepticism, we may have to settle for something rather less than the absolute certainty Descartes wanted. If we must begin by assuming something, one could certainly do worse than to start by assuming that we may rely upon what we perceive clearly and distinctly; but that is an assumption, even though we may have to make something like it to get off the ground at all.

Mind and body

I now turn to Descartes's understanding of his own nature (which is supposed to be our nature too) and of the relation of the mind to the body, and his reasons for taking the position he does on these matters. But this is not the question he poses at the beginning of the Second Meditation. This issue only comes up at this point because his general program of a reconstruction of our knowledge in such a way that it will be completely certain, and his methodological strategy of systematic doubting, compels him to turn his attention to thinking activity and the thinking mind. It is only here, he feels, that he will be able to lay the foundations which ultimately will support the structure of our knowledge of God and the world in general.

He begins the Second Meditation where the First leaves off, saying: 'I shall proceed by setting aside all that in which the least doubt could be supposed to exist . . . until I have met with something which is certain' (149). For if he were to start with something which is *not* certain, nothing he based upon it would be certain either. But he is very optimistic about what he will be able to achieve if he *can* find something which is certain; he says: 'I shall have the right to conceive high hopes if I am happy enough to discover one thing only which is certain and indubitable' (149). This is a little rash of him, since it might turn out that nothing at all would follow from the one certain indubitable thing discovered. If one were to start with a simple statement of self-identity, for example, such as 'A = A' or 'I am I' or 'a rose is a rose,' one might feel that one had latched on to something certain and indubitable; but one wouldn't be able to get much mileage out of it by itself. In short, Descartes's 'high hopes' are really based on his hindsight (or so at least he supposes) that the certainty *he* comes up with enables him to carry out his program of reconstruction.

It is rather astonishing, given the importance of this first step, how little discussion Descartes devotes to it, either in the *Meditations* or in the *Principles*. Virtually all he says in the *Principles* is this:

13

We cannot doubt our existence without existing while we doubt. . . . For there is a contradiction in conceiving that what thinks does not at the same time as it thinks, exist. And hence this conclusion, *I think, therefore I am* [cogito, ergo sum], is the first and most certain of all. . . . (221, Princ. VII)

He says a little more, but only a little more, in the Second Meditation, referring to his worry in the First Meditation that there might be some all-powerful evil genius employing all of his powers to deceive me. He says:

without doubt I exist also if he deceives me, and let him deceive me as much as he will, he can never cause me to be nothing so long as I think that I am something. . . . We [thus] must come to the definite conclusion that this proposition: I am, I exist, is necessarily true each time that I pronounce it, or that I mentally conceive it. (150)

This is all he says; and upon this rock (so to speak) he proceeds to build his system. He doesn't say more because he thinks his point is so obvious that it doesn't require further discussion. To be sure, in Principle X, he does acknowledge that in order to make any sense of this,

we must first of all know what is knowledge, what is existence, and what is certainty, and that in order to think we must be, and such like; but because these are notions of the simplest kind . . . I did not think them worthy of being put on record. (222)

Now this is a much more serious problem than Descartes seems to think it is; and his cavalier way of dismissing it, by saying that these concepts are such simple ones that they are scarcely even worth mentioning, is far from satisfactory. Unless the notion of 'existence' is explicated, it is not clear what it means to say 'I exist' and whether one is saying anything important when one says this. And one cannot simply pass over the questions of what account is to be given of knowledge and certainty, without either leaving us in the dark about what Descartes is trying to achieve, or assuming things which by his own criterion one has no right to assume at the outset. Take knowledge, for example. Knowledge is often construed (and is more or less conceived by Descartes) in terms of a correspondence of our ideas about the world with the way the world really is. But to construe knowledge in this way is to construe

14

it in terms of certain assumptions about ourselves and the world and our relation to the world – assumptions which on Descartes's own grounds we are not initially entitled to make. Descartes might reply to objections of this sort that he can get around these problems; but even if he can – and philosophers are by no means agreed that he can – he at least ought to recognize that he is under an obligation to *show how* one can get around them.

But let us assume that he can get around them. His main point in relation to the evil-genius hypothesis is that even if he is being deceived consistently in what he thinks about things and mathematics and the like, he is still *thinking*; he is still having thoughts, even though they may correspond to nothing at all. And as long as he is thinking, it cannot be true that he does not exist, since then he would not be able to think.

This sounds plausible enough; though one might think that Descartes should have said that he has now discovered *two* indubitable truths – the first being that whenever he thinks something, then deceived or not, *he is thinking*; and the second, derived from the first, that when he is thinking, he must exist. (It should be observed that he is using the term 'thinking' very broadly, to refer, as he says explicitly in Principle IX, to 'all that of which we are conscious as operating in us,' including all instances of 'understanding, willing, imagining, [and] feeling,' the last term comprehending 'external' sensations (sense-perceptions) as well as 'internal' ones; all of these being construed as events or experiences in our stream of consciousness.)

But now another question arises, with potentially serious consequences. What justification does Descartes have for taking as his starting point the proposition that '*I* think'? It is true that our grammar is such that predicates require a subject; and that it is customary to hold that if there is thinking going on, there must be someone doing the thinking. It is a long-standing philosophical assumption that there can be no activity without an agent. But is Descartes entitled to accept this assumption? He should not accept it, given his intention to accept nothing that is not completely certain, unless there would be some contradiction involved in assuming its contrary, or unless he perceives the subject doing the thinking with the same self-evidence that he perceives the conscious events occurring. And one might certainly challenge him on both counts. It is not obvious that the notion of activity without an agent is self-contradictory. And it might be suggested (as Hume subsequently did) that when you restrict yourself to a description of what you are conscious of, you will come up with all sorts of things – shapes, colors, concepts, pains, desires, and so on – but *not* with any sort of 'I' or 'mind' or 'self' who is perceiving the shapes and colors, thinking the concepts, feeling the pains, and having the desires. In short, it may be certain and indubitable that 'thinking' in Descartes's broad sense is going on; but is it certain that 'I am thinking'? One might want to say here that as soon as you say *that*, you make an assumption about this thinking going on that you are not entitled to make if you accept Descartes's requirement of rejecting everything which is not absolutely indubitable.

Still, it is true that what Descartes says here has a good deal of commonsense appeal. And he suggests that if you are willing to follow him this far – as no doubt many will be inclined to do – then you get some very interesting results. Supposing that he has established *that* he exists, *that* he is, he turns to the question of *what* he is. And his answer to this question follows more or less directly from what he has already said. (I say 'more or less directly' because his conclusions do rest upon several other rather important assumptions as well.) It is important to keep in mind that Descartes sets the same standards in his discussion of the nature of the 'I' that has been found to exist, as he does when he first raises the question of what we can know: namely, complete certainty and indubitability. He says:

> I shall consider anew what I believed myself to be . . . ; and of my former opinions I shall withdraw all that might even in a small degree be invalidated by the [programmatic and methodological] reasons I have just brought forward, in order that there may be nothing at all left beyond what is absolutely certain and indubitable. (150)

Descartes began with a commonplace understanding of his nature much like that which most people today have. We talk about ourselves as having bodies and as having minds; and we tend to think of ourselves as some sort of unity of the two. So Descartes says:

> In the first place . . . , I considered myself as having . . . all that system of members composed of bones and flesh . . . which I designated by the name of body. In addition to this I considered that . . . I walked, that I felt, and that I thought, and I referred

16

all these actions to the soul: but I did not stop to consider what the soul was. (151)

Unlike some philosophers, Descartes does not end up reducing either the mind to the body or the body to the mind. Rather, he maintains that we do indeed have both minds and bodies – and that the two are *not* ultimately one and the same thing, but rather are radically and irreducibly different *sorts* of thing, which exist in an intimate union. This position – which may or may not still be part of the commonsense view, but which certainly is the traditional Christian view – is customarily referred to as *dualism*. And Descartes goes one step further, in effect saying that this union is *not* a partnership of equals; for while he insists upon the reality and irreducibility of the body, he also holds that the body is only something I *have*, whereas the mind or soul and that alone is what I *am*. Or at least it is his contention that the 'I' which purportedly has been shown to exist by means of the *cogito* is essentially mind and mind alone, separate and distinct from the body, and (another point of agreement with the traditional Christian view) capable of existing independently of it.

His conclusion to this effect is based on several assumptions, one of which has already been mentioned. First, it is inconceivable to him that there could be an activity without an agent, thought without a thinking subject – or as he often says, a thinking thing or substance.

Second, he assumes that mere matter, or extended substance, is incapable of thought. If something is mere extended substance, it seems self-evident to him that one could not say of it that it thinks or imagines or conceives or wills. And conversely, it seems self-evident to him that something which has been shown to think cannot be a mere extended substance, but rather must at a minimum be a thinking substance as well.

Third, he assumes that, if two things can be *conceived* independently of each other, then it is *possible* for them to *exist* independently of each other; that if they can be conceived independently of each other, then *they are* different from each other. In his words, 'it suffices that I am able to apprehend one thing apart from another clearly and distinctly in order to be certain that the one is different from the other' (190).

These are his basic assumptions; and if one grants them, then his argument is quite sound. It runs as follows: From the fact that I think, it follows that I exist. But it only follows that I exist *as a*

17

thinking thing, or a conscious subject. For though I may think that I have a body, it is conceivable that I am deceived about this. It is possible, for example, that I in fact am nothing more than a thinking thing, but that the evil genius or some unknown power within my thinking being causes me to have those experiences on the basis of which I conclude that I am also an extended thing, i.e., have a body. So it does not follow with complete certainty from the fact that I think, that I have a bodily as well as a conscious existence. And since this does not necessarily follow, and since Descartes will 'not now admit anything which is not necessarily true,' he concludes: 'to speak accurately I am not more than a thing which thinks, that is to say a mind or a soul . . .' (152).

It is possible for me to conceive of a thinking thing or substance which is not extended, i.e., has no bodily existence; there is nothing self-contradictory about such a notion, and there is nothing in the notion of a thinking thing which presupposes extended existence. My senses tell me that I have an extended existence; but they are not to be trusted, for reasons discussed in the First Meditation, and again in the Sixth. In short, it is not part of the notion of a thinking thing that it must also be extended. And since it is possible to conceive of a thinking thing which is not an extended thing, and since 'it suffices that I am able to apprehend one thing apart from another clearly and distinctly in order to be certain that the one is different from the other,' it follows that the 'I' I have discovered to exist is essentially a thinking thing, period. Or, in Descartes's words:

> Therefore, just because I know certainly that I exist, and that meanwhile I do not remark that any other thing necessarily pertains to my nature or essence, excepting that I am a thinking thing, I rightly conclude that my essence consists *solely* in the fact that I am a thinking thing, or a substance whose whole essence or nature is to think. (190)

It *may* be *true* that I have a body; and in fact, Descartes goes on to argue that at least in this world it *is* true that I have a body. 'Yet,' he says,

> because, on the one side, I have a clear and distinct idea of myself inasmuch as I am only a thinking and unextended thing, and as, on the other, I possess a distinct idea of body, inasmuch as it is only an extended and unthinking thing, it

is certain that this I . . . is entirely and absolutely distinct from my body, and can exist without it. (190)

So much for the argument. It is, as I have suggested, a valid argument, *if* one grants that the 'cogito' establishes that I exist as a thinking subject, and *if* the assumptions I mentioned are also allowed. If the argument is to be criticized, therefore, it is Descartes's assumptions, rather than the logic of his reasoning, which must be examined. I have already mentioned the kinds of questions which might be raised with reference to the *cogito*. It remains to say a word about his other assumptions. And here it might be said that while Descartes professes in the First Meditation to make a clean sweep of all of his earlier opinions, and to doubt everything which it is possible to doubt, he in fact has not done so. For one might wish to suggest that each of the assumptions I mentioned at the very least stands in need of justification and is not just self-evidently true, and therefore should be placed in question along with the other things he *does* place in question. And of course if one places *them* in question, then the argument does not go through, and one is left with the bare '*cogito, ergo sum*,' if even that.

Descartes did not question these assumptions, not because he was deliberately trying to cheat, but rather because they were such fundamental assumptions of medieval thought that it simply did not occur to him that they *were* assumptions standing in need of justification, and perhaps untenable ones. Descartes broke rather significantly with medieval philosophical thought in his program and proposed method; but he still took for granted a number of very basic axioms of medieval reasoning. (One encounters more examples of this sort of thing in his proofs of the existence of God.) It remained for subsequent philosophers to notice that the method he proposed, and the standards of knowledge he set, would undercut not only the claim of many of our commonsense opinions to be genuine knowledge, but also many of these basic axioms of assumptions which he still retains. This does not establish that they are actually *wrong*; it only shows that his proposed method and standard had consequences he did not foresee.

It is conceivable, of course, that these assumptions are correct, even if incapable of the kind of justification Descartes demands. And it is also open to us to reject the attempt to achieve complete certainty, and the decision to treat as if false everything that is not absolutely indubitable. We might set our sights a little lower, on the ground that the standards of geometry ought not be applied to our knowledge of reality. This at least might open the way to the readmission of the kind of assumptions Descartes needs. But it might also turn out that, while we simply have to make certain basic assumptions, we might not decide to make the ones he makes. If one *is* willing to make them, one may wind up agreeing with Descartes's conclusions after all; but if one is not, then one may reach others.

Let me now turn briefly to Descartes's picture of the way in which the mind and the body are related, within the context of his view of them as essentially distinct substances, the one an unextended thinking substance, and the other an unthinking, extended substance, each capable of existing independently of the other. Descartes regards the body as a kind of machine; he explicitly uses the term 'machine' to characterize it at several points in the *Meditations*. The body is a thing essentially similar to other things in the world, the existence and nature of which are established along the same lines and at the same time as are those of other things in the world. (I will consider his argument for the existence of the body when I discuss the way in which he reached the conclusion that extended substances generally exist, later in this chapter.) These two substances – mind and body – are, he allows, 'very intimately conjoined' (190). When we talk about the nature of 'man', it is to this conjunction of a mind and a body that we are referring; so Descartes speaks of 'the nature of man, inasmuch as it is composed of mind and body' (198). It is not just an accident that I – my mind – happens to be connected with a body; in this life, at any rate, God has ordained it that I do not exist except as conjoined to a body.

But it should be obvious that there is something of a problem here, of which Descartes is aware, and with which he tries to deal. If a human being is the conjunction of these two distinct substances, one extended but unthinking, and the other thinking but unextended, and if they affect each other, as Descartes recognizes they do, how is it possible that they affect each other? How does something that goes on in the mind bring about a bodily movement? And how does something that affects the body result in something happening in the mind? The problem is particularly acute because of Descartes's characterization of the two in terms which explicitly exclude the fundamental qualities of the other. His famous – or infamous – solution is rather ludicrous: he holds that the two have a point of contact in the pineal gland, in which the

20

mind gives subtle pushes to the organism which result in nerve impulses and ultimately in bodily movement, and in which subtle physical impulses are transmitted to the mind. This solution is rendered untenable by the fact that nothing but a machine can move a machine; and that if the mind really is unextended, then nothing the machine does can touch it. Descartes was forced to go to these absurd lengths because he had to account for the interaction of mind and body. If no better account of the interaction can be found than this, however, the fact of interaction would be a virtually conclusive argument against the kind of radical dualism Descartes embraces.

The nature and existence of God

Having established to his satisfaction *that* he is, and *what* he essentially is (a thinking thing), Descartes sets out in the Third Meditation to extend his knowledge further. But immediately he encounters a problem; for unless he can rely upon his clear and distinct ideas, he *cannot* extend his knowledge further. The hypothesis of the evil genius has not yet been laid to rest, and the reliability of his clear and distinct ideas has not yet been established. So, Descartes says,

> I must inquire whether there is a God as soon as the occasion presents itself; and if I find that there is a God, I must also inquire whether He may be a deceiver, for without a knowledge of these two truths [i.e., that God exists and is not a deceiver], I do not see that I can ever be certain of anything [i.e., anything other than that I exist and am a thinking thing]. (159)

Descartes thus maintains that his entire enterprise of a reconstruction of our knowledge depends for its success on his ability to prove that God exists and is not a deceiver. How he supposes this will enable him to succeed in carrying out this program is something I will discuss later. First, however, I will consider his arguments concerning the existence and nature of God. It is essential to his program that these arguments be absolutely certain and indubitable proofs; for nothing which follows from the supposition of God's existence and goodness can be certain unless God's existence and goodness can be shown to be certain. And it is certainty in the whole of our knowledge that Descartes is seeking. This is why, much to the displeasure of some people like Kierkegaard, Descartes places so much emphasis on *proving* God's existence.

21

Descartes offers three such proofs, two in the Third Meditation, and one in the Fifth. I will consider them in the order in which he presents them; and then I will turn to the proofs he gives relating to God's nature. My main strategy will be to uncover the crucial assumptions upon which his proofs depend for their validity, leaving it to the reader and the philosophers I will be discussing subsequently to evaluate the soundness of these assumptions. Many of these assumptions are ones which may seem rather strange; for they are not ones we are accustomed to making. But here again, they were so completely taken for granted by Descartes's predecessors and contemporaries that it did not occur to him that he was assuming anything that was the least bit problematical.

First proof

Descartes begins by distinguishing between *ideas* of things and *judgments* concerning things. I may have an idea of a centaur, for example, without making any judgment concerning the existence or non-existence of centaurs. An idea, considered simply as such, is neither true nor false, and the possibility of deception and error does not arise insofar as I merely have it in my mind. This possibility arises only when I venture to make some judgment concerning the existence of that of which I have an idea, its relations to other existing things, and so forth. And among the ideas Descartes reports having, along with those of centaurs and men and rocks and chairs, is the idea of God as a supremely perfect being. These ideas are simply given; the existence of the corresponding objects is as yet uncertain, but he is certain that he has these ideas.

Are these ideas all on a par with each other? Descartes contends that they are not. And here he does not mean simply that they differ in their particulars, as the idea of a horse is different from the idea of a cow. He rather means that some of these ideas differ *essentially* from others, in that some of them 'contain ... more objective reality within them' than others do; and in particular, that the idea of

> a supreme God, eternal, infinite, immutable, omniscient,
> omnipotent, and Creator of all things which are outside of
> Himself, has certainly more objective reality in itself than those
> ideas by which finite substances [such as men, rocks, trees,
> and centaurs] are represented. (162)

Now this notion of 'objective reality', along with the view that some ideas 'contain more objective reality in themselves' than others do, is an unfamiliar one to most people today, and requires some explanation. 'Objective reality' is not to be confused with 'formal (or actual) reality.' It is *formal reality* which pertains to real existence; to judge that something has *formal* reality is to judge that it actually exists. But *objective reality* does not of itself pertain to actual existence. All actually existing things have one degree or another of objective reality; but an idea can have a certain degree of objective reality too, even though it is doubtful or even not true that there exists such a thing in the world. *Objective reality* pertains to something about the essence of a thing, which may either be manifested in an actual instance of it or simply grasped in an idea of it. And what it pertains to is the *perfection* of the thing actually existing or represented in the idea. Consider, for example, the idea of an angel and the idea of a centaur. One might want to say that neither angels nor centaurs exist; neither has formal (actual) reality. But the idea of an angel has greater *objective* reality than does the idea of a centaur, because the idea of an angel is the idea of a more perfect being than is the idea of a centaur. That is precisely what it *means* to say that the former 'contains more objective reality in itself' than does the latter.

If one can keep in mind these terminological conventions, one should be able to make sense of what Descartes says when he says that the idea of God has more objective reality in itself than do the other ideas I have, which are ideas of finite substances; even though nothing has yet been said about the *existence* of anything other than the thinking thing which I am. It may be observed, however, that there is a problem here, in that Descartes has not explained how the relative perfection of different things is to be measured. Given that the greater the perfection, the greater the objective reality, how do we *know* what constitutes a greater perfection and what a lesser one? It is simply self-evident to Descartes that the idea of God is the idea of a more perfect being than is the idea of any other thing, and that the idea of a stone is the idea of a less perfect being than is that of a man; but one determined to doubt everything that is not absolutely certain might have reservations about these rather intuitive estimations. It is not enough to point out that God is to be conceived as infinite, and man as finite; for it is meaningful to ask whether infinity is necessarily a perfection.

This is a relatively uncontroversial assumption, however, in comparison with the next assumptions Descartes makes: first, that the ideas I have must have causes; second, that the ultimate cause, at least, of an idea must be something with *formal* reality – something actually existing; and third, that, in his words, 'there must at least be as much reality [objective as well as actual] in the efficient and total *cause* as in its effect.' These assumptions together entail that the cause of each of my ideas must ultimately be something actually existing with a perfection at least equal to that of the idea in question. 'What is more perfect,' Descartes says, 'cannot proceed from the less perfect. And this is not only evidently true of those effects which possess actual or formal reality, but also of the ideas in which we consider merely what is termed objective reality' (162). In other words, everything, whether its reality is actual or simply objective, *must* ultimately have as its cause something actually real which is at least as perfect as it is.

Descartes supposes that this follows from the principle of *sufficient reason*; that is, the principle that an effect cannot contain more than its cause. This would seem sensible enough in general. However, he considers this principle to apply to the amount of perfection a thing has, so that a thing cannot be more perfect than its cause. It therefore follows, he holds, that if I have any idea which contains more objective reality – more perfection – than I myself do, then I cannot be that actual reality which is its cause. Rather, there would have to exist some actual reality other than myself, with a perfection comparable to that of the idea in question. Its cause cannot simply be some other objective reality, and the cause of that some further objective reality, and so on to infinity; for that would mean that it would exist without an actually existing cause, which would be the same as something spontaneously coming to exist from nothing; and that, Descartes assumes, is impossible.

It should be clear where all of this is leading. I have the idea of God; and the objective reality – the perfection – of this idea greatly exceeds my own. Consequently, there must actually exist something in addition to myself, something, in fact which has as much perfection as is associated with God in my idea of God. And this something, which has all of the perfections associated with God in my idea of God, is obviously God himself. Thus the actual existence of God is purportedly demonstrated.

Now let us grant Descartes's initial premises: that he exists; that he is not a perfect being; and that he has the idea of God or a perfect being. What must then be considered is the tenability – indeed, for Descartes's purposes, it must be the indubitability – of the axioms he employs in reaching his conclusion: that (a) for every actual or objective reality, there must ultimately be an actually real

24

cause; and (b) there must be at least as much contained in a cause – including perfection – as there is in its effects. I would simply ask: are these axioms as indubitable as Descartes seems to think? And even if he feels that he has a clear and distinct idea that they are valid, does he as yet have the right to rely upon his clear and distinct ideas as a guarantee of truth? Or didn't he say, in the First Meditation, that God's existence and goodness would have to be proved, before his clear and distinct ideas could be relied upon?

Finally, one more question: is an idea of a perfect being itself perfect? After all, I don't actually have a perfect being in my mind when I think of a perfect being; and, poor mortal that I am, my idea of God surely is inadequate to his infinite perfection. It is only if there is *a perfect idea* in my mind, however, that Descartes would be justified (granting the validity of his axioms) in concluding that there must exist a perfect being who is its cause. So it might be asked whether there isn't a difference between the idea of perfection and a perfect idea, and whether Descartes isn't confusing the two. And if there *is* a difference, and if he *is* confusing the two, then if the idea of perfection I have is itself no more perfect than my idea of a stone or a chair – which Descartes allows I *could* be the cause of *myself*, for all that we know so far – then this whole proof fails to get off the ground.

Second proof
Descartes offers another proof of God's existence, proceeding along different lines, shortly after proposing this one. His strategy in this proof is to try to show that the existence of God is necessarily presupposed by his own existence, which has already been established. This is a perfectly legitimate strategy; and it has the advantage of being free from any possibility of the sort of confusion just suggested in connection with the first proof.

So Descartes proposes to inquire 'whether I . . . can exist if no such being [as God] exists.' He begins by asking: 'From whom do I then derive my existence?' He suggests that there are three other possibilities in addition to God: himself, his parents, and 'some other source less perfect than God' (167). And his strategy more specifically is to argue that it cannot be true that he derives his existence from any of these three, and that therefore by elimination his existence must derive from God, who therefore must exist, since he does.

He rejects the suggestion that his parents could be the cause of his existence, on the grounds that they can at most be said to be the cause of the existence of his body; whereas the 'I' whose existence is under consideration is a thinking thing, a substance distinct from and independent of extended substance in general and the body in particular. My parents may be the cause of that extended substance which is my body; but they cannot be said therefore also to be the cause of that thinking substance which differs from my body and which is what I have discovered myself truly to be – 'there being no relation,' Descartes says in a different edition, 'between the bodily activity by which I have been accustomed to believe I was engendered and the production of a thinking substance.' (It should be observed that this line of reasoning makes the validity of this proof of God's existence depend upon acceptance of Descartes's contention that the mind is a substance distinct from and independent of the body. For if this contention is not accepted, then the suggestion that my parents are the cause of my existence cannot be ruled out in this way.)

I will pass over what Descartes has to say about the idea that the cause of my existence might be something greater than myself or my parents, but less perfect than God, and will restrict myself to his treatment of the rather more interesting suggestion that I could be the cause of my own existence. The argument against this suggestion runs roughly as follows:

(1) I, a thinking substance, exist.

(2) I have not always existed.

(3) When a thinking substance comes to exist, something comes into existence out of nothing.

So (4) When I came into existence, something came into existence out of nothing.

(5) Causing something to come into existence out of nothing requires powers greater than those necessary to achieve a knowledge of all things, and indeed greater than those necessary to achieve all other perfections.

So (6) If I had caused myself to come into existence, I would have been capable of bestowing all perfections upon myself.

(7) If one can bestow all perfections upon oneself, one will do so.

So (8) If I could have bestowed all perfections upon myself, I would have done so, and would now have all perfections.

(9) I am imperfect in a number of ways.

So (10) I have never had the power to bestow all perfections upon myself.

So (11) I have never had the (still greater) power to cause myself to come into existence out of nothing.

So (12) I cannot have been the cause of my own existence. (Q.E.D.)

If this argument is valid, then assuming that one can rule out one's parents and other things greater than oneself but less than God as possible causes of one's existence, it will follow that only God could be the cause of one's existence, and therefore must exist. But are the premises Descartes employs in this argument valid? One might question the premise that, if one can bestow all perfections upon oneself, one will do so; but I am inclined to let that pass. The more controversial premise is that, when a thinking being comes to exist, something comes into existence out of nothing. That would seem to presuppose the validity of Descartes's radical distinction between the mind and the body as distinct substances, and more besides. And the validity of what is thus here assumed is at the very least questionable.

One might also question the premise that I have not always existed. Descartes recognizes this, and provides another argument to show that even if I *have* always existed, my existence *still* would presuppose the existence of something like God. This argument runs as follows:

(1) Time may be divided into an infinite number of parts, each independent of the others.

So (2) Duration through time is tantamount to recreation from nothing at each instant.

(3) I lack the power to cause anything to come into existence out of nothing even once, let alone repeatedly (for the reasons outlined above).

So (4) I cannot be that being which brings it about that I endure through time (for an unlimited or limited period).

And from this Descartes concludes that even if I have always existed, there still must exist a power external to myself – God – in order to account for my continued existence. What is dubious, or at least less than 'clear and distinct' here, is of course the first two steps. But since few people are likely to maintain seriously that they have always existed, it is perhaps unnecessary to pursue this criticism further.

The most fundamental objection one might raise to the whole basic argument under consideration is that it assumes that, for everything that exists (with the exception of God himself), there must also exist a cause of its existence. And of course, if *this* assumption is questioned, then the whole argument fails. The issue is not whether this is a fairly reasonable assumption, but rather whether it is *inconceivable* that anything could exist without a cause. For remember: complete certainty is Descartes's own requirement. *Is* this something completely indubitable? Finally, there is the recurring problem of the status and reliability of Descartes's (or our) clear and distinct ideas, of which he constantly makes use in the course of his argument. Is he entitled to do so, given the doubts he raises about them in the First Meditation, before he has established God's existence and goodness?

Third proof
Let us now turn to Descartes's third proof of God's existence, which is to be found in the Fifth Meditation. This is the famous so-called 'ontological argument.' It has the advantage of presupposing neither that everything must have a cause, nor that the perfection of the cause must equal or exceed the perfection of the effect – which perhaps accounts for its greater appeal to more recent philosophers.

This proof can be stated relatively simply. It runs as follows:

(1) If I clearly and distinctly see that it is part of the concept A that A is B, then it is in fact the case that A is B. (I.e., if B is entailed *logically* by A, then B is *in reality* entailed by A.)

(2) I 'find the idea of God, that is to say, the idea of a supremely perfect being, in me.' (180)

(3) A being which lacked any perfection would not be a supremely perfect being.

So (4) It would be self-contradictory to conceive of God, a supremely perfect being, as lacking any perfection.

(5) Existence is a perfection.

So (6) To lack existence is to lack a perfection.

So (7) It would be self-contradictory to conceive of God, a supremely perfect being, as lacking existence (i.e., as not existing).

So (8) It is part of the concept of idea of God that he exists.

So (9) God must, in reality, exist. It is in fact the case that God exists.

This is the argument. Clearly the crucial premises are the first and the fifth. With regard to the first: while we might in general be willing to grant it, the old problem again arises, concerning the reliability of our clear and distinct ideas, *prior to* the demonstration that God exists and that he is good. But even if this problem is set aside, a crucial problem remains with regard to the contention that existence is a perfection. Whether existence is a perfection – and whether existence is something that can be included in the very idea or definition of something – is an issue that has been contested by philosophers ever since. I won't attempt to answer the question; many of the philosophers to be considered subsequently will have things to say about it. I will only say this: Think of God existing. Now think of God with all of the characteristics you have just imagined, only not existing. Have you conceived of his *nature* any differently in the two cases? Or have you simply thought of a being with one and the same nature in both cases, only in the one case you have also imagined that *there is* such a being?

God's nature

Let us now assume for the sake of argument that it has been established that God exists, and turn briefly to the question of his nature. Descartes's argument that God must be omnipotent, omniscient, etc., has roughly the form of the argument for his existence I have just outlined; only in each case the premises 'omnipotence is a perfection,' 'omniscience is a perfection,' and so on, replace the premise 'existence is a perfection.' And since these are relatively uncontroversial premises, his arguments would appear to be sound enough. In each case the point is that God could not lack these qualities and still be the supremely perfect being which he is by definition. The same sort of argument is used to show that all of these perfections must be united in one being, rather than divided up among a number of beings each of which had only one or a few of them. For it is Descartes's contention that without this unity of all perfections, no such being would be supremely perfect, and therefore would not be the God who has been shown to exist. Without possessing all of these perfections, God would not be the supremely perfect being he is by definition.

Finally, Descartes argues in a similar manner that God cannot be a deceiver, like the evil genius he imagines. The argument runs as follows (in the Third Meditation):

(1) God is a supremely perfect being.

(2) A supremely perfect being has no defects or imperfections.

So (3) God has no defects or imperfections.

(4) 'Deception necessarily proceeds from some defect' or imperfection (171).

So (5) God 'cannot be a deceiver' (171).

Deception, in short, would be inconsistent with God's all-perfect nature. God cannot be all-perfect if he is not good; and he would be not good but evil if he used his powers to deceive – or at least, he would be less good than he might be if he used his powers to deceive, and hence he would be less than completely perfect if he did so. But he is completely perfect; hence he is no deceiver. At *this* point Descartes would perhaps be justified in laying to rest his doubts about the reliability of his clear and distinct ideas. Once again, however, it is difficult to see how he could *get* to this point without making use of them. At any rate, we next will see how far he thinks he can get with respect to knowledge of things other than his own and God's existence and nature, now that he feels he has established that his clear and distinct ideas may be relied upon.

The world and things

Convinced that he has proven that God exists and is no deceiver, in the Third Meditation, Descartes says, early in the Fourth: 'It seems to me that I now have before me a road which will lead us from the contemplation of the true God . . . to the knowledge of the other objects of the universe' (172). He says this because he feels he can *prove* the soundness of our judgments, provided that we restrict them to matters which do not exceed our understanding. And if he can prove this, then given the validity of the arguments about the mind and God discussed previously, he thinks he will be able to carry out the reconstruction of knowledge to which he aspires. The proof he offers to establish the reliability of proper judgments runs something like this:

(1) All capacities I have, I have received from God.

(2) I have a capacity of making judgments about things.

So (3) My capacity of making judgments is given to me by God.

(4) God would do nothing which would cause me to be deceived or to err, since he is no deceiver.

So (5) God would not have given me a faculty which would 'lead me to err if I use it aright' (172).

So (6) My capacity of making judgments will not lead me into error if I use it properly.

So (7) If I use my capacity of judging properly, then what I *judge* to be the case *really is* the case.

Before considering what it is to judge properly, I will comment briefly on the premises of this argument. Premise (2) is quite uncontroversial; we do make judgments about things, and the fact that we do so shows that we have the capacity of doing so. Premise (4) depends upon the soundness of the reasoning discussed above; if it is disallowed, the argument fails, and Descartes's attempted reconstruction of knowledge along with it. The only other premise is (1), the assumption that all of my capacities are capacities which have been given to me by God. This premise too is essential; reject it, and Descartes would contend that we can never have any knowledge of the world that is worthy of the name. He does not argue for this premise here, because he feels that he has already established it, when he argued (in the second proof of the existence of God) that God alone can be the cause of my existence as a thinking and hence judging substance. If one accepts that argument, one will have no trouble here. If one rejects that argument, however, or if one finds it plausible but less than an indubitable proof, then this proof is likewise undercut or weakened; and in either of these cases, it would no longer do the job Descartes feels must be done if our knowledge of the world is to be guaranteed.

But let us grant the argument, and briefly consider Descartes's account of what is it to judge properly. On his analysis, an act of judging or passing judgment about something (e.g., that it exists, or that it has this character rather than that) involves the use of the two faculties – the understanding, by which I conceive of things, and the will, by which I (among other things) affirm or deny that they exist or have the character I conceive them to have. Both of these faculties are God-given; but my understanding is limited in a way in which my will is not; namely, I am able to affirm things even when I do not understand them clearly and distinctly, whether through inattention or through limitations of my intellect. When I do this, as I have an unfortunate inclination to do, I fall into error. This is judging *im*properly. But when I affirm only what I understand clearly and distinctly, I judge properly, and discover what is really the case; I attain true knowledge. For since God is not a deceiver, and since God has given me my faculty of understanding, what I understand clearly and distinctly *must* be true; otherwise I could not help being deceived, and this would mean that God would be a deceiver.

Here I would point out that Descartes is continuing to make use of the conclusions from previous arguments I have discussed; and further that his analysis of judgment is something worth thinking about. For it depends upon a sharp separation of understanding from willing or affirming, which may have been taken for granted for a long time before him and after him, but which has been challenged by many more recent philosophers. I do not suggest that one reject his analysis just because this separation has been challenged; but one should keep in mind that its tenability is open to question.

At any rate, Descartes concludes at the end of the Fourth Meditation that, 'as often as I so restrain my will ... that it forms no judgment except on matters which are clearly and distinctly represented to it by the understanding, I can never be deceived' (178). 'Now,' he says, at the beginning of the Fifth, my principal task is to endeavour ... to see whether [anything] certain can be known regarding material things' (179). He does not really get to material things, however, until the Sixth Meditation; for he first turns his attention to the truths of mathematics. And he thinks they can be dealt with relatively simply, since the only reason he could think of to doubt them in the First Meditation was that his clear and distinct ideas might be untrustworthy. But since he now has satisfied himself that they are trustworthy, he concludes that any idea pertaining to numbers (e.g., $2 + 3 = 5$) or to geometrical figures (e.g., what the properties of a triangle are) which he perceives clearly and distinctly is true. He does not claim that mathematical entities like numbers and triangles have a real existence in a physical sense. He does want to claim, however, that the idea of a certain number or geometrical figure is not simply an empirical idea derived from experience, but rather has 'a certain determinate nature, form, or essence, which is immutable and eternal, which I have not invented, and which in no wise depends on my mind' (180).

He argues that this is so on the grounds that most of the truths of arithmetic and geometry are truths which we discover through the use of reason alone, rather than through the senses; and that we *discover* these truths, which must be presumed to have been true all along, rather than *invent* them, as we invent the ideas of imaginary beings like centaurs. Arithmetical and geometrical truths are not true because physical objects have the properties they do. They are true independently; and knowledge of them would be attainable even if a knowledge of the existence and natures of material things were unattainable. We do not know that $2 + 3 = 5$, or that the sum of the angles of a triangle is 180 degrees, by *induction* from a variety of specific perceptions of physical objects. Rather, we know it by virtue of what we discover when we think about numbers, triangles, and the like.

But now: what about material objects? It is to this question that Descartes turns in the Sixth Meditation, saying: 'Nothing further now remains but to inquire whether material things exist,' not simply 'as the objects of pure mathematics,' but as concretely existing things. And the first question one might raise is whether it is *possible* that such things should exist, independent of and external to the thinking substance which is my mind, and the ideas of such things I have. Descartes's answer to this question is affirmative. 'For,' he says, 'there is no doubt that God possesses the power to produce [anything] that I am capable of perceiving with distinctness . . . , unless I [find] a contradiction in attempting to conceive it clearly' (185). But the idea of independently existing material objects is not self-contradictory; hence they are possible. The point here can be stated more simply, without making reference to God; and it is a point to which few people would object: anything logically possible is actually possible. Material objects are logically possible, hence they are actually possible. Though of course it does not follow simply from this that they actually do exist, as Descartes himself would be the first to insist.

So: *do* they actually exist? I will skip over the argument for the existence of the body, based on the existence of the power of imagination which Descartes finds he has (pp. 186–7); because as he himself recognizes, the existence of this power of imagination (together with the idea one has of one's bodily existence) does not enable one to 'derive any argument from which there will necessarily be deduced the existence of body.' And since it is this kind of argument which must be found if his program of a reconstruction of knowledge is to be extended to material things, he is forced to try another tack to get results amounting to more than a 'conjecture with probability' (187).

The proof he comes up with (187f.) runs something like this:

(1) I have ideas of various material things.

(2) It is impossible for anything by itself to come into existence out of nothing.

So (3) These ideas have been formed and produced by some existing thing.

(4) There are four and only four existing things possible that could have produced these ideas: myself, God, actual material things, or some being higher than myself but less than God.

(5) I am as I am because God so created me.

(6) I have a strong inclination to believe that these ideas of material things issue from actual material things.

So (7) I have this inclination because God caused me to have it.

(8) If these ideas issued from myself, God or some other being higher than myself but less than God, this inclination would result in my being deceived.

So (9) If these ideas issued from any of these three sources, God would be a deceiver.

(10) God is not a deceiver.

So (11) These ideas do not issue from any of these three sources.

So (12) These ideas must issue from actual material things.

So (13) Actual material things must in fact exist.

This argument could be slightly simplified by deleting all reference to other possible sources of my ideas of material things, without significantly altering it. In either case, it comes down to the contention that, since I cannot help believing that actual material things are the source of the perceptions of material things I have, and since God who is not a deceiver made me that way, material things must actually be the source of these perceptions, and must therefore actually exist.

The argument obviously will not go through if one rejects Descartes's arguments for God's existence and goodness; but it depends upon more as well. Does it in fact follow, given that God exists and is the cause of my existence, that he must be the cause of my inclination to believe that the source of my perceptions of material things is actual material things? After all, Descartes recognizes that we also have the inclination to make judgments about things which we do not understand clearly and distinctly;

yet he attributes *that* inclination to ourselves, not to God. Why are the two cases different? Let it be granted that I may be sure I am not being deceived if I affirm only that which I clearly and distinctly understand – which is all that Descartes previously said follows from God's not being a deceiver. Surely I do not clearly and distinctly understand that actual material things are the source of my ideas of them, simply without further ado; otherwise the sort of proof Descartes offers would not be necessary. But if I do not immediately see clearly and distinctly, simply from examining my ideas of material things, that they have as their source actually existing material things, why am I not obligated to withhold my judgment about the matter?

To repeat: to proceed differently in this matter than in other cases in which I am inclined to affirm more than I clearly and distinctly understand, it would be necessary for Descartes to show that there is something special about my inclination to believe that actual material things are the source of my perceptions and ideas of material things, such that it makes sense to attribute *this* inclination to God, while attributing other, seemingly similar inclinations to excesses on the part of my own will. This is an internal criticism, which is quite independent of criticisms which might be directed at Descartes's previous arguments. And it is not clear that he has any convincing answer to it. If he cannot provide one, however, the proof doesn't go through, and thus he is left without the possibility of extending his reconstruction of knowledge to matters pertaining to the supposed external world of material things.

But now: supposing that the *existence* of material things has been established, what can we know of their *natures* – their qualities? Most people no doubt are convinced that there are material objects, even though one may not think that Descartes's argument for their existence is sound. And his answer to the question of what we can know of their qualities is of some independent interest, since he does not use the above line of reasoning to argue that material things do in fact have all the qualities we are inclined to think they do. He does reason along these lines to conclude that, when our perceptions vary, '*corresponding variations*' must be occurring in the material things themselves, accounting for the variation in our perceptions. But he contends that a number of the qualities we ordinarily take to inhere in the objects themselves cannot in point of fact really be said to do so. These are the so-called 'secondary qualities' – for example, heat, color and taste. These qualities, just as we perceive them, cannot be taken to be qualities of things themselves, since it is easy to show that our perceptions of these qualities are conditioned by our senses, and vary with the states of our sense organs. He holds that, when the state of our sense organs remains constant and we still perceive a change of color or temperature or the like, some 'corresponding variation' must be occurring in the object; but it may not be possible for us to discover precisely what this is.

While we may not be able to discover *precisely* what corresponding variation is occurring, however, Descartes feels that it is reasonable to assume that it is a matter of some change in *another* set of qualities, which (at least generally speaking) we both can perceive and may take to be actual qualities of things themselves. These are the so-called 'primary qualities', such as shape, motion and number. Descartes contends that qualities such as these are not conditioned by our senses in the way in which color, taste and the like are; and that therefore when we determine, e.g., the shape of an object, we are discovering an actual characteristic of it. He accounts for changes in the secondary qualities we perceive in terms of minute changes in the primary qualities of a thing. Given this way of viewing the matter, it should be obvious why the terms 'primary' and 'secondary' have come to be used to refer to the two sorts of qualities. Primary qualities are qualities things themselves have, more or less as we perceive them to be; whereas the secondary ones are qualities things do not really have as we perceive them to be, but rather are sensations in us to which things give rise, as the result of the interaction of their primary qualities with our sense-organs.

Descartes's answer to the question of what we can know of material things is thus as follows: we can know what their primary qualities are, when these are of a sufficient magnitude to be perceptible by us. Of these qualities we can form clear and distinct ideas; and since our clear and distinct ideas have been shown to be trustworthy (for reasons relating to God's existence and goodness), we can know that things have those qualities of which we can form clear and distinct ideas. Our knowledge is limited, however; and in particular, with regard to those features of things associated with our perception of secondary qualities, we can know only that things *have* some such features which 'arouse' these perceptions in us. We may suppose them to be configurations of imperceptible primary qualities; but we cannot form clear and distinct ideas of precisely what those features are, and so we cannot have true knowledge of them.

Let us now recall the three reasons Descartes originally gave for doubting the testimony of the senses, which he recapitulates in the Sixth Meditation, and see how he handles them, in such a way that he now feels warranted in accepting the testimony of the senses within these limits. The three reasons pertained (a) to the fact that I am often deceived by my senses; (b) to the possibility that at any given moment I might be dreaming, and therefore not perceiving the real world at all; and (c) to the possibility that I might be systematically deceived through being so constituted as always to fall into error.

The last of these reasons Descartes feels he has eliminated by his arguments that God exists and is good and that, as his creature, I cannot be so constituted as constantly and inescapably to fall into error. With regard to the first: while he recognizes that it is still possible that my senses may deceive me upon occasion, he feels that he has shown error from this source to be *avoidable* through the proper use of the faculty of judgment and the pooling of the evidence of the various senses, together with the assurance that God is good and therefore has given me faculties which are trustworthy if used properly. And finally, with regard to the possibility that I might be dreaming, Descartes feels that I can set aside my doubts deriving from this possibility if I take care to observe whether what I think I am experiencing can be integrated into the rest of my experience; for he maintains that if it can be, I may be sure that I am not dreaming. He says:

> I find a very notable difference between [dreaming and waking],
> inasmuch as our memory can never connect our dreams one
> with the other, or with the whole course of our lives, as it
> unites events, which happen to us while we are awake. . . .
> When, without any interruption, I can connect the perceptions
> which I have . . . with the whole course of my life, I am
> perfectly assured that these perceptions occur while I am
> waking and not during sleep. . . . For because God is in no
> wise a deceiver, it follows that I am not deceived in this. (199)

With this, Descartes feels that the reconstruction of our knowledge which he set out to achieve has at least in principle been accomplished. What remains is only to set out and – within the restrictions he has placed upon our judgments – determine what characteristics particular types of existing things have. Our knowledge will never be as complete as that of God himself; but we purportedly will wind up knowing with certainty virtually everything we thought we knew and could know in the first place; only now we really know it, whereas formerly we could not be said to have true (i.e., certain) knowledge.

The general picture of reality which emerges from Descartes's discussion is very much like the traditional view of it, and is also fairly similar to the view many people hold today. First, there is a world made up of material things – extended objects with various shapes, some in motion and some at rest, in great numbers. These objects are simply there, with their various primary qualities making them similar and different in various ways, independent of our thoughts about them and our perceptions of them. Certain of these extended objects are associated with things of a different sort, which we call minds or souls. These minds or souls are not identical with these objects or human bodies, but rather differ from them and are essentially distinct from and independent of them; even though in this world the two are intimately connected. Thus there are two basic kinds of things or substances in the world – extended substances which do not think, and thinking substances or minds which are not extended.

Finally, there is something further: God, an all-perfect being, who has brought everything else into existence, and who has given each mind and each extended object the qualities it has. The extended objects, which are incapable of thought, merely interact physically with each other. The thinking things or minds, on the other hand, are capable of achieving a considerable (if ultimately limited) knowledge of themselves, of the other thinking things and extended objects in the world, and even of the existence and nature of God himself, thanks to God who has provided them with the faculties of perception and understanding and whose goodness ensures the reliability of these faculties. In short, Descartes, who began by determining to doubt everything, wound up denying practically nothing of the traditionally accepted world-view. Only he felt that at the end he was no longer merely accepting this world-view on faith, but rather had achieved certain knowledge of its validity.

Thus, as I suggested at the outset, Descartes's conclusions were hardly revolutionary. What was revolutionary was his demand that traditional assumptions must be subjected to the test of rational analysis; and that they must be denied the status of knowledge if it is found that they fall short of complete certainty, or cannot be demonstrated with complete certainty to be valid. He provided arguments which he thought showed that the traditional world-view was essentially correct. Subsequent philosophers had doubts about some of his arguments; and when they questioned them, they came up with results which differed in varying respects from his. But they proceeded in the spirit of Descartes, however much they may have disputed his arguments and his conclusions. They too were motivated by a desire to determine what can be *known* about reality, and a readiness to reject traditional beliefs if the results of their inquiry showed that traditional beliefs could not be rationally justified. And if sound reasoning should lead to the conclusion that reality is constituted very differently than has traditionally been believed – well then, so much the worse for our traditional and ordinary beliefs. That is how Descartes himself would have had it.

CHAPTER II

LEIBNIZ

Leibniz was born in 1646, four years before Descartes's death. He was a contemporary of both Spinoza and Locke; in fact, he was some years younger than either of them, and outlived both of them. When he died, in 1716, Berkeley was just about to take his first teaching position at the age of 22. And since Hume was born in 1711, all of the philosophers considered here, with the exception of Kant, were alive during Leibniz's lifetime; and Kant was born only eight years after his death.

Unlike Berkeley and Kant, but like the rest of these men, Leibniz never held a teaching position in philosophy in a university; though like most of the others, he could have had one if he had wanted one. He was something of a prodigy, publishing substantial philosophical essays while still in his teens, and earning both his bachelor's degree and a doctorate of law by the time he was 20. He had one of the most brilliant philosophical minds in the course of the whole history of philosophy; and many of his ideas – concerning, for example, logic, computer theory, and the creation of an ideal language – continue to be of interest today. Unfortunately, he rarely worked out his philosophical ideas systematically and in detail, and published relatively few philosophical works. Most of his writing took the form of correspondence with other men. And when he did write for publication, it was usually in the form of short essays, few of which are representative of his thought or are worked out in enough detail to be readily comprehensible. This means that the demands placed upon someone who studies him are much greater than those made by Descartes and by most of the other writers to be considered. But one has to make do with what there is.

Like Descartes, Leibniz held theological views which do not differ greatly from those of traditional Christian theology. Indeed, he hoped that his philosophy would contribute to the elimination of skepticism with regard to the basic tenets of Christian thought, and also to the resolution of the theological conflicts which had plunged Europe into decades of religious wars. But it would be inaccurate to characterize his program merely as an apology for traditional Christian theology. He did not simply set out to construct a philosophical defense of it; and his program is of interest in its own right, even if Christian theology is completely removed from the picture.

Program and method

Leibniz also shared Descartes's concern with what he calls 'the improvement of the sciences' (11) – meaning the advancement of knowledge generally, and the provision of a foundation of knowledge which would render it secure against the possibility of serious doubt and error. Like Descartes, he felt that the various sciences and our so-called knowledge generally are not properly grounded, and lack the certainty and freedom from the possibility of error which they must have if they are to deserve the name of knowledge. And he further felt that this is a matter of considerable practical as well as theoretical importance, since if the possibility of error is not removed, we may take something to be true which is not, and may therefore be led to do things which will have harmful practical consequences. In the spirit of Descartes, therefore, he sought 'the true organon [i.e., method] of a general science of everything that is subject matter for human reasoning, [which] would be endowed throughout with the demonstrations of an evident calculus' (19).

As Descartes had been, Leibniz was very much impressed with mathematics, and with the degree of certainty and the exactness of reasoning that is to be found in mathematical demonstrations. The philosophical method he proposes is modeled on the mathematical, in the hope of securing a comparable exactness and certainty of our reasoning about reality. It was with this goal in mind that he came up with the suggestion of an ideal language or 'characteristic' to replace natural languages such as those we ordinarily speak. He says:

> The natural languages are of very great value in reasoning, but full of innumerable equivocations and unable to function in a calculus; for if they were able to do this, errors in reasoning could be uncovered from the very form and construction of the words. . . . Hitherto only the arithmetical and the algebraic notations have offered this admirable advantage. (18)

This idea of an ideal language – which would be free of the

41

equivocations which plague ordinary language and in which our reasoning could proceed free from the problems which these equivocations raise – has exerted a strong influence on the thinking of such recent philosophers as Bertrand Russell and the early Wittgenstein, and continues to have influential adherents today. The movement given the label 'Logical Atomism,' so powerful earlier in this century, was something of a Leibniz revival. The basic idea of Logical Atomism is similar to that of Leibniz when he says:

> all human ideas . . . can be resolved into a few as their
> primitives. . . . If characters were assigned to these primitives,
> characters for derivable notions could be formed therefrom,
> and from these . . . it would be possible to find correct
> definitions and values, and hence, also the properties which are
> demonstrably implied in the definitions. (18–19)

> Once this is achieved, anyone who in his reasoning and writing
> is using characters of this kind, will either never fall into error,
> or, if he does, he will always discover his errors by himself by
> the simplest examinations, as anybody else will; and
> moreover, he will find the truth which is implied in the available
> data. (19)

Leibniz's program would seem to be essentially similar to that of Descartes, though given this original twist. In fact, however, Leibniz is critical of Descartes's method and procedure on a number of counts. First, he contends that if one is determined to place in question absolutely everything one can conceive of even the slightest reason (such as the evil genius hypothesis) for doubting, then one will never get anywhere at all. He recognizes that, in order to get out of the predicament Descartes gets himself into through his systematic doubting, Descartes is forced to rely upon certain assumptions which he has no right to assume if he is *really* going to doubt everything that is less than certain. The conclusion Leibniz draws, however, is not that we can never know anything, but rather that we should not be deterred from making a few basic assumptions on the wild supposition that something like Descartes's hypothesis might be the case, provided that the assumptions we make are assumptions no one in his right mind would really question. And he believes that it is necessary to make only two such assumptions, or to take for granted the validity of only two such fundamental principles, in order to get results.

Our reasoning is founded on two great principles; the first is the principle of *contradiction*, by virtue of which we consider as false what implies a contradiction and as true [anything the denial of which is] contradictory or false.

The second is the principle of *sufficient reason*, by virtue of which we hold that no fact can be true or existing and no statement truthful without a sufficient reason for its being so and not different. (153)

From these principles Leibniz contends that 'the rules of *common logic*' may be derived; and thus any 'solid demonstration' of some point – that is, 'one which respects the forms prescribed by logic' – is sufficient to determine 'the truth of propositions' (8). When we follow these rules, we may be sure that our conclusions are true. In this way, knowledge having the requisite degree of certainty may be attained. 'To avoid all errors,' he says, 'nothing more is required . . . than to use the most common rules of logic with great constancy and rigor' (40). It is not necessary first to prove the existence and goodness of God, which would not be possible without these rules anyhow. The fact that these rules presuppose the validity of the two basic principles mentioned is no cause for worry; and the fact that they themselves cannot be proven valid is no reason to retreat into skepticism. The better course is simply to lay our basic assumptions on the table, observe the absurdity of questioning their validity, and then get on with the business of seeing what follows from them together with our immediate experience.

In this connection it should be noted that for Leibniz we do have something more to go on than just these two principles – and indeed something more to start with than Descartes himself explicitly acknowledges: the particular contents of our immediate experience. What is immediately given is not simply that I think (and exist), but also that I have the particular thoughts or perceptions I do. They do not guarantee that there exists anything independent of them corresponding to them; but they themselves are not subject to doubt. So Leibniz says:

Descartes' thesis that the 'I think therefore I am' is one of the primary truths is excellent. But it would have been only fair not to neglect other truths of the same kind. . . . There are as many primary truths of fact as there are immediate perceptions. . . . For I am conscious not only of my thinking self, but also of my thoughts, and it is no more true and certain that I think [and therefore exist] than that I think this or that. (25)

This is surely reasonable enough, and is only what Descartes himself should have said. While Leibniz does criticize Descartes on this point, however, he does not criticize the 'cogito' argument for the existence of the 'I' or self, but rather accepts it. This is a point on which, if Descartes is to be criticized, Leibniz is as well.

Truth and knowledge

From the fact that Leibniz criticizes Descartes for carrying his systematic doubting farther than it is reasonable to carry it, one might expect him to say that Descartes should not have expressed the doubts he does about his 'clear and distinct' ideas in the First Meditation, but rather should have felt free to rely upon them. Leibniz does not say this, however – not because he agrees with Descartes that the evil genius hypothesis renders them at least initially untrustworthy, but rather because he contends that Descartes has no satisfactory criteria of what it is for an idea to be clear and distinct. He observes that 'frequently what appears to be clear and distinct to people who judge superficially is actually obscure and confused.' And he concludes that Descartes's principle that 'whatever I perceive clearly and distinctly of a thing is true and can be predicated of it' is 'useless, unless we add *criteria* of clearness and distinctness' (8). This is a point with which one cannot but agree.

Rather than simply abandoning all talk of clearness and distinctness, however, Leibniz attempts to give these notions more precise meaning (in the first pages of 'Reflections on Knowledge'), in order to render them more serviceable. 'All knowledge,' he says, 'is either obscure or *clear*, and clear knowledge is again either confused or *distinct*; the distinct in its turn is either inadequate or *adequate*, and again either symbolic or *intuitive*. The more perfect knowledge is that which is both adequate and intuitive' (3). Before going any further, it should be observed that it would seem rather odd to speak of 'knowledge' which is neither adequate nor distinct nor even clear as *knowledge* at all. But it may simply be that Leibniz is here trying to sort out the various modes of apprehension which are at one time or another *taken* to be knowledge, and to indicate the degree to which they fall short of or approach being genuine knowledge. And genuine or perfect knowledge – knowledge which is most worthy of the name – is held not only to be clear, and not only distinct as well, but also completely adequate and intuitive.

But what do these terms mean? Leibniz suggests that I do not apprehend something *clearly* unless I am able to distinguish it from other things which resemble it. This is the criterion of clarity. Next, I do not apprehend something *distinctly* unless I am able to identify the various features of a thing which distinguish it from other things. This is the criterion of distinctness. And this involves more than clarity; for I may be able to distinguish something from other things which resemble it without being able to identify the features in virtue of which it differs from them.

The notion of *adequacy* is really only an extension of the notion of distinctness. The possibility of inadequate apprehension arises only in connection with things having a complex nature; if I only apprehend some of the components of a complex thing distinctly, but not others, my apprehension of the complex thing falls short of complete distinctness, and so is inadequate. If, on the other hand, I apprehend all of its components distinctly, then my apprehension of the complex thing is *adequate*.

Finally, Leibniz distinguishes between symbolic and intuitive apprehension. If a thing is relatively simple, I may have no trouble directly envisaging each of its distinguishing features simultaneously when I think of it. In such a case, my apprehension is intuitive. But because most things are very complex indeed, and because my ability to envisage different features simultaneously is limited, I very commonly must make use of symbols to (as it were) hold the places of some of the component features of things when I think of them. When I focus my attention on some specific feature, I may be able to dispense with the symbol I use to refer to it, and to envisage it directly. But when I think of the entire complex thing, the most I commonly can do is to think of it in terms of a set of these symbols. An animal, for example, is something very complex. I may be able to state what it is; but in doing so, I make use of many words (or symbols) the precise meaning of each of which I am not able to envisage or intuit simultaneously when I think of what it is. In such cases, my apprehension is not intuitive but symbolic. Symbolic knowledge is the sort of knowledge we often must settle for; and it is quite good enough, and respectable enough, provided that we are able to conceive clearly and distinctly of each of the features involved when we turn our attention to them. But such knowledge is less perfect than a completely intuitive or non-symbolic knowledge of the same thing would be. Such knowledge, however, in the case of most things, is possible for God alone.

And our disadvantage is even more serious than this, according to Leibniz. For on his view, a truly *complete* specification of the nature of most existing things would require an infinitely long analysis or specification of features; since a complete specification of the nature of an existing thing would require a specification of its relation to everything else in the universe. We can get along quite well for practical purposes with much more limited specifications; but this is what a complete knowledge of a thing would involve. And since our powers are limited, we could not perform an infinitely long analysis even in the whole of our lifetime, let alone all at once, in a given moment, grasping each feature simultaneously. God alone is able to do this; and so, once again, for even more compelling reasons, perfect knowledge is in most cases something reserved to God alone. We can have perfect knowledge of what Leibniz calls 'primitive notions,' and of very simple complexes formed from primitive notions; but for the rest, the most we can attain is knowledge that is less than perfect – symbolic knowledge, and symbolic knowledge that is far from complete at that. So Leibniz says:

> I would not . . . dare to affirm that it will ever be possible for men to perform a perfect analysis of notions. . . . For the most part we must content ourselves with gathering the reality of certain notions from experience and compounding them afterward into others. (7–8)

But this does not mean that we are incapable of achieving the true knowledge of anything. It only sets limits on what we can know of the natures of particular existing things and types of existing things. It compromises our empirical knowledge; but Leibniz has a rather low opinion of the importance of empirical knowledge. He speaks of 'mere factual truths,' and is not greatly disturbed by the fact (which he readily acknowledges) that 'for mere factual truths,' the 'art of computation' he advocates 'is not competent' (14). He is much more interested in what can be discovered about the general nature of things through the use of reason alone; and this, he contends, is something about which we can discover a great deal, merely by considering the logical consequences of the several basic principles with which he begins, together with the few 'primary truths of fact' which it is within our power to discover. So he says, at the beginning of 'On the Universal Science': 'Let us at present disregard experiments . . . , and let us concentrate on that improvement of the sciences which is *based on reason*' (11). It is this main reliance upon reason as opposed to experiment, and his conviction that reason can reveal to us the basic structures of reality despite the limitations applying to empirical knowledge, which accounts for the traditional designation of Leibniz and Spinoza (who proceeds along similar lines) as *rationalists*.

There are, according to Leibniz, 'two kinds of truths; those of *reason*, which are necessary and of which the opposite is impossible, and those of *fact*, which are contingent, and of which the opposite is possible' (153). This is a distinction which applies primarily to our knowledge; for at least a great many things which are contingent truths for us, given the limitations upon our cognitive abilities, are necessary truths for God. This holds, for example, where the natures of particular things and their relations to each other are concerned. If we knew what God knows, we would see that these things are not simply matters of fact, contingently true, but rather are necessarily true. As things stand, however, it is only within a relatively limited (but important) class of cases that we can see that certain things are necessarily true. But where we *do* see that something is necessarily true, because its opposite is impossible, then we can rest assured that it *is* really true; and neither God himself nor Descartes's evil genius could cause matters to be otherwise. So whatever we discover to be necessarily true about the world, through the use of our reason, we know actually to be true about the world. And through the discovery of such necessary truths, Leibniz holds that we can come to know a good deal about the basic structures of reality.

At this point mention must be made of some Leibnizian terminology. To say that something is known *a priori* is to say that it is a truth of reason, discovered by the operation of reason alone, either by drawing a logical consequence of some principle of reason, or by the logical analysis of some concept. To say that something is known *a posteriori*, on the other hand, is to say that it is a matter of fact, discovered in the course of experience. So, for example Leibniz says:

> Possibility can be known either *a priori* or *a posteriori*; it is known *a priori* when we resolve the notion [the possibility of which is in question] into its requisites . . . , and when we find

it in no [logical] incompatibility. . . . We know the possibility *a posteriori* [on the other hand] when we know by experience that the thing actually exists; for whatever actually exists or has existed is certainly possible. (7)

Finally, one other bit of terminology. In the same passage Leibniz says: 'It is also evident . . . which *ideas* are *true* and which *false*. An idea is true when the notion is possible and false when it involves contradiction' (7). Now we do not ordinarily consider something to be true just because it has been shown to be possible. But here Leibniz is speaking of 'true *ideas*', rather than of 'the truth of propositions' which pertains to actual existence, as he does elsewhere; and in *this* context, the term 'true' has a rather special meaning: namely, an idea is said to be 'true' if only it is not logically self-contradictory – if only it is logically possible. 'True' in this context *means* simply 'logically possible.' A 'true idea' is thus simply something like a logically sound idea. But it does not follow, just because an idea is 'true' in this sense, that there actually exists something answering to that description. And with this I now turn to what Leibniz feels he can establish *does* exist; and first of all, to the question of the existence of God.

God and the world

Because Leibniz does not think it is reasonable to push the matter of systematic doubting as far as Descartes does, he has rather more to start with than Descartes did at the outset of his metaphysical inquiries. He does not have a great deal more, since he too feels that most of our ordinary opinions must be placed in question and must not be granted the status of knowledge unless they can be proven by rational arguments presupposing nothing that is not indubitable. But he considers a few more things to be indubitable than Descartes did. With Descartes, he considers it indubitable that I think, and therefore also that I exist. And he points out that within the general broad category of 'thinking', there are essentially three basic types of conscious activities we may observe going on in ourselves: perceiving, conceiving and willing. This is quite consistent with Descartes; whatever the character of the world may be, it is quite certain that I perceive various qualities, that I conceive various ideas or concepts, and that I will various things. And from this it follows that at least while I am engaged in these kinds of conscious activities, I exist. This would seem quite reasonable; but one should recall the kind of question that might be raised about the justifiability of concluding, from the fact that there is perceiving, conceiving and willing going on, that *I* am doing these things, and that therefore *I* exist. Since I have already considered this point, I will not pursue it. Suffice it to note that the same remarks apply here as well.

Further, Leibniz follows Descartes in taking it to be given that among the ideas he has is the idea of an all-perfect being; though it remains to be seen whether such a being exists. He regards several other things as given at the outset as well. First, there are the two fundamental principles of reasoning I mentioned earlier; the principle of non-contradiction and the principle of sufficient reason. And it should be observed that for Leibniz the principle of sufficient reason is rather more general in its formulation than the principle that, for everything that has come into existence, there must be a cause of its existence which contains in itself at least as much as the thing in question. Leibniz's more general principle is that, for everything that exists, even if it is eternal and therefore has not at a given point come into existence, there must be some *reason* for its existence, so that it is possible to answer the question of *why* it exists. To Leibniz, it is simply obvious that things cannot just *happen* to exist. If they exist, there must be a *reason* for their existence as opposed to their non-existence. In most cases, or for most practical purposes, it suffices to cite their cause as the reason, and so this extra twist is taken care of; but there *must be* an explanation, whatever the case may be. This is an idea which most people are inclined to accept in ordinary life and in science as well. And Leibniz is suggesting that it *always* applies; he feels it would be *irrational* to stop demanding an answer to the question 'why?' at any point, where the existence of anything short of a necessarily existing being is concerned.

Finally, Leibniz regards two other things as indisputable. First, there are the truths of mathematics (and of arithmetic and geometry in particular) and the rules of 'common logic,' which he calls 'eternal truths,' since he holds them to be necessarily and universally valid. On his view they are just as certain as are the two fundamental logical principles of reasoning, and therefore are no more to be doubted and in need of external justification than are these principles – or rather, the only external justification they require is provided by the indubitability of these fundamental principles themselves.

Second, there is the existence of the world. For Leibniz, this is not something it makes sense to doubt; though the true *nature* of the world is at the outset a very open question. If 'the world' is conceived in terms of Descartes's 'material things,' then its existence is by no means immediately certain; but that is because this involves a particular conception of the *nature* of the world, and the *nature* of the world is something that remains to be determined. Leibniz has rather unkind words for Descartes's attempted proof of the existence of the world conceived in terms of material things, saying, 'The argument by which Descartes tries to demonstrate the existence of material things is very weak indeed; it would have been better had he not tried' (41). But this does not mean that he is a skeptic with regard to the existence of the world, or that he thinks he has a better *proof* of its existence than Descartes does. He thinks he has a better conception of what its *nature* is; but that the world exists – that there is something rather than nothing, whatever its true nature may be – is a point he regards as just as indubitable from the outset as is his own existence.

In short, the resources Leibniz takes himself to have at his disposal as he begins his metaphysical inquiries are: the two fundamental principles of reasoning, the 'eternal truths' of mathematics and 'common logic,' the idea of an all-perfect being, and the 'primary truths of fact' of his thinking (perceiving, conceiving, willing), his existence, and the existence of the world. And the first task he sets for himself is to prove the existence of God, starting from some of these 'givens,' and making use of others – but of nothing else – along the way.

Like Descartes, Leibniz offers three proofs of God's existence; but none of them is identical with any of Descartes's three proofs, all of which he criticizes. Two of his are similar to two of Descartes's, but his third proof is quite different. He attempts no proof even resembling Descartes's first proof, which argues from the fact that we have the idea of an all-perfect being that there must exist an all-perfect being as its cause. He finds that proof defective to the point that he feels that not even some modified form of it will work. He does believe, however, that modified versions of Descartes's other two proofs are sound; and that a third, based on the so-called 'eternal truths' of mathematics and logic, is also possible.

His version of the 'ontological argument' differs from Descartes's only in that he feels that one further step is needed in order for it to be valid. With Descartes, he holds that (a) if A logically or analytically entails B, then, given A, B must *in fact* be the case;

that (b) he has the idea of God as an all-perfect being; and that (c) existence is a perfection. For Descartes, it followed without further ado that God must in fact exist, since the idea of God not existing would be the idea of an all-perfect being which lacked a perfection, which would be self-contradictory. For Leibniz, however, the matter is not quite this simple. He says:

> It ought to be realized that from this argument only the following conclusion can be drawn: If God be possible, it follows that he exists. For we cannot use definitions to draw conclusions with certainty before we know that the definitions [themselves] . . . involve no contradiction. (6)

Leibniz's point is that we have no right to conclude from the definition of God that God exists unless it can be shown that the definition of God is internally consistent, and contains no hidden contradiction. 'To demonstrate geometrically the existence of God,' he says, 'it remains . . . to demonstrate the [logical] possibility of God accurately and with geometrical rigor' (29). But this is something which he thinks can be done; Descartes's only fault was to fail to see that it must be done (and to do it).

Leibniz's argument that the idea of God is logically sound runs roughly as follows: first, aside from existence, the perfections attributed to God ultimately reduce to three: omnipotence, omniscience, and omnibenevolence. So he writes:

> In God there are his *power* which is the source of everything, his *knowledge* which contains the particulars of the ideas, and finally his *will* which is the source of change or production and acts according to the principle of the best possible. (155)

These three characteristics are all logically compatible with each other, and also with the idea of existence. And, second, it follows from the very idea of such a being as a being who is the source of all that exists that there could be no limitations upon him which would be inconsistent with his omnipotence and omniscience. Consequently, the idea of God is logically sound; it involves no self-contradiction. And now, Leibniz says, we *may* conclude with certainty that God does in fact exist – indeed, that he *necessarily* exists, since the idea of his not existing would be self-contradictory.

Leibniz here has called attention to an important defect in Descartes's version of the ontological argument. and his resolution of the problem would seem to be sound. The only thing I would point out is that his version of this proof still involves regarding existence as a perfection, and therefore as something that can be treated as a quality or characteristic feature of a thing – something that can be predicated of it. And if this is questionable in the case of Descartes, then it is questionable here as well. So once again, it must be asked: can existence be regarded as a predicate? Is it legitimate to treat existence as a perfection, and therefore as one of the essential features of the very idea of God?

Leibniz's other two proofs are essentially two versions of a single general proof, which differ only in that which is cited as something presupposing and therefore entailing the existence of God. These proofs are to some extent similar to Descartes's proof which argues that the existence of God is entailed by *my* existence; my existence must have a cause, and the ultimate cause of my existence must be God, who must therefore exist, since I do. Leibniz's arguments differ from this one in that they are cast in terms of 'sufficient reason' rather than 'ultimate cause'; and also in that it is not the 'I' or self for whose existence a sufficient reason is sought. Rather, in one proof it is the world, and in the other the 'eternal truths' of logic and mathematics, the existence of which is said to require the existence of God. Since the argument is essentially the same in both cases, and since it is developed at greater length (and is also easier to understand) in the case of the world, I will confine myself to considering this version of the proof.

This proof is commonly known as the 'cosmological argument'; and it is presented in greatest detail in Leibniz's essay 'On the Ultimate Origination of the Universe.' He simply takes it to be a 'fact' that 'something rather than nothing exists' (86). And this 'something,' he says, he will call 'the World' which for the time being may be characterized non-committally as 'the aggregate of finite things' (84). It may then be asked: 'Why is there something rather than nothing at all?' Why is there a world, rather than no world at all? This question, sometimes called 'the ultimate Why?' is one which many contemporary philosophers find meaningless, and therefore decline to try to answer. But for Leibniz, it is not a meaningless question; and it must have an answer, for according to the principle of sufficient reason, there must be some reason or other for everything that is so. Nothing simply *happens* to be the case. It cannot be, therefore, that there simply *happens* to be something rather than nothing – that there just *happens* to be a world.

Now Leibniz holds that it is *not* the case that there *must* be a world. He says: 'The world is not necessary, metaphysically speaking, so that the contrary would imply contradiction or logical absurdity' (88). In other words, one cannot explain the existence of the world as the existence of God was explained in the ontological argument, by pointing out that its existence is entailed by its essence. The world is not an all-perfect being, and therefore there is no self-contradiction in the idea of the world not existing. But it *does* exist; so how is its existence to be explained? What is the reason sufficient to account for its existence, given that, in accordance with the principle of sufficient reason, 'there is a reason why there exists something rather than nothing' (87)?

The next contention Leibniz advances is that 'the reason for any existent can only be another existent' (86). His thinking is apparently that if the reason for some existent were *not* another existent, this would amount to something existing without any real reason for its existence, which would be incompatible with the principle of sufficient reason. Just as Descartes had argued that something cannot come into existence out of nothing by itself, so Leibniz here argues that something whose essence does not entail its existence could not exist without a reason for its existence embodied in something really existing.

At this point the most natural explanation of the existence of the world as we find it might be that the sufficient reason for its existence is the world itself as it existed previously. The world now existing exists as the result of the world existing a moment before that, and so on to infinity. The world existing a moment ago was an existent; and so the requirement just mentioned, that 'the reason for any existent can only be another existent,' would seem to be satisfied. Leibniz, however, rejects this explanation, even though he is willing to allow, at least for the sake of argument, that the world might be eternal. He says:

> You may well suppose the world to be eternal; yet what you thus posit is nothing but the succession of states, and you will not find the sufficient reason in any one of them nor will you get any nearer to accounting rationally for the world by taking any number of them together: the reason must therefore be sought elsewhere. (85)

Leibniz's point is that it is not just the world at the present moment the existence of which must be explained, but rather the whole succession of world-states, even if this succession should never have had a beginning. For the non-existence of the whole succession still would not be self-contradictory; and so its existence still remains as something to be explained. And if the reason for its existence is not to be found in it itself, then, given that there must be a reason for its existence, and given that this reason must be located in something really existing, it must be located in something existing outside of the world of finite things itself. And it cannot be located in something whose existence is not necessary, since then the existence of *that* thing would remain to be explained. In short, somewhere along the line one must come to an existent whose existence is necessary (i.e., whose non-existence would be impossible), in order to bring this series to an end. In order to give a satisfactory explanation of the existence of the world, in other words, one must ultimately assume the existence of a necessarily existing being; and the only possible being who can satisfy this description is God. 'Hence,' Leibniz says, 'it is evident that even by supposing the world to be eternal, the recourse to an ultimate cause of the universe beyond this world, that is, to God, cannot be avoided' (85). He sums up the argument as follows:

> Since . . . the ultimate root of the world must be in something which exists of metaphysical necessity, and since furthermore the reason for any existent can only be another existent, it follows that a unique entity must exist of metaphysical necessity, that is, that there is a being whose essence implies existence. Hence there exists a being which is different from the plurality of beings, that is, from the world, for it has been granted and proved that the world does not exist of metaphysical necessity. (86)

This is a very powerful argument. As Leibniz formulates it, it requires that one grant the legitimacy of the idea of a being whose essence entails its existence. But one can get along without having to do so, by simply stipulating that God is the only being for whose existence an explanation or reason need not be sought. If one makes this move, then provided that one is willing to accept the principle of sufficient reason as applying to everything short of God himself, the argument would seem to be sound. And I think it must be admitted that all of Leibniz's assumptions are quite plausible ones. If there is any place at which one might reasonably attack the argument, it would seem to have to be at the assumption (and very broad application) of the principle of sufficient reason. The argument rests heavily on this principle; and if one were to reject it, the argument would fail. But this is a principle Leibniz contends it would be absurd to reject. And it is also one of the most fundamental principles of rational thought. In trying to decide what to make of this argument, therefore, one must consider whether one is willing to give up the general applicability of this principle. Some people have reasoned as follows: God does not exist. If the principle of sufficient reason were sound, it would follow that God exists. Therefore, the principle of sufficient reason cannot be sound. This, it seems to me, is not the way to decide the matter. It is by no means clear, however, how one *should* go about deciding it.

At any rate, Leibniz concludes by means of these two arguments – the ontological and the cosmological – that God exists. I have already suggested what he takes God's nature to be. God for him is an all-perfect being – omnipotent, omniscient, and omnibenevolent – and the creator of all other existing things. This includes everything in the world, whatever the particular natures of the things making up the world might be. And from this Leibniz draws another conclusion, which he proceeds to apply in describing the nature of the world. For if God has created everything that exists, then from the fact that he is omnibenevolent, it follows that he has created the world in such a way that the greatest possible perfection obtains within it, appearances to the contrary notwithstanding. One could deny that the greatest possible perfection obtains in the world only by denying either that God created everything in it, or that he is omnipotent, or that he is omniscient, or that he is omnibenevolent. But all of these things, by previous arguments, are out of the question. In describing the nature of reality, therefore, we may not only make use of the two fundamental logical principles and the rules of common logic, but also the principle of greatest perfection, which while not a fundamental principle of reasoning is at any rate a logical consequence of God's nature. It might seem to us that it would have been possible for the world to have been made better than it is; but that is only because we do not know the whole picture. Out of all of the possible worlds God might have created, he created this one. And why this one, rather than some other? Leibniz says:

> Since in the divine ideas there is an infinity of possible universes
> of which only one can exist, the choice made by God must
> have a sufficient reason which determines him to the one rather
> than another. This reason can be found only in . . . the degree
> of perfection contained in these worlds. . . . This is the cause
> for the existence of the best, which is disclosed to [God] by

his wisdom, determines his choice by his goodness, and is produced by his power. (156)

So while we as yet know little about the particular natures of finite things (ourselves included) we already know *a priori* that the world has a rational structure according with the principles of non-contradiction, sufficient reason, and the greatest perfection. Whatever these principles logically imply must also in fact be true of the world. And Leibniz feels that it is possible to come to know a good deal about the world simply by applying these principles to the few 'primary truths of fact' which are at our immediate disposal, without undertaking the kinds of investigations empirical scientists undertake. If it should turn out that these principles (together with 'primary truths of fact' discoverable from our immediate experience) lead to conclusions about the natures of things which run contrary to our ordinary or even scientific beliefs about them, then Leibniz feels that we can only conclude that these beliefs are mistaken. For when it comes to a choice between what common sense would seem to indicate and what reason tells us is the case, then if we are concerned to achieve a knowledge of what things *really* are like, we ought to hold to what reason tells us. For, as even the scientist agrees, reason is a much more trustworthy guide to the truth than are our ordinary observations and our traditional beliefs. It therefore remains to consider some of the conclusions Leibniz reaches concerning the natures of things in the world generally, and of ourselves in particular.

Finite things

Given that the world consists of 'the aggregate of finite things,' the question for Leibniz now is: What are these things? Given that there is a God, what else is there? What are the basic natures of those finite things which make up the world God has created? Descartes had held that there are basically two sorts of finite substances: thinking substances (which are not extended), and extended substances (which do not think). Thinking (in Descartes's broad sense) is precisely the essence of substances of the first sort; while the sole and entire essence of substances of the second sort is extension. All of the properties or characteristics of thinking substances are simply various modes of thought; and all of the properties or characteristics of extended substances are simply various modes of extension. All finite things other than man (including animals) are merely extended substances – more or less complicated configurations of extended substance, in some cases static structures, and in other cases complex machines. It is only in conjunction with that complex machine we call the human body that thinking substance is to be found in this world; but this conjunction is not a necessary one, for each kind of substance is capable of existing independently of the other.

In place of Descartes's division of finite things into thinking substances and extended substances, Leibniz proposes a distinction between *souls* or 'spiritual substances' (better: 'psychic substances,' since the term 'spirit' is used to refer to a special sort of 'soul') and *bodies* or 'corporeal substances.' This is not simply a matter of substituting one set of terms for another; for Leibniz's application of these terms is also rather different. First, Leibniz holds that souls and bodies do not and cannot exist independently of one another; 'God alone,' he says, 'is entirely bodiless' (160). For the rest, there are no bodies without souls – 'nothing . . . dead in the universe' (159) – 'nor are there any totally separate souls' (160).

It should be obvious that Leibniz is using 'soul' in a very general way, to refer not only to the human mind, but more generally to what might be termed the 'life-principle,' as Aristotle used the term *anima*. And this is another difference between his use of the term 'soul' and Descartes's use of the expression 'thinking substance.' According to Leibniz, animals and plants as well as human beings may be said to have 'souls'; for they too are to be characterized not merely in terms of their material characteristics, but also in terms of a life-principle. And Leibniz goes even further than Aristotle, who had said as much, and says that something like this life-principle must be ascribed even to what we call inorganic things; though of course it is not the same in them as it is in what we distinguish as *organic* things.

It follows from this that 'thinking', even in Descartes's broad sense of the term, does not adequately express the nature of 'soul.' 'Thinking' even in this broad sense only characterizes certain kinds of 'souls' – and not only human ones at that, at least where some of the activities subsumed under it are concerned. What distinguishes human souls from others generally, and from animal souls in particular, is that they have a feature which others lack: they are capable of attaining a knowledge of necessary truths. Leibniz says: 'Knowledge of necessary and eternal truths . . . distinguishes us from mere animals. . . . This possession is what is called our reasonable soul or *spirit*' (152). And it is interesting to notice that Leibniz considers us to differ from animals only insofar as we are capable of *this sort* of knowledge – *a priori* knowledge, rather than empirical knowledge. Empirical knowledge is something he feels that even animals are capable of attaining, at least to some degree. For he holds that empirical knowledge is basically a matter of memory, which animals have. And so he says: 'Men act like animals in so far as the succession of their perceptions is brought about by the principle of memory. . . . In fact, we are mere empiricists in three quarters of all our actions' (152). From which it follows that, to the extent that we are mere empiricists, we are essentially no better than mere animals. (A slur on empiricists which was by no means unintentional.)

The other side of the coin, however, is that Leibniz *denies* that either empiricists or mere animals are nothing but lifeless machines. For a being which lacks or fails to actualize this special ability of attaining knowledge of necessary truths still has a soul, even if not that special sort of soul which Leibniz designates as 'spirit.' Reason is not a defining feature of soul; it is only a special feature of a certain class of souls.

Turning to Leibniz's notion of 'body,' he holds that 'extension' does not adequately express *its* essential nature any more than 'thinking' adequately expresses the essential nature of soul. This is one of his main points in the essays 'On the Improvement of Metaphysics' and 'What is Nature?' He contends that 'body' is adequately characterized only if reference is also made to 'force.' 'This force of action,' he says, 'is inherent in all substance . . . ; corporeal substance itself . . . is never inactive. This does not seem to have been sufficiently understood by those who considered mere extension . . . as the essence of matter' (83). According to him, 'The very substance of things consists in their force of acting and being acted upon' (102). He feels that it is simply impossible to give an adequate account of the behavior of things in terms of their extension or geometrical qualities alone. Bodies move; and their movements can be explained neither by reference to the activities of souls, nor by reference to an initial impetus given to them externally by God when he created the universe. Their movements can be explained only by assuming that a certain active force was implanted in them as part of their very nature when they were created. And subsequently, they move in accordance with laws different from those which govern the activities of souls – which shows that souls themselves do not *constitute* the very force which impels bodies to action or movement. So Leibniz says:

The souls act according to the laws of final causes, through appetitions, ends, and means. The bodies act according to the laws of efficient causes, that is, of motion. . . . Bodies act as though there were no souls . . . ; and . . . souls act as though there were no bodies. (161)

So, while there is no soul without a body and no body without a soul, the two operate distinctly, without interacting with each other, at the pineal gland or elsewhere. They *do* have something in common for Leibniz (as opposed to Descartes, for whom thinking substance and extended substance had no common feature): both are *active* – both are to be characterized in terms of the concept of *force*. And this is something more in common than the fact that the term 'substance' may be used to refer to both – as 'corporeal substance' and 'spiritual' or 'psychic substance.' For it is of the essence of both sorts of substance that they involve a kind of force; though in the one case it is a force which issues in bodily motion, and in the other case it is a force which issues in a succession of psychic states, such as perceptions and appetitions.

Now every finitely existing thing, according to Leibniz, consists of a unity of 'corporeal substance' or body and 'spiritual substance' or soul. In fact, this must be so, given that neither body nor soul is ever to be found without the other. This is not to say that the same soul is always to be found united to the same body. One soul does not move from one entire body to another; but the body with which one soul is associated gradually changes as time passes, so that eventually it might happen that all of the original parts of the body have been replaced with others. 'You must not imagine,' Leibniz says, 'that each soul has a mass or portion of matter forever belonging or attached to it. . . . For all bodies are, like rivers, in a perpetual flux; small parts enter and leave them continually. Thus the soul changes its body bit by bit' (159–60).

One might well wonder, however, how there can be any correspondence between what goes on in the soul and the movements of the body, given that Leibniz has said that each acts according to its own laws, and acts as though the other did not exist. Leibniz does not deny that there is a correspondence between them; we are inclined to believe that there is such a correspondence, and we are right. 'The two realms,' he says, 'that of efficient causes and that of final causes, are in mutual harmony' (161). But we are mistaken in thinking that they actually influence each other, and that this mutual interaction is what explains the correspondence.

Leibniz grants that 'both act as though the one influenced the other' (161); but in fact they do not. They do not because they *cannot*; Descartes's recourse to a point of interaction in the pineal gland is absurd. They cannot interact because bodies can only move and be moved by other bodies; and perceptions and desires can only be stimulated by and give rise to other perceptions and desires. Interaction between the two would seem to be ruled out in principle. Bodily movements can only be explained – and are completely explainable – in terms of the movements of other bodies. And things like thoughts and intentions can only be explained – and are completely explainable – in terms of things like inclinations and dispositions, which are psychic rather than physical or bodily.

Still, it is true that when I write something, for example, I have a certain thought, and my hand makes certain movements; and so we say that I wrote down what I had in mind. Leibniz grants the existence of the correspondence which leads us to say this. But he claims that different explanations must be given for my having the thought and for the movement of my hand. He says:

> There is an infinity of figures and movements, past and present, which contributes to the efficient cause of my presently
> writing this. And there is an infinity of minute inclinations and dispositions of my soul, which contribute to the final cause of my writing. (153)

In short, Leibniz, like Descartes, is a dualist. But while he grants that there is a correspondence of states of the body and states of the soul, he also contends that never the twain shall meet. And there is a further difference between him and Descartes; for he holds that precisely the same situation exists where *all* finite things are concerned, and not just in the case of man; for the same duality of body and soul exists in all cases.

So once again: how is the correspondence of states of the body with states of the soul to be explained? The principle of sufficient reason entails that there must be an explanation. One can't say that the two simply *happen* to correspond. Further: the correspondence cannot be due to the action of anything in the world – any finite existing thing; for finite things *are* just this duality of body and soul, and neither their corporeal nor their psychic aspects are able to bring it about that the other corresponds to it.

It would be conceivable (i.e., logically possible) for this correspondence not to have existed. The idea of bodily states *not* corresponding with states of the soul is not self-contradictory. So the correspondence is not a logical necessity, but rather a contingent truth, which cannot be explained simply by the law of non-contradiction. But it *can* be explained by means of the principle of the greatest perfection. Leibniz holds he has established *a priori* that the greatest possible perfection prevails in the world, since God has created it, and since he is omnipotent, omniscient, and omnibenevolent. It would be possible to imagine a world in which this correspondence did not exist; but such a world, he contends, would clearly be far less perfect than one in which this correspondence *did* exist. And since it was within God's power to create a world in which it does exist, his omnibenevolence led him to do so. The correspondence exists because God has so made the world that it does exist. And the fact that God (in accordance with his omnibenevolent nature) has so ordained things is the sufficient reason for its existence. Thus, Leibniz says, we have

a natural explanation for the union or conformity of the soul and organized body. The soul follows its own laws, and so does the body. They meet by virtue of the pre-established harmony prevailing among all substances. . . . (161)

This may seem to be far-fetched. But certainly it cannot be denied that if God has created all things and is omnipotent, omniscient, and omnibenevolent, he *could* have brought it about that such a pre-established harmony exists. And Leibniz has the merit of recognizing that, if one holds to a dualism of the sort he or Descartes maintains, one cannot consistently contend that soul and body or thinking substance and extended substance can actually interact; and that therefore if there is a correspondence between the states of each – as there undoubtedly is – some explanation of it of a rather extraordinary nature will be required. He contends (and he may well be right) that the only alternative is to reject the dualism which gives rise to the problem in the first place. But he feels that this dualism cannot be denied; the case for it, on his view, is irrefutable. You cannot reasonably reject it simply because you may feel uncomfortable about the conclusion to which it leads. If you reject it, you ought only to do so on the basis of being able to show what is wrong with the case he makes for it.

Now living beings, according to Leibniz, and extended objects generally, are composed of parts, even though as a whole they may form a functional unit, or a single complex 'machine,' to use his rather figurative expression. In fact, they are composed of infinite numbers of parts, since anything extended is infinitely divisible. And each part may itself be viewed as a functional unit or smaller 'machine'; so that, in his words, 'The machines of nature (namely, the living bodies) are . . . machines even in their smallest parts without any limit.' He continues:

> Hence it can be seen that in the smallest portion of matter there is a world of creatures, living beings . . . , and souls. But these living beings most frequently are so minute that they remain imperceptible to us. (159)

As a whole, each functional unit such as an animal or human being has what Leibniz calls a 'dominant soul'; otherwise it would not be a functional unit at all. 'But,' he says, 'the limbs of this living body are full of other living beings . . . , each of which again has its . . . dominant soul' (159).

But despite this infinite divisibility of everything extended, Leibniz considers it to be self-evident – in fact, logically necessary – that there must be some ultimate irreducible elements out of which all compound substances are formed. These he calls *simple monads*. They are not something one could ever discover (e.g., by continuing to divide complex substances) through empirical analysis; their existence is simply a logical necessity, which one discovers by the use of reason alone. It is a logical necessity that every existing complex substance must ultimately consist of real, simple elements. Leibniz says: 'There must be simple substances, since there are composites' (148). His initial definition of a monad is simply that it is such a simple substance: 'The *monad* is . . . a simple substance, which enters into composites; "simple" meaning, which has no parts' (148). The monad in his metaphysics is similar to the point in geometry. You will never arrive at a single geometrical point by dividing lines into smaller and smaller segments; but still, where there is a line, there are points – though an infinite number of them.

Many of the things Leibniz goes on to say about monads are merely logical consequences of the fact that, as completely simple substances, they can have no parts. Only that which has parts is destructible, since destruction involves the separation of parts; therefore monads cannot be destructible. Everything that is extended, has figure or shape, or is divisible, must as such have parts; therefore, where simple monads are concerned, 'neither extension, nor figure, nor divisibility is possible.' (148) Nothing which does not have parts can be affected by the action of something else, since to be affected means at a minimum to have the arrangement of one's parts altered; therefore monads cannot be affected by anything external to them. This holds even in the case of perceiving what is going on around one; for to be able to receive impressions from sources external to one, one must have parts which are affected (that is, moved) in some way by these impressions. So Leibniz says: 'The monads have no windows through which anything could come in or go out' (148). Each monad is thus completely self-contained, and has no way of interacting with any other monad.

Yet the monads must have qualities; 'otherwise,' according to Leibniz, 'they would not even be beings' (148). This is reasonable enough; for if something has no qualities at all, it would be meaningless even to talk about it. Further, Leibniz holds that each monad must differ in at least some of its qualities from every other. For in logic it is a principle that no distinction can be drawn between what are purported to be two things if their complete descriptions are entirely identical. Logically, if their descriptions are identical, then *they* are identical, one and the same. This is the so-called principle of the identity of indiscernibles; and since it is logic which leads Leibniz to conclude that monads exist, he feels it to be necessary to follow the rules of logic in inferring what their natures are.

Next, Leibniz says: 'I take it for granted that all created beings, consequently the created monads as well, are subject to change, and that this change is even continual in each one' (149). This is not a logical conclusion derivable from the idea of a monad alone; it follows only if one accepts certain presuppositions about what distinguishes God's nature from the natures of things he creates. It was long customary to assume that *immutability* is a perfection possessed by God alone; and from this it follows that things less perfect than God cannot be immutable, and therefore are subject to change. This is a view one might wish to challenge. Leibniz, however, accepts it; and much of the rest of what he says presupposes it.

If something is subject to change, and yet cannot be affected by anything external to it, it follows that the changes it undergoes must be due to some '*internal principle*' (149). And this internal principle can only be the particular configuration of qualities which defines the particular monad and sets it apart from others. It cannot be a matter of the parts of the monad rearranging themselves; for they have no parts. All of the changes a monad undergoes thus must be simply the result of the unfolding of its own inner nature. But its inner nature is simply its specific particular character. A complete description of the particular character of a given monad, therefore, would be a complete description of the entire sequence of states through which it passes. Leibniz calls the particular states in this sequence 'perceptions'; and he calls the principle which determines 'the passage from one perception to another . . . *appetition*' (150).

Now 'perception' and 'appetition' and the other terms Leibniz uses in this connection, 'apperception or [self-]consciousness,' are obviously terms borrowed from our descriptions of the various types of our own mental processes. And it is not clear what his justification is for applying these terms to the internal changes of state in monads, which are something logically inferred rather than something which we discover ourselves to be. Leibniz may be reasoning that, since these are what *our* internal states are, and since monads are the simple substances of which we are ultimately constituted, these must be what *their* internal states are too. If these states are found in us, then they must also be found in the ultimate constituents of all compound substances, since otherwise we could not account for the existence of these internal states of perception, appetition and self-consciousness in ourselves.

There may be something to this line of reasoning; but I have my doubts. Leibniz would hold that the psychic phenomena associated with the soul cannot be explained if something similar does not go on in the monads. But it is one thing to say that *something similar* must go on, and another to say, as he does, that 'there is nothing else to be found in the simple substance but perceptions and their changes' (150). For this would seem to be to regard the monads as much more similar to *little souls* of the sort we attribute to animals and ourselves than we have any right to do, at least without further argument, which Leibniz does not give.

At any rate, these monads for Leibniz are the simple elements of which all finite things are complexes. They are what God created, when he created the world. And when he created them, he created them in such a way – one might say, he 'programmed' them in such a way – that they relate to each other as they do, and form the complexes they do, in a pre-established harmony. Since they are incapable of really interacting with each other, the order which exists among them cannot have come about in any other way. Leibniz says that the 'influence of one monad upon the other . . . can take effect only through the intervention of God'

(156). But this does not deter him from regarding the relations of the monads to each other as very complex indeed. Although it happens only by means of the pre-established harmony, he contends that this harmony is so extensive that every monad in the universe stands in a relation to every other.

But there is one final twist. No monad – and therefore no soul – is capable of being affected by anything external to it. And so, while Leibniz speaks of 'perceptions' in both cases, no monad – and no soul – is really perceiving anything external to it when it perceives. Each is like a person alone in his own movie theater. What each sees correlates with what every other sees, because the movies they are all seeing are correlated. But the perceptions of each are really only the unfolding of the inner nature of each. To change the metaphor, each sees only what it has been programmed at the outset to see; only, in creating the world, God has correlated the programs in such a way that the program of each is integrated with the programs of all.

Of the many strange things Leibniz is led to assert, this would certainly seem to be the strangest of all. Yet here, as elsewhere, he took his conclusion to be an inescapable one – a logical consequence of premises and principles which no reasonable person could deny. But there sometimes comes a point when seemingly sound premises and principles yield such strange conclusions that it is good policy, not simply to reject the premises and principles out of hand, but rather to take another look at them, and reconsider whether they are really as sound as they may at first have seemed.

CHAPTER III

SPINOZA

It would be hard to think of two philosophers whose lives were more different than Leibniz's and Spinoza's. They were contemporaries, and discussed their work with each other on several occasions; but it is not difficult to see why a close relationship between them did not develop. Leibniz was a man of the world, who moved easily in European society, cultivated relationships with everyone of any importance, and was anything but disdainful of wealth, power, fame and the pleasures of life. Spinoza, on the other hand, lived in almost complete isolation from the European establishment and high society. This was owing partly to the fact that he was a Jew, in a society in which Jews generally were more or less outcasts; and partly also to the reputation he acquired of being a heretic and an atheist, which led virtually everyone to repudiate and vilify him. It seems odd to us that he was considered an atheist, since God figures so centrally in his philosophy; but he certainly was heretical, even to the Jews. For he rejected the traditional Judeo-Christian conception of God, and went so far as to speak interchangeably of 'God or nature' – which, to those who held that nature was God's *creation*, amounted to a denial of the existence of God as traditionally conceived.

But Spinoza's isolation was not solely due to his rejection by European society. It was also of his own choosing. As the first pages of his essay *On the Improvement of the Understanding* make clear, he not only did not desire wealth, power and fame, but moreover regarded them (and sensual pleasure as well) as things which could only interfere with the highest good in life, which for him was something very personal and inward. He once was offered a professorship at Heidelberg University, but declined it on the grounds that it would have interfered with his independence and with the tranquility and solitude which he felt the highest good in life required. While Leibniz constantly interjected his personality into his work, Spinoza sought complete anonymity, and published virtually nothing under his own name in his lifetime. He was not independently wealthy, but rather earned his livelihood as a lens-grinder, and lived very ascetically. He received a large inheritance from his wealthy father, but renounced it, on the grounds that it would have imposed responsibilities on him which he did not want, and would have compromised his independence. He died in 1677 – at the age of only 45 – of consumption, despised as a dangerous heretic by both the Christian and Jewish communities of Europe; and it was only after more than a century had passed that people began to revise their opinion of him, and to see his true greatness.

Leibniz may have been more brilliant; but he applied himself to too many different things, and never had the patience to work out his system in detail, and to resolve the many problems which arose because of his piecemeal approach to it. Spinoza's *Ethics*, on the other hand, is one of the most remarkable metaphysical systems in the entire history of philosophy. It is all-encompassing in its scope, and worked out – in elaborate detail – with the greatest rigor and precision, leaving no loose ends. In these respects it makes the work of Descartes and Leibniz look feeble by comparison.

Yet, curious as it may seem, Spinoza's motivation in constructing this system was a very 'existential' one. The concern which led him to undertake its development was a very passionate personal one, which – oddly – was very similar to the basic concern of the most vehemently anti-systematic philosopher of all: Kierkegaard. One can even use Kierkegaard's expression to describe it: a profound desire for an 'eternal happiness' – a happiness so secure that no change of worldly fortunes could shake it, and so great that no worldly loss could undermine or overwhelm it. So Spinoza says that he began by attempting to determine whether 'there might be anything of which the discovery and attainment would enable me to enjoy continuous, supreme and unending happiness.' (3)

Like Kierkegaard, Spinoza holds that experience shows that 'all the usual surroundings of social life are vain and futile' where this is the issue (3), whichever of them one might consider: wealth, honor, fame, sensual pleasure, or anything else which consists in 'the love of what is perishable' (5). And, like Kierkegaard, his disillusionment with all attempts to achieve an enduring happiness which involve the pursuit of anything 'perishable' leads him to look beyond what is perishable, to what is eternal. Thus, as Kierkegaard does, Spinoza winds up concluding that only 'the love of God' can enable one to achieve such a happiness, and that this is an entirely inward thing. Only, unlike Kierkegaard, God for him is not something distinct from the world itself, but rather is identical with the underlying structure of the world, or 'nature'. Further-more, unlike Kierkegaard, he holds that the proper relationship to God is to be attained not through the renunciation of reason and by a 'leap to faith,' but rather through the most rigorous employ-ment of pure reason conceivable. 'The chief good,' he says, 'is the knowledge of the union existing between the mind and the whole of nature. This, then, is the end for which I strive' (6).

Since this end consists in the attainment of the highest and truest sort of *knowledge*, it becomes necessary to determine what method must be followed in order to achieve it. Such knowledge, if it is to *be* such knowledge, must be both completely certain and completely clear and adequate to its objects. So, Spinoza, says, 'A means must be devised for improving the understanding and purifying it . . . , so that it may apprehend things without error, and in the best possible way' (7). This is his project in the essay *On the Improvement of the Understanding*; the 'method' he discusses there is to be the 'means' he speaks of. In the *Ethics*, he presents the results he achieves by means of it, and their conse-quences. One should always keep in mind his reason for under-taking the entire enterprise. In his words:

> love towards a thing eternal and infinite fills the mind wholly with joy, and is itself unmingled with any sadness, wherefore it is greatly to be desired and sought for with all our strength. (5)

With this in mind, one can understand how Spinoza was able to renounce his inheritance and positions of honor and influence, to endure his ostracism by Jews and Christians alike, and to accept the fact that he had no followers, and what must have seemed the likelihood that his writings would never achieve any recognition. These things meant nothing to him. He wrote only because he wished to help anyone he could to attain to the inner joy he had found. The fact that others rejected his views made him sad – not for himself, however, but for them. For his own part, he needed nothing more than the knowledge he felt he had achieved to be supremely happy. What may seem to us to be an incredibly abstract metaphysical system with little 'relevance' to our lives was to him something *personally* more important and more valuable than anything else it is within our power to achieve. The relevance, he would insist is there, and is enormous – if only you have the eyes to see it.

Program and method

Spinoza's philosophical program is at one level similar to that of Descartes and Leibniz, and at another level different. It is different in that, for Spinoza, what might be called 'the existential stakes' are greater than they are for either of the others, even though they too felt that their philosophies were of more than merely theoretical importance. For Spinoza, the attainment of an unshakable and enduring happiness depended upon the completion of his program. Descartes and Leibniz still had faith to fall back on for this; but Spinoza did not. If the 'existential stakes' are set aside, however, his program does resemble Descartes's and Leibniz's; for it involves the attempt to achieve an all-inclusive system of knowledge relying primarily on reason rather than empirical data, which would be entirely certain from its foundations to its particular conclusions.

Spinoza agrees with Descartes and Leibniz that we cannot be said to have any knowledge that is truly worthy of the name unless complete certainty is attainable. To know something is either to know it with complete certainty or not really to know it at all. But under what conditions is complete certainty possible? Spinoza is by no means satisfied with a subjective kind of certainty. Merely 'feeling sure' is not enough; for everyone has had the experience of feeling sure that something is the case, only to find out that the matter is otherwise than one thought. There is only one criterion of genuine certainty: logical necessity. Only logically necessary propositions are absolutely certain; and therefore only logically necessary propositions, or propositions logically deduced from logically necessary propositions or simple definitions, qualify as genuine knowledge. Spinoza says:

> I call a thing *impossible* when its existence would imply a contradiction; *necessary*, when its non-existence would imply a contradiction; *possible* . . . , when the necessity or impossibility of its nature depends on causes unknown to us. . . . (19)

Of those things of which (so far as we can tell) neither the existence nor the non-existence would imply a contradiction – either a self-contradiction or a contradiction with something previously established – we can have no genuine knowledge. We can truly be said to know something only when we can demonstrate the existence of some state of affairs is either logically necessary or logically impossible. Otherwise, any assertion we make, however plausible it may seem, may turn out to be wrong, and so cannot qualify as knowledge. The first criterion to be satisfied, therefore, is that of logical necessity. Knowledge of the world must be as certain as is knowledge of a theorem in geometry, or else it is not knowledge at all. And it is not enough simply to have true belief about something that happens to be logically necessary; one cannot be said to know it unless one sees the logical necessity. If you have been told and believe that the sum of the squares of two sides of a right triangle is equal to the square of the hypotenuse, you are right, but you cannot be said truly to *know* it unless you know the proof.

But certainty is not the only criterion of genuine knowledge for Spinoza. There is also another: if knowledge is genuine, it must be *adequate* to the thing known. It is not enough to see the logical necessity with which one proposition follows from another; one must also have a completely adequate grasp of the natures or essences of the things referred to in them. For example, if you are told that all animals are mortal, and that all men are animals, and that therefore all men are mortal, you may perceive the logical necessity of the conclusion, since you may know that all syllogisms of that form are valid; but your knowledge will be less than adequate if you do not have an adequate grasp of the essences of the things mentioned.

So when Spinoza proposes to list what he calls 'all the modes of perception,' with a view to determining which of them will be the one to rely upon for the attainment of the result he has set out to achieve, it is obvious which one he will select. He finds that there are basically four such 'modes of perception':

I. Perception arising from heresay. . . .
II. Perception arising from mere experience. . . .
III. Perception arising when the essence of one thing is inferred from another thing, but not adequately. . . .
IV. Lastly, there is the perception arising when a thing is perceived solely through its essence, or through the knowledge of its proximate cause. (8)

Hearsay obviously is not to be relied upon; the so-called knowledge it yields is neither certain nor adequate. And the same holds true of mere experience, and the so-called empirical knowledge resulting from it; for while it may teach us that certain particular events have occurred, it neither establishes the necessity of any connection of one type of thing with another, nor shows us the essential nature of anything. Spinoza says:

Its results are very uncertain and indefinite, for we shall never discover anything in natural phenomena by its means. . . , unless the essence of the things in question be known first. Wherefore this model also must be rejected. (11)

What distinguishes the third and fourth modes of perception Spinoza mentions from each other is the matter of adequacy of the grasp of the essences of the things in question: 'The fourth mode alone apprehends the adequate essence of a thing without the danger of error' (11). His examples of knowledge of this sort – genuine knowledge – are: 'When, from knowing the essence of mind, I know that it is united to the body. . . ; that two and three make five, or that two lines each parallel to a third are parallel to one another, etc.' (9). It is interesting to notice that two of these examples are drawn from arithmetic and geometry; for this illus- trates the fact that for Spinoza, as for Descartes and Leibniz, mathematics provides the epistemological standard for metaphysics.

How, according to Spinoza, is one actually to proceed? Here it is necessary to distinguish two methods – one which must be employed at the outset of metaphysical inquiry, and the other which may be employed once certain crucial results are achieved, to bring the whole of knowledge into an orderly system. The first, which might be called the *ascending* method, is that upon which Spinoza concentrates in *On the Improvement of the Under- standing*. Its purpose, as this title suggests, is to improve the under- standing of the individual to the point that a knowledge of the most fundamental matters of metaphysics is achieved. In describing it, Spinoza says:

The intellect, by its native strength, makes for itself intellectual instruments, whereby it acquires strength for performing other intellectual operations, and from these operations gets . . . the power of pushing its investigations further, and thus gradually proceeds till it reaches the summit of wisdom. (12)

This 'summit of wisdom,' which is reached at the end of the method or process of 'ascent,' consists principally in a knowledge of the nature of God and his identity with the world, insofar as we are capable of such knowledge. But this is not how Spinoza proceeds in the *Ethics*. There his method might be described as the *descending* method. In this case he begins by stating these truths about God and the world in the form of definitions, and proceeds to draw out their logical implications for more particular matters. These two methods do not contradict each other; on the contrary, for Spinoza they complement one another. The method of ascent takes us to the point that we can grasp the validity of the basic premises from which all else is then deduced in accordance with the method of descent. The former is that with which metaphysics begins; the latter is that with which it is completed. I will be dealing mainly with the *Ethics*, and this will mean working within the framework of the definitions and axioms Spinoza there sets out. But it is important to see that these definitions and axioms are not ones he simply adopts arbitrarily. On the contrary, he considers their validity to be established by the method of ascent which he describes in the essay I am now considering.

Spinoza agrees with Leibniz in rejecting Descartes's suggestion that we cannot rely upon any of our ideas without a demonstration of their reliability, which Descartes tries to give by proving that God exists and is not a deceiver. Like Leibniz, Spinoza agrees that many of our ideas – and in particular, those which derive from sense-experience – are not to be taken as certain. But also, like Leibniz, he recognizes that by placing *all* of his ideas in question, Descartes gets himself into a skeptical predicament which he then cannot legitimately get out of; for to do so, he must make use of some of the very kinds of ideas he has placed in doubt. Spinoza holds that either we possess some ideas the truth of which is unquestionable and not to be doubted, or else all genuine knowledge is impossible. And he contends, with Leibniz, that the former is the case. It is simply a fact, in his words, that 'we possess a true idea.'

His use of the particular article is somewhat misleading, in that it suggests that he has in mind Descartes's *cogito ergo sum*. What he really has in mind is that we have some ideas which are based simply on logical principles, and in particular, upon the law of non-contradiction. And he holds that the law of non-contradiction is something which simply is not to be questioned. Anything which is just a matter of logic may be accepted as true without the slightest hesitation. And anything which follows logically from the definition of something is valid – provided, of course, that the definition is itself logically sound. In short, we may proceed without having first to prove that there is no evil genius who might be leading us to think that something logically follows whereas in fact it does not. If this involves making an assumption, very well; Spinoza is prepared to make it. Only he would add that making it is the presupposition of attaining any knowledge whatsoever, and that anyone who refuses to make it is not to be taken seriously. He says:

> If there yet remains some sceptic, who doubts of our primary truth, and of all the deductions we make, taking such truth as our standard, he must either be arguing in bad faith, or we must confess that there are men . . . [of] complete mental blindness, either innate or due to misconceptions. (17)

The first part of the method Spinoza is describing consists simply in recognizing that we have ideas which are logically necessary, that logical necessity is precisely the standard of truth, and that any idea which is logically necessary is true, while any idea we may have which falls short of logical necessity also falls short of truth. The next steps are to sort out those of our ideas which are logically necessary from those which are not; and then to proceed to increase our store of logically necessary ideas by analysing complex ideas into their components, logically deducing their consequences, and determining their logical interrelations. In this way, fiction may be set aside, false ideas exposed and laid to rest, and doubts dispelled.

The second part of the method Spinoza is describing does not come after the first, but rather goes along with it. It concerns fixing upon 'good definitions,' so that the criterion of adequacy as well as that of logical necessity will be satisfied.

> The best basis for drawing a conclusion will be either some particular affirmative essence, or a true and legitimate definition. . . . Thus the true method of discovery is to form thoughts of some given definition. . . . Wherefore, the cardinal point of all this second part of method consists in the knowledge of the conditions of a good definition, and the means of finding them. (34–5)

Now it is obvious that here something over and above the law of noncontradiction is involved; for a good definition is more than simply a non-self-contradictory one. Spinoza says: 'A definition, if it is to be perfect, must explain the inmost essence of a thing, and must take care not to substitute for this any of its properties' (35). And here, at least to some extent, it is necessary to rely upon experience in addition to logic. For it is only through experience that we get the ideas of the things whose 'inmost essence' our definitions are supposed to state. But this does not mean that we determine this essence through empirical investigations. We have ideas of things; and we have the ideas we do because these things – or at least the simple things of which they may be compounds – in reality exist. But the way to determine their essences, once we have the ideas, is through what might be called conceptual analysis, rather than data-gathering in the manner of the empirical scientist.

In this connection, there are several important points to be made. On one level, Spinoza may be said to hold to a *coherence* theory of truth. That is, he holds that the only way to determine whether an idea is true is to see whether it is consistent with certain other ideas we have. The criterion of its truth is not whether it happens to correspond to some actual state of affairs, but rather whether (if it is a complex idea) it is a logical consequence of other, simpler ideas; or whether (if it is a simple idea) it is logically consistent with and connected to our other simple ideas. The objective of metaphysics is to achieve a complete system of ideas which forms a logically related totality; and to say that an idea is true is ultimately to say that it occupies a place in this logically coherent system.

But on another level, Spinoza subscribes to a *correspondence* theory of truth; for while the criterion of the truth of an idea is not its correspondence to some particular actual state of affairs, he holds that this logically coherent system of thought corresponds to the actually existing world. It is not within the power of the mind, he contends, spontaneously to generate the ideas it has. The soul cannot, 'by its unaided power, create sensations or ideas unconnected with things' (22). On the contrary, he holds that at least for every simple idea we have, there is some actually or objectively existing thing of which this idea is a subjective representation. 'As regards a true idea,' he says, 'its subjective effects in the soul correspond to the actual reality of its object' (32). In his view, ideas are nothing but subjective reflections of objectively existing things; and it is simply absurd to suppose them to have any reality or existence independently of existing things.

This may be seen, he maintains, if one analyses the essence of an idea. Of course, we may think of something which is not now present, and we may invent ideas of things which have never existed; but we can do so only by drawing upon ideas which we have previously experienced, which *did* reflect existing things. 'The idea in the world of thought,' he says, 'is in the same case as its correlate in the world of reality' (15). It is important to add that

74

he is *not* holding that things exist independently of our *perception* of them just as we *perceive* them to be; he is not a naive realist. His point is that things have the same *essential structures* in reality as they have in our thought. But he takes it to follow from this that since 'an idea must, in all respects, correspond to its correlate in the world of reality,' our ideas may 'reproduce in every respect the faithful image of nature' (15–16). And by means of this assumption, Spinoza bridges the gap between his system and reality.

God, nature, substance

The first part of Spinoza's *Ethics* is entitled 'Concerning God'; but it might just as well have been entitled 'Concerning Nature,' since for him the two terms turn out to be interchangeable. And it would have been still better if it had been entitled 'Concerning Substance'; for this term is the most basic of the three. Indeed, it develops in the course of the discussion that there is but one true substance, which may alternatively be designated either as 'God' or as 'Nature.' One might wish that Spinoza had avoided speaking of 'God' altogether, since as he himself points out, this term has associations which must be rejected. He retains the term because the 'substance' he conceives to exist does have a significant number of features common at least to the scholastic theological conception of God; and he applies the term 'God' to this 'substance' because on his view there is nothing else to which to apply it. But he avails himself of it at the cost of no little confusion on the part of anyone who is not careful to keep in mind precisely what he means by it.

Before getting into his discussion, it is necessary to say a few words about his notion of 'cause.' While his use of this term is not completely different from ours, it does differ from our ordinary use of it today to some extent. When Spinoza speaks of 'cause,' he has in mind roughly the same thing Leibniz does when he speaks of a 'sufficient reason.' What one does when one states the 'cause' of something is to give an *explanation* of the fact that it exists and has the character it does. To say that there must be some cause of everything that exists and every state of affairs in the world is to say that there is an explanation for everything being the way it is. Spinoza, like Leibniz and their predecessors, takes it for granted that this is so.

In this connection, he distinguishes conceptually between two classes of things. We can conceive of things whose existence and characteristics and particular states are to be explained in terms of things other than themselves. And we can also conceive of things whose existence and characteristics and states may be explained by reference to themselves alone. Things of the latter sort may be termed *causa sui* – causes of themselves; while things of the former sort are not their own causes. Something is *causa sui* only if its existence and *all* of its characteristics and *all* of its particular states follow from its own essential nature. If it is capable of being affected in any way by anything other than itself, or if its existence presupposes the existence of anything else, it is not *causa sui*. Leibniz's monads satisfied the first of these criteria; but none of them, with the exception of the supreme monad, God, satisfied the second. The other monads were said to have 'no windows through which anything can either come in or go out'; but their existence was explained by reference to something other than themselves: namely, to God. An adequate conception of a monad, therefore – one which said everything needing to be said about it to explain it completely – would be independent of the conception of any other created monad; but it would of necessity make reference to the conception of something other than itself – that is, God.

Now as has been observed, the central notion in the first part of the *Ethics* is that of 'substance.' Traditionally, in philosophy, substances have been conceived as things capable of existing independently of other things – as opposed to qualities, for example, which cannot exist simply by themselves. The crucial notion here is tht of independent existence. And philosophers' ideas about what things are and are not substances have varied, depending on what things they have taken to be capable of independent existence, and also on how strictly they conceived 'independence.' For example: what about ordinary physical objects? In some loose sense, they are capable of independent existence. Yet they are affected by each other; and many of their particular states and characteristics are the results of their interactions with and relations to other objects. This has led some philosophers to conclude that they cannot strictly be considered substances, since they do not really exist entirely independently of each other.

Further: what about the fact that ordinary objects are capable of dissolution and destruction? It might be thought questionable whether things capable of dissolution should be termed substances, strictly speaking, since their existence as units is only a more or less temporary affair, and is not really independent, but rather is dependent upon favorable conditions. So, for example, Leibniz concluded that the only true substances in the world are the simple monads, which are neither affected by each other in any way, nor capable of dissolution.

But if one *really* presses the point, and carries the requirement of independence to its logical conclusion – as Spinoza does – one must deny the term 'substance' to anything which is not *causa sui*. For something cannot be said to be truly independent of everything else unless its very existence may be explained solely by reference to its own nature, rather than by reference to something other than itself. In other words, for Spinoza, neither Descartes's finite extended and thinking substances nor Leibniz's created monads could truly be said to be substances. But the only kind of thing whose existence may be explained solely by reference to its own nature would be a thing the non-existence of which would logically contradict its own essential nature. Either there is such a necessarily existing being, therefore, or there is no true substance at all. This much follows simply from a strict construal of the notion of a substance. But notice that, as yet, nothing has been said to establish that *there is* a substance (or are substances) in this strict sense of the term.

The same point may be made in connection with Spinoza's introduction of the term 'God' into the discussion. He does so in a definition – Def. VI: 'By *God*, I mean a being absolutely infinite – that is, a substance [in the above sense], consisting in infinite attributes.' So far, nothing has been said about whether such a substance exists. And this point also applies when Spinoza goes on to argue that one substance cannot be produced by another substance, and that there cannot be two or more substances having the same attribute or essential characteristic. This is all a matter of drawing out the logical consequences of the definitions. And notice that it follows from the proposition that there cannot be two or more substances having the same attribute, that *if* there *is* a 'substance consisting in infinite attributes,' then this would exclude the possibility of there being any substances other than God, strictly as a matter of logic. Other substances could not exist, because if they did, they would have to have some attributes, and these would be the same as some of God's; and such a situation has already been ruled out. So, once he has given his proofs that such a God exists, Spinoza immediately draws the consequences that 'Besides God no substance can be granted or conceived' (I: Pr. XIV); and that, accordingly, 'Whatever is, is in God' (I: Pr. XV).

It is in Prop. XI that Spinoza asserts that God, or a substance consisting of infinite attributes, exists, and moreover necessarily exists. In supporting this proposition, he refers to an earlier one, which states that 'Existence belongs to the nature of substance' (I: Pr. VII). The first proof of God's existence he offers runs as follows: (1) To conceive of God is to conceive of a substance. (2) Existence belongs to the nature of substance. Therefore (3) God cannot be conceived except as existing; to conceive him as not existing would be absurd – it would involve a self-contradiction to deny that he exists. Therefore he exists.

As it stands, this is a good argument – precisely because the main problem is supposedly already taken care of; that is, it supposedly has already been established that 'Existence belongs to nature of substance.' But has it? What is Spinoza's argument for it? The proof he gives certainly does not do the job, for it consists merely in arguing that since a substance by definition cannot be produced by anything external to itself, it must, if it exists, be *causa sui*; its existence would have to follow from its very nature, since it could not, *qua* substance, be dependent upon something other than itself for its existence. But does it follow, from the fact that I have the idea of a being which is *causa sui*, that such a being actually exists? When Spinoza says, in Axiom VI, that 'A true idea must correspond with its ideate or object,' this might be taken to mean that he would hold there must be an object corresponding to my idea of a necessarily existing being, accounting for my idea of it; this would be an argument similar to Descartes's first argument for God's existence. But Spinoza does not actually argue in this way. This may be either because he simply takes the result for granted, as obvious, or because he does not wish to argue in this way. If he does not wish to argue in this way, however, it is difficult to see how he can use Prop. VII to establish that God exists.

Some light is shed on this problem by Axiom VII, which states: 'If a thing can be conceived as non-existing, its essence does not involve existence.' This would seem quite reasonable. And it has important implications for the issue under consideration. For Spinoza asserts in Prop. VII that it is part of the idea of a substance that it exists; he says, 'its essence necessarily involves existence.' And this would seem to imply that he holds that one cannot conceive of a substance as non-existing. And from this it would follow that if it is possible to conceive of a substance – as Spinoza obviously holds it is – then it must be conceived as actually existing. This is rather like Leibniz's version of the ontological argument. It does not involve treating existence as a *perfection*; but it does involve treating it as a predicate, which may be included in the definition of a substance. Here again, therefore, we have proof of God's existence which stands or falls with the legitimacy or illegitimacy of regarding existence in this way.

Spinoza has several other proofs of the existence of God or a 'substance consisting of infinite attributes.' The second of his proofs involves a rather strange premise: namely, 'A thing necessarily exists, if no cause or reason be granted which prevents its existence.' Given this premise, then, Spinoza says, one may reason as follows:

> If, then, no cause or reason can be given, which prevents the existence of God, or which destroys his existence, we must certainly conclude that he necessarily does exist. If such a reason or cause should be given, it must be either drawn from the very nature of God, or be external to him. . . . But substance of another nature could have nothing in common with God (by Prop. II), and therefore would be unable either to cause or to destroy his existence. . . . God's own nature . . . [does not] involve a contradiction. . . . Therefore, God necessarily exists. (52)

Now this argument may go through, once the initial premise is granted; but why should it be accepted? It would not seem to follow from Spinoza's more basic premise (which is essentially the principle of sufficient reason) that, 'Of everything whatsoever a cause or reason must be assigned, either for its existence, or for its non-existence.' This may be granted, and yet it may still be doubted whether 'A thing necessarily exists, if no cause or reason be granted which prevents its existence.' For this to follow, we would have to posit a Leibnizian striving for existence on the part of all possibles, for which Spinoza provides no argument. If the premise is modified by substituting the word 'substance' for 'thing,' so that it states, 'A substance necessarily exists, if no cause or reason be granted to prevent its existence,' then it becomes more reasonable. And this is really all Spinoza needs, since it is a substance whose existence is in question. But then it becomes clear that this second proof is really simply a restatement of the first, and stands or falls with it.

Spinoza's third proof is stated in two versions; and in both versions it is very obscure indeed. One version is *a posteriori*; that is, it makes reference to a fact of experience – namely, our own existence. The other version is *a priori*. It is the less complicated of the two; but it is none the clearer for that. It is stated as follows:

> As the potentiality of existence is a power, it follows that, in proportion as reality increases in the nature of a thing, so also will it increase its strength for existence. Therefore a being absolutely infinite, such as God, has from himself an absolutely infinite power of existence, and hence he does absolutely exist. (I: Pr. XI. N).

It would not be particularly fruitful to spend the time necessary on this proof in order to clarify it. I will only observe that it involves the very questionable assumption that every possibility strives for existence, with a strength proportionate to the relative perfection of the possibility. I know of no way to make this assumption seem plausible; and so I will conclude that if Spinoza has a valid proof of the existence of God, or of a 'substance consisting of infinite attributes,' it is the first; and if that proof is not valid, then he fails to establish that there is a substance which satisfies his definition. (Consider, however his Prop. I: 'Substance is by nature prior to its modifications.' Given that there are things which are not substances, and given that things which are not substances are modifications of substances, and given also this proposition, it could be argued that it would follow *a posteriori* that at least one substance must exist. But Spinoza does not argue in this way.)

If Spinoza's proof (or some other) is accepted, however, some very remarkable conclusions follow. In particular, it turns out to be necessary to revise both our ordinary notion of what God is like, and our ordinary notions of what the world is like and what its relation to God is. In connection with the first point, I would call attention to the Appendix to the first part of the *Ethics*. Spinoza's discussion of the origins of our traditional conception of God leaves very little to be added; and it is astonishing that such seemingly modern insight was possible in the seventeenth century. Spinoza was determined to base his understanding of what he calls 'God' solely on rational argument, and to reject any part of the traditional conception of God that is inconsistent with the understanding of God's nature he achieves through reason and logical argument. And this meant rejecting some very basic things, such as the notion of God as a *personal* God who cares about each individual, the notion of a divine plan for the individual and for the world, and the idea that God is capable of acting as he pleases, suspending the laws of nature for his purposes.

In place of this familiar God, Spinoza speaks of a God who is not to be distinguished from the world as a whole, which traditionally was regarded as God's free creation. In place of a God whose intellect, will and goodness could be understood as analogous to our own (only much greater), he says that these terms cannot be applied to the God of which he speaks in anything like the senses in which we apply them to men. In place of a God who acts according to what we call 'freedom of the will,' Spinoza argues that God is determined in all that he does by the necessity of his essential nature, and could not act any differently. He does call God 'free,' and in fact says that God 'is the sole free cause.' But what this means, as he goes on to say, is that 'God alone exists by the sole necessity of his nature . . . , and acts by the sole necessity of his nature' (I: Pr. XVII: Cor II). God is free only in the sense that he is not determined by anything external to himself; though he *is* free in *that* sense, since he (and he alone) is *causa sui*. But he has no freedom in the sense of caprice; all of his actions are strictly determined, even if what determines them are the laws of his own nature.

Translated into terms of the world, Spinoza is saying that nothing whatsoever happens in the world that is not strictly determined in accordance with laws. He claims to show, 'more clearly than the sun at noonday,' that 'there is nothing to justify us in calling things contingent' (I: Pr. XXXIII: N.I). Everything that happens, he holds, is logically necessary, either with respect to its essence or with respect to its existence or with respect to its cause. It is only 'in relation to the imperfection of our knowledge' that we take some things to be contingent. Spinoza sums up what he has to say about 'the nature and properties of God' at the beginning of the Appendix to Part I:

I have shown that he necessarily exists, that he is one: that he is, and acts, solely by the necessity of his own nature; that he is the free cause of all things, and how he is so; that all things are in God, and so depend on him; lastly, that all things are pre-determined by God, not through his free will or absolute fiat, but from the very nature of God. . . .

The world and things

If, as Spinoza argues, there *is* one substance, and if there cannot
be two or more substances, then it follows that everything that
exists must in one way or another be a part of that one substance.
For if there were something that were independent of that one
substance, it would have to be another substance or part of another
substance; but since there cannot be two or more substances,
everything that exists must be a part of the one substance. And
since this one substance can be called either God or Nature, one
can therefore say either that 'Whatever is, is in God,' as Spinoza
does in I: Pr. XV, or that everything is a part or aspect of Nature.
This last way of putting the point may sound quite uncontroversial;
but one must keep in mind that for Spinoza Nature must be
conceived as one and indivisible – a single substance, rather than
a collection of distinct and independent substances.

This has several important consequences. First, any form of
ontological dualism is ruled out; for dualism is the thesis that there
are two distinct and irreducible types of substance or kinds of
being – for Descartes, thinking substance and extended substance;
for Leibniz, body and soul. But any such dualism is obviously
excluded if there is one and only one substance.

Second, it follows that, since thought and extension or soul and
body are not distinct substances, they must be simply two different
aspects of the one true substance – or, in Spinoza's words, two
'attributes of God [or nature]' (I. Pr. XIV: Cor II). It is quite true
for Spinoza that, as both Descartes and Leibniz observed, thought
or ideas are not to be reduced to extension or things, and vice
versa; and that the existence of a particular thought is to be
explained solely by reference to other particular thoughts, and that
the existence of particular things or states of affairs is to be
explained solely by references to other particular things or states
of affairs. But on his view it does not follow from this that we are
dealing here with two different kinds of substance. This does not
follow, because that conclusion or interpretation was ruled out
along with the possibility of two or more distinct substances. Given
that there is just one substance, only one interpretation is possible:
namely, that we are here confronted with two irreducible attributes
of a single substance, which is simply being regarded in two
different ways. So Spinoza says: 'Substance thinking and substance
extended are one and the same substance, comprehended now
through one attribute, now through the other' (II. Pr. VII: N.).

Third, it follows from this that there is no problem about the interaction or correspondence of thought and extension or soul and body. For they are not two different things, but rather merely two different aspects of one and the same thing. Descartes, with his pineal gland, and Leibniz, with his pre-established harmony of soul and body, were driven to these lengths because they wrongly concluded that thought and extension or soul and body represented two different substances, and then found themselves faced with the difficult problem of how to put them back together again. For Spinoza, on its own terms the problem is insoluble; but it is only a pseudo-problem, which is to be *dis*solved, rather than solved, by seeing that it arises only because of an error. And he would deny that a similar problem arises in his own case, of accounting for the correspondence of thought and extension viewed as two aspects or attributes of the one substance; for this would be a problem only if it were possible for them to vary independently of each other. Things can vary independently of each other, however, only if they *are* independent of each other; and they cannot *be* independent of each other unless they are distinct substances. But thought and extension are not distinct substances. Therefore they *necessarily* correspond to each other; and so their correspondence is nothing problematical, and requires no further explanation.

Fourth, this enables one to see why Spinoza holds that there is no problem about the relation of our ideas to things. But he stipulates that 'By ideas I do not mean *images* such as are formed at the back of the eye, or in the midst of the brain, but perceptions of thought.' (II: Pr. XLVIII: N). He states that they correspond in an axiom (I: Ax. VI): 'A true idea must correspond with its ideate or object.' But he could just as well have stated this as a corollary to the proposition that 'Substance thinking and substance extended are one and the same substance.' For our ideas are precisely instances of the 'thinking' he is talking about when he argues that thought and extension are but two attributes of the same substance which necessarily correspond.

For Spinoza it is not necessary to prove that God exists and is good before one may conclude that our ideas correspond with things, as it is for Descartes; or to prove that a pre-established harmony prevails between states of the soul and bodily states before one may arrive at the same conclusion, as it is for Leibniz. All that is necessary is to observe that, since there can be but one substance, and since it must be all-inclusive if it is to *be* the only substance, it follows that thought in general – and our ideas in particular – cannot be regarded as possibly distinct from it. The suggestion that our ideas might not correspond to the way the world really is, is a suggestion which presupposes the independence of thought from the world. If thought were something independent of the world, however, there would have to be more than one substance. But there cannot be two or more substances. Therefore, our ideas *must* correspond to the rest of the world. Or, at least, our 'true ideas' must. Spinoza does not mean to deny that some or even many of our ideas are inaccurate. He is speaking only of ideas which conform to the standards of 'good definitions' and logical soundness. But this is not to say that our erroneous or fictitious ideas have some other source. Their components, at least, correspond to things too; the only trouble with them is that they are either confused or compounded in ways that are not logically sound.

In connection with this general line of argument, I would simply make the following comment. Given that there is only one substance, and that therefore everything – thought included – must be regarded as some attribute or some modification of an attribute, it *would* seem to follow that our distinct and logically sound ideas would correspond to things. But the same line of reasoning *cannot* legitimately be used to establish that, since it follows from Spinoza's definitions and axioms that there is only one substance, there really is only one substance. You cannot assume that there is only one substance in your proof that there is only one substance. And Spinoza does not do this. He rather relies simply upon the logical consistency of his definitions and axioms and propositions, and upon the claim that his definitions satisfy the criteria of good definitions, and are the only consistent set capable of providing us with a coherent account of reality. They *would* appear to be logically consistent. In evaluating them, therefore, one must consider, first, whether his further claims about them are sound; and second, if so, whether it follows that reality must actually have the character they suggest.

But now let us return to the further implications of Spinoza's basic contentions for the nature of what we ordinarily call the physical world, or the world of *things*. (The term 'world,' as used here, is to be distinguished from his term 'Nature,' which is more comprehensive in that it is synonymous with 'God' or the one substance, and so comprehends thought as well as things.) It is quite legitimate, according to Spinoza, to speak of 'things,' as long as one does not make the mistake of construing them as distinct substances. The world for him is not 'the aggregate of finite things' *as opposed to* God who created them, as it is for Leibniz (and Descartes). Rather, it is the one substance considered under the attribute of extension; and all 'things' in the world are in fact particular modifications of the single all-embracing substance considered under the attribute of extension.

As such, the world cannot be considered God's *creation*, if this is taken to imply that it is something distinct from God himself. Rather, the world *is* God himself, considered under the attribute of extension. It may be said to be God's creation only in a figurative sense, in which this is understood to mean that the existence and natures of particular things are determined by the laws of God's nature; but these are simply the laws immanent in the world itself, or in the one substance itself *qua* extended. God may be said to be the 'cause' of the world; but this is not to be taken to mean that he is the *first cause* of the world, who brought it into existence by an act of will. Rather, it should be understood to mean that God is the *explanation* for the world being as it is; and *this* is to be understood to mean that the explanation for the world being as it is is to be found in the fact that God (or the one true substance) is determined by the set of laws whch define or follow from his (or its) essential nature.

In point of fact, Spinoza holds that the world cannot really be said to have been 'created' at all, if this is taken to imply that there was some time at which the world did not exist. On the contrary, he holds that it must be eternal, since God's nature must be considered eternal, and since God's nature entails the existence of the world. One cannot conceive of God existing without the world existing, according to Spinoza, if one understands the meaning of these terms properly. So he says: 'God did not exist before his decrees, and would not exist without them' (I: Pr. XXXIII: N. II). For him no less than for Leibniz, the existence of the world requires an explanation. But that explanation is not that at some point God, who is distinct from the world, created it. Rather, the explanation is that the existence of the world is entailed by the nature of the one substance or God, whose existence is logically necessary. In short, for Spinoza, the ontological argument for the existence of God is precisely an argument for the existence of the one substance, which, under the attribute of extension, just *is* the world.

On this view of the world, a number of things logically follow. First, the world must be considered infinite in extension. For, according to Def. II in Part I, something may be considered '*finite after its kind*' only if 'it can be limited by another thing of the same nature.' Thus particular extended things will be finite, since they are limited by the existence of other things of the same nature. But the world itself, which by definition is the one substance considered under the attribute of extension, cannot be 'limited by another thing of the same nature,' since there cannot be 'another thing of the same nature.' This follows from the fact that there can only be one substance. But the world is not infinite without qualification; it is only infinite with respect to extension. It would be infinite without qualification only if extension were the only attribute of substance. The substance itself *is* infinite in this way, in that there is no positive attribute which it lacks; and so it is not limited in the sense of there being attributes which do not apply to it. But there *are* attributes which do not apply to the world as such, since only the attribute of extension applies to it: in particular, the attribute of thought. So we may say that the world is infinite 'after its kind,' though not without qualification.

Second, contrary to Leibniz, Spinoza holds that particular things *may* be said to interact. Since he does not conceive of the world as consisting of an infinite number of windowless monads or discrete substances which by nature *cannot* interact, he has no need of the idea of a pre-established harmony to account for the appearance of interaction. He considers the interaction of particular things to be possible – and, in fact, necessary – precisely because they *are not* and do not consist of distinct substances, but rather are interconnected and interdependent modifications of a single substance or continuum of extension. What is impossible in *his* view is *not* that they interact (which is what Leibniz held to be impossible), but rather that they act independently of each other. For the premise that all things are simply particular modifications of a single all-embracing substance entails that none of them is in any way independent of the rest. If any feature or action of a thing were not completely explainable in terms of its antecedents and associations in the rest of the system, it would have to be explained by saying that the thing is a substance unto itself. But this would mean that there would be more than one substance; and this, according to Spinoza, is a logical impossibility.

At this point it should be acknowledged that his position on the status of particular things *is* rather counter-intuitive. The thesis that all particular things are in fact not independent of each other, but rather really constitute so many different modifications of a single substance, certainly seems strange from the standpoint of common sense. It seems just as strange in its way as does Leibniz's thesis that the whole created world is made up of monads which never affect each other; only the problems in the two cases are almost opposite. For here the problem is not how to deal with the appearance of mutual influence and connection, but rather, how to deal with the appearance of separation and discontinuity.

What makes the problem seem even more difficult is that Spinoza denies that extended substance is divisible (I: Pr. XIII: Cor), and that it is composed of parts (I: Pr. XV: Cor). 'Extended substance,' he says, 'can only be conceived as infinite, one and indivisible' (I: Pr. XV: Cor). This certainly makes it easier to see how he can treat extension as an attribute of God; and it also makes it easier to see how he can treat particular extended things as modifications of a single substance, one of whose attributes is extension. But the problem still remains of dealing with ordinary experience, which would seem to show the world of extended things to be anything but 'one and indivisible.' Spinoza attempts to deal with the matter in the following way:

> If we regard quantity as it is represented in our *imagination*, which we often and more easily do, we shall find that it is finite, divisible, and compounded of parts; but if we regard it as it is represented in our intellect, and conceive it as substance, which it is very difficult to do, we shall then, as I have sufficiently proved, find that it is infinite, one, and indivisible. This will be plain enough to all, who make a distinction between the intellect and the imagination. . . . Matter is everywhere the same, [and] its parts are not distinguishable, except in so far as we conceive matter are diversely modified, whence its parts are distinguished, not really, but modally. (I: Pr. XV: N.)

Now this does not really reconcile our ordinary view with that which Spinoza is proposing. It is only to propose that we distinguish between the imagination – which we employ in forming our ordinary notions or mental 'images' on the basis of our sense-perceptions – and the intellect or reason, which we employ in figuring out logically how things really must be. And Spinoza is saying that we shouldn't be surprised if the two give rise to differing pictures; and that it is by no means a serious matter that they do, as it would be if reason itself came up with these different conclusions on different occasions. Reason is that which we should rely on, since it informs us of what *must*, of logical necessity, be the case. And to the extent that the imagination (which is largely based on the senses) suggests a different picture, that different picture is not to be taken as authoritative. What the senses do is to enable us to make various discriminations which are useful in life; but in order to do this, they need not provide us with an accurate picture of things, so long as they merely enable us to make the discriminations we need to make. In this case, they apparently represent what are actually merely modal variations of a single undivided and unified substance as though they were discrete entities. But how they actually work is of little importance, where knowledge of the basic nature of things is concerned; for that is to be obtained by reason alone.

In short, Spinoza does not even *try* to reconcile our ordinary view of the extended world with his account of it. Rather, he contents himself with showing how it is that the two might differ, and with suggesting that our ordinary view does not have very strong credentials in comparison with those of his account. When it comes to a choice between the imagination and reason, he takes it to be obvious which we ought to accept when knowledge is our concern.

A further logical consequence of the premise that there is but one substance, and that therefore all particular things are simply modifications of this one substance considered under the attribute of extension, is that every existing thing and state of affairs in the world is logically necessary, or completely determined; or, in Spinoza's words: 'Nothing in the universe is contingent, but [rather] all things are conditioned to exist and operate in a particular manner by the necessity of the divine nature' (I: Pr. XXIX). Nothing happens merely by chance; this follows from the principle of sufficient reason. Therefore everything that exists and everything that happens in the world of things must be explained either by reference to its own nature or by reference to God's nature – that is, to the nature of substance under the attribute of extension. But if the existence or nature of something is explainable by reference to its own nature, it is a substance. There can be only one substance; therefore the existence and natures of all particular things are to be explained by reference to God's nature. And they must follow logically and necessarily from God's nature (or the nature of substance), considered under the attribute of extension. For if the explanation of something were to fall short of logical necessity, an element of indeterminacy would be introduced – it *might* have been otherwise – which would be incompatible with the principle of sufficient reason.

Approaching the matter from the opposite direction, Spinoza holds that the one substance or God necessarily exists; that it (or he) necessarily, not contingently, has the attributes it does; that the modes associated with a given attribute follow necessarily (not contingently) from it; and that the particular modifications or forms assumed by these modes are necessarily (not contingently) determined by their natures. Given that this is so, and that particular things are nothing more and nothing less than these modifications, it follows that the existence of these particular things and everything pertaining to them is determined with the strictest necessity. Grant Spinoza's premises, and this conclusion is inescapable.

Spinoza goes on to say, in a manner reminiscent of Leibniz, that 'things have been brought into being by God in the highest perfection' (I: Pr. XXXIII: N. II). In a sense, he is agreeing with Leibniz that this is the best of all possible worlds. But he differs from Leibniz in the way in which he reaches this conclusion. For on his view it is the best possible world because it is the *only* logically possible world; and it possesses the highest perfection only because it 'necessarily followed from a most perfect nature.' According to Leibniz, there were many logically possible worlds any one of which God could have created, logically speaking; and he chose to create this one because his goodness led him to choose the best one possible. Spinoza rejects this whole way of viewing the matter. On his view, if this world were anything less than logically necessary, the principle of sufficient reason would be violated. God had no choice; the existence and nature of this world are strictly determined by the laws of his nature.

How are particular things to be characterized, in relation to each other? According to Spinoza, not only in terms of their figures or shapes, but also in terms of 'motion and rest.' These are the basic 'modes' which qualify extended things. Spinoza says: 'Bodies are distinguished from one another in respect of motion and rest, quickness and slowness, and not in respect of substance' (II: Pr. XIII: N. Lemma I). The degree of motion and rest (or amount of energy) which characterizes a particular single body is a function of its interactions with other bodies. But it is only the simplest bodies which are characterizable in terms of their relative energy alone. More complex bodies must be characterized not only in terms of the relative energies of their components, but also in terms of the relations of their components to each other. Spinoza offers the following definition of a complex body or 'individual':

> When . . . [the] mutual movements [of certain simple bodies] should preserve among themselves a certain fixed relation, we say that such bodies are in union, and that together they compose one body or individual, which is distinguished from other bodies by this fact of union. (II: Pr. XII: N. Lemma III)

Certain relatively simple complex bodies or individuals may combine to form more complex ones; the human body, for example, is held by Spinoza to be a very complex one indeed. But one need not stop with things like the human body; thus he suggests that the whole world may be regarded as 'one individual, whose parts, that is, all bodies, vary in infinite ways, without any change to the individual as a whole.' (II: Pr. XII: N. Lemma. VII: N)

In this way, Spinoza links his view of the constitution of complex individuals out of simpler bodies with his general view of the whole of the world of extension as 'one and indivisible.' One *may* – and perhaps must, for purposes of analysis – regard things like particular human bodies and cells and rocks and microscopic particles as 'individuals' which ultimately consist of simple components. But in reality, these simple components are not discrete, separate, independent substances, such as Leibniz's monads were said to be. Rather (and here, in a way, Spinoza anticipated the conclusions of modern physicists), these simple components have the character of centers of energy, constantly affected by each other, and making up a single system encompassing the whole of the world of extension. This system as a whole neither increases nor decreases, but rather constitutes a single stable unit. Thus it is unitary. And it is indivisible, in that within it there are no parts which are not interconnected with each other. Any division of it into distinct parts is arbitrary and merely conventional, and does not affect the fact that the whole system is a continuum. Within this continuum there are concentrations of centers of energy which we call, and perceive as, particular things; but we should not be misled by the appearance of discontinuity into denying that the continuum exists. And now I would ask: Is Spinoza's conception of the world really so implausible? To the theoretical physicist, at any rate, it might well not seem to be.

Mind and body

In the Preface to Part III of the *Ethics*, Spinoza says: 'Most writers on the emotions and on human conduct seem to be treating rather of matters outside nature than of natural phenomena following nature's general laws.' The same might be said of most writers on our human nature generally. But Spinoza rejects any such way of regarding ourselves, as though we were wholly or partly of supernatural origin; just as he rejects any way of conceiving of God, such that God is thought to be a being radically distinct and apart from Nature as a whole. He goes on to say that there is 'one and the same method of understanding the nature of all things whatsoever, namely, through nature's universal laws and rules.' Man, in other words, is to be conceived in no terms other than those which are applicable to the rest of the nature. We are a part of nature, and nothing besides.

Spinoza thus is committed to what might be termed a 'naturalistic,' as opposed to a 'supernaturalistic,' view of man's nature. His 'naturalism,' however, is not to be confused with 'materialism,' or the view that everything that exists is completely describable in terms of physical properties, such as extension and motion. For there is more to Nature as he conceives of it than extended things in motion, which constitute the 'world' as I spoke of it earlier. The 'world' of things in motion is identical with Nature only insofar as Nature is considered under *one* of its attributes – namely, under the attribute of extension. But it has another attribute – namely, thought; and this attribute is not reducible to that of extension, even though it is not a substance which is capable of existing independently of Nature considered under the attribute of extension. As has already been observed, Spinoza holds that 'substance thinking and substance extended are one and the same substance, comprehended now through one attribute, now through the other' (II: Pr. VII: N.). Thus it is necessary to make reference to thought, as well as to extension, in any complete characterization of Nature in general, and of man in particular.

Given that thought or ideas and extension or things are simply 'one and the same substance, comprehended now through one attribute, now through the other,' it follows, as Spinoza says, that 'The order and connection of ideas is the same as the order and connection of things' (II. Pr. VII). This means that for every thing or modification of extension, there is associated with it an idea or modification of thought, and vice versa. But this does not mean

91

that there are two different orders of *entities*, ideas and physical objects, between which there is a one-to-one correspondence. On the contrary, according to Spinoza, it follows from the fact that thought and extension are simply two different attributes of one and the same substance, that 'a mode of extension and the idea of that mode are one and the same thing, though expressed in two ways' (II: Pr. VII: N.). In the cases of many objects, the associated ideas are consciously apprehended neither by the objects themselves nor by us; that is, they are not self-conscious. But Spinoza holds that all of these ideas must be in God or substance considered under the attribute of thought, just as all of these objects are in God considered under the attribute of extension. God or substance may have other attributes, but these are the only two known to us; which is to say that everything of which we have any experience is either a modification of extension (a body or object or thing) or a modification of thought (an idea), which can only be an idea of some body or object or thing.

It was no less common in Spinoza's time than it is today to think of a human being as a union of a body and a mind. Spinoza is willing to grant this – *provided* that the natures of 'body' and 'mind' and of their union are properly understood. And they are properly understood, in his view, only if they are construed in terms of the foregoing general analysis. Let us consider first the body, then the mind, and then the nature of their union.

With regard to the body: Spinoza does not consider it necessary to *prove* that one's body exists. If I exist, my body exists. For if my thinking establishes that I exist, it also establishes that my body exists. This follows from the proposition that there can be no modification of thought where there is no modification of extension, since the two are simply one and the same thing considered under different attributes. My existence is itself not necessary; as Spinoza states in the first Axiom of Part II: 'The essence of man does not involve necessary existence, that is, it may, in the order of nature, come to pass that this or that man does or does not exist.' But if in fact I do exist, the existence of my body as well as the existence of my thinking is established by the general proposition that thought or thinking things are not substances in themselves, but rather are an attribute (or modifications of an attribute) of a single substance, another attribute of which is extension. And this in turn follows from the proposition that there can be but one substance, and that both thought and extension are attributes of this one substance.

Given that my body exists, Spinoza holds quite reasonably that the same account is to be given of it as is to be given of the nature of bodies or extended things generally. In particular, he makes the following observations, in Postulates in Part II:

> The human body is composed of a number of individual parts, of diverse nature, each one of which is in itself extremely complex. (I)

> The individual parts composing the human body, and consequently the human body itself, are affected in a variety of ways by external bodies. (III)

> The human body stands in need for its preservation of a number of other bodies, by which it is continually, so to speak, regenerated. (IV)

> The human body can move external bodies, and arrange them in a variety of ways. (VI)

And to these points, Prop. VI of Part III should be added: 'Everything, in so far as it is in itself, endeavors to persist in its own being.' In other words, all particular things – human bodies included – have a certain *conatus* or impulse for self-preservation. But like all other particular things, the human body, owing to its dependence upon other things, is destructible or perishable. It persists as long as the order among its parts can be preserved; and it perishes when this order is sufficiently disrupted. All of these claims are contentions with which virtually no one would take issue. Spinoza further holds that the greater the complexity of a certain kind of body is, the greater individuality particular things of that kind will be capable of, and the greater also will be the variety of ways in which it will be capable of being affected by other things. And he contends that the complexity of the human body is perhaps greater than that of any other kind of existing body. Men may not be the largest existing things; but this claim could be substantiated by reference to the complexity of our bodily organs, and in particular, of our brain. It is for these reasons, he suggests, that men are more individuated than are other kinds of things, and that men are capable of greater knowledge than are other kinds of things. But the very complexity of our bodies, which in these respects constitutes an advantage, is in another respect a disadvantage; for it means that we are also more vulnerable than other kinds of things. The more complex an organism is, the more ways there are in which it can be disrupted.

If this is the basic character of the human body, however, what is the nature of the human mind? It is simply self-evident, for Spinoza as for Descartes, that we *think*. 'Man thinks' in his second Axiom in Part II. But what follows? It does not follow, according to Spinoza, that there therefore exists a thinking substance, whose sole and whole essence it is to think. What I discern, when I observe that I think, is what Spinoza calls certain 'modes of thought' – certain ideas. But I do not in addition observe a certain thinking thing, distinct from my body, which is doing the thinking. Spinoza takes this to be so obvious that he simply states as an Axiom that 'We feel and perceive no particular things, save bodies and modes of thought' (II: Ax. V). And he goes on to suggest that there is nothing whatever to warrant the suggestion that in addition to bodies and modes of thought or ideas, there is some third thing, which *has* the thoughts or ideas, and which is conjoined to, or in pre-established harmony with, a particular body. There is no reason to stop speaking of the 'mind' altogether; but, given that all that exists in nature are modifications of extension or bodies and modifications of thought or ideas, our understanding of 'mind' must be modified accordingly.

In particular, this means abandoning the conception of the mind as a substance unto itself, and construing it rather *as* a modification of thought, or idea: a very complex idea, to be sure, but an idea nonetheless, as opposed to something that *has* ideas. We may still say that *man* thinks, and exists in the world; that a man has a body, and has ideas. But this should not be taken to mean or imply that a human being is anything over and above body and idea. What a man really is, strictly speaking, is a certain modification of the one substance; and as the one substance has the attributes of thought and extension, so a man is one thing with the two attributes of thought and extension, idea and body, the two being simply two different aspects of one and the same thing. Indeed, the same may be said of all existing things. Like Leibniz, Spinoza rejects Descartes's contention that all things other than man may be completely characterized simply in terms of extension. Every existing thing, as a particular modification of the one substance, may be considered under the two attributes of extension and of thought. 'The propositions we have advanced,' he says,

> have been entirely general, applying not more to men than to other individual things, all of which, though in different degrees, are animated. For of everything there is necessarily an

idea. . . , in the same way as there is an idea in the human body. (II: Pr. XIII: N.)

This would seem logical, if also rather strange. I will say more about it a little later, to try to render it understandable.

First, however, more requires to be said with respect to our own nature. It is not Spinoza's position that what I call my mind consists of *all* of the ideas I have; for many of these ideas I have are ideas of other things which can in no sense be said to be part of *me*. Every idea has an object, or is the idea of some object. And the object of which my mind *is* the idea is nothing other than my body. In Spinoza's words: 'The object of the idea constituting the human mind is the body, in other words a certain mode of extension which actually exists, and nothing else' (II: Pr. XIII). My mind is nothing in itself, apart from my body; it is simply the idea of my body, as opposed to the ideas of other bodies or things. And it is not something that exists alongside my body, conjoined to it but distinct from it, and capable of existing independently of it, as Descartes took the mind to be. Spinoza says: 'The idea of body and body, that is, mind and body, are one and the same individual conceived now under the attribute of thought, now under the attribute of extension' (II: Pr. XXI: N.). And the fact that I can have an idea of my mind does not mean that it must therefore be something other than an idea. Thus Spinoza continues:

> The idea of the mind and the mind itself are one and the same thing. . . . Strictly speaking, the idea of the mind, that is, the idea of an idea, is nothing but the distinctive quality of the idea in so far as it is conceived as a mode of thought without any reference to the object. (II: Pr. XXI. N.)

Spinoza is not contradicting himself when he later says, in Part III, that 'Body cannot determine the mind to think, neither can mind determine the body to motion or rest. . . .' (III: Pr. II). For his point here is simply that, since the two are really one and the same thing conceived under different attributes, it does not make any sense to speak of either determining the other to do this or that. It only makes sense to speak in this way of things which are to some extent distinct from each other – one body, for example, determining another to move in a certain way. But since mind and body are not distinct individual things, they cannot be said to affect each other at all.

It should now be clear how Spinoza deals with the problem of the interaction of mind and body, which is such a difficult one for Descartes and Leibniz. He does not *solve* the problem, but rather *dissolves* it, by arguing that there is no problem here at all, once one sees that mind and body are one and the same thing. A problem arises only if one mistakenly takes mind and body to be two different things. One may speak of the 'union of mind and body' (Spinoza himself does so); but this union is not a union of distinct substances. It is rather a *unity* – a unity of inseparable attributes of a single individual.

Now just as the human body is very complex, the idea which is the human mind is also very complex. Or, as Spinoza says: 'The idea, which constitutes the actual being of the human mind, is not simple, but compounded of a great number of ideas' (II: Pr. XV). This may go some way toward making Spinoza's contention that the mind is the idea of the body seem more reasonable; and it becomes more reasonable still when he speaks of the human mind as 'the very idea *or knowledge* of the human body' (II: Pr. XIX: Proof). The matter might be put in this way: when we speak of our minds, we can mean nothing other than *ourselves*, insofar as we have knowledge of ourselves. And what we have knowledge *of*, when we have knowledge of ourselves, is our bodies – not simply the perceivable physical features of our bodies, but more importantly the various capacities we have, in virtue of having the bodily structure we do. It is no objection against this view that we know ourselves to be capable of doing a great many things which we cannot begin to account for in terms of our present physiological theories. Our theoretical ignorance does not prove that the activities our philosophical theories do not enable us to explain must have some non-philosophical explanation. To be sure, it may seem odd of Spinoza, given our present relative philosophical ignorance, to speak of the mind in terms of the 'knowledge of the human body.' But there is a very legitimate sense in which one can say that we know what we are capable of doing, even if we cannot explain precisely how it is that we are capable of doing it. And given that there is no justification for conceiving of the mind as anything other than the idea of the body, it is quite reasonable to go on to say that the object being described when we describe what we are capable of doing is just the body, and nothing else.

On this view, the ideas we have at various times are simply subjective reflections of changes in our bodily states. If my bodily state changes in some way, and if my mind is but the complex idea of that complex thing which is my body, then it is only to be expected that this change in bodily state would be reflected in some change in that complex idea which is my *mind*. And this, according to Spinoza, is just what happens in *perception*. Things other than my body impinge upon my body in various ways; and my ideas are modified accordingly. So he says: 'The human mind is capable of perceiving a great number of things, and is so in proportion as its body is capable of receiving a great number of impressions' (II: Pr. XIV). The greater the complexity of the body, the greater the number of ways in which it may be affected will be – and therefore the greater the variety of its perceptions will be. This is at least one respect, on his view, in which 'the human mind differs from other things, and . . . surpasses them.' For, he observes,

> in proportion as any given body is more fitted than others for doing many actions or receiving many impressions at once, so also is the mind, of which it is the object, more fitted than others for forming many simultaneous perceptions. . . .
> (II: Pr. XIII. N.)

This also helps render comprehensible the suggestion that in the case of every existing thing (and not simply ourselves), there is an idea of that thing which stands to it as that idea which is the human mind stands to the human body, in spite of the obvious differences between men and other things – if one takes into account the further proposition that 'The human mind has no knowledge of the body . . . save through the ideas of the modifications whereby the body is affected' (II: Pr. XIX). For the same would hold true of other things as well. And this would account for the great difference between men, with their considerable awareness of themselves; animals, with their much more limited consciousness; and inorganic things, which cannot be said to be conscious at all. For if a thing's 'knowledge of itself' is proportional to the degree to which it is capable of being affected by other things, and if self-consciousness presupposes a very great capacity of this sort indeed, then it is only to be expected that relatively simple things like inorganic objects will not be self-conscious, and that self-consciousness is only to be found in any significant degree in man, whom Spinoza considers to be much more complex than such objects (or mere animals) are. If this does not seem to be an entirely satisfactory explanation of man's relatively unique degree of self-consciousness, one might ask oneself how one could account for it without resorting to some supernatural explanation of the sort that Spinoza rejects. And in this way, he is able to account for man's relative uniqueness in this respect, without having to relinquish either the claim that some modification of the attributes of both thought and extension must apply to every existing thing, or the claim that the human mind just is the idea of the human body.

But it is not only in terms of man's greater power of perception that Spinoza distinguishes man from other things. 'Our mind,' he says, 'is in certain cases active, and in certain cases passive' (III: Pr. I). It is passive to the extent that our particular ideas follow one upon another solely as the result of the operation of external stimuli, or 'according to the order of nature.' It is active, on the other hand, to the extent that the succession of our particular ideas is determined *logically*, in accordance with the laws of logic. The mind can be active in this way only in a state of relative organic equilibrium. Even when in a state of organic equilibrium, most of us (perhaps all of us most of the time), like animals generally, do not really think at all. But the important thing is that, in such a state, the human mind is at least capable of logical reasoning, of arranging its particular ideas in logical rather than merely natural sequence. And in such a case, one achieves a degree of self-determination which is quite unique.

To be sure, this is self-determination in a very restricted sense. All it implies is a degree of freedom from external stimuli. It does not imply that in such states thought is to be regarded as independent of our bodily states. On the contrary, Spinoza holds that even in cases of this sort, our ideas are subjective reflections of our bodily states – and in particular, as philosophers are inclined to say today, of our brain-states. But this physiological basis even of logical thinking does not make it any less true that it is logical rather than determined by external stimuli.

To the extent that mind can become active in this way, it achieves the only kind of freedom Spinoza considers it possible for us to achieve. This freedom is freedom of bondage to external stimuli and natural impulses pertaining to the preservation of our bodily existence. But it is not freedom in the sense of complete spontaneity, or in the sense of the absence of determination by any laws whatsoever. Freedom of that sort, for Spinoza, is a myth; not even God is free in that sense. Our ideas are ordered either by external stimuli and psychological laws, or by the laws of logic. To the extent that they are ordered by the laws of logic, however, we achieve at least an approximation of the kind of freedom enjoyed by God himself. We do not become the causes of our own existence; but just as God is said to be free because he is determined solely by the laws of his own rational nature, we become free to the extent that our ideas are ordered by these same laws. And this *is* a kind of freedom because these laws are not the laws of the nature of a being who is alien to ourselves. For just as Spinoza holds that our bodies are particular modifications of the one substance considered under the attribute of extension, so also he holds – quite logically, given his premises – that our minds cannot be anything other than modifications of the same single substance considered under the attribute of thought.

In conclusion, I would pose two questions. First: It may be that the applicability of Spinoza's initial definitions and axioms and postulates to the actual world is more problematical than he thought. But even if one is inclined to question their applicability to the actual world, on what grounds could one dispute it? And second: If one does so, does this mean that the various particular points he makes are to be rejected? If some of them seem appealing and if one nonetheless rejects the basic principles *he* uses to argue for these points, can they be salvaged and defended by means of different arguments drawing upon different assumptions and principles?

CHAPTER IV

LOCKE

John Locke was a contemporary of both Leibniz and Spinoza. In fact he was born in 1632, two years before Spinoza, and fourteen years before Leibniz. And his most important work, the *Essay Concerning Human Understanding*, was published in 1689 – twelve years after the publication of Spinoza's *Ethics*, but some years earlier than the *Monadology*. Leibniz was by no means unaware of Locke's claims and arguments; in fact one of his longest works (*New Essays on the Human Understanding*) was written directly in response to Locke's *Essay*, arguing against many of Locke's claims. He certainly did not think that Locke's arguments were superior to his own; and one would do well to keep in mind that fact that, to so astute a philosopher as Leibniz, the kinds of considerations presented by Locke were by no means sufficient to undermine the kind of philosophical program he (and the other rationalists) had undertaken. Locke's approach to philosophical problems, and the similar approach of Berkeley and Hume after him, certainly differs from theirs; but the question of which is superior is hardly one which can be answered simply in terms of which came first and which came later (let alone which lived on which side of the English Channel).

It is also of some interest to observe that, of the three, Leibniz and Spinoza were indisputably the more brilliant, and the more original. Their conceit, and Locke's modesty, both had some foundation in reality, even if both were also rather exaggerated. It is hard to imagine either of them saying, as Locke does in his 'Epistle to the Reader,' that for himself 'it is ambition enough to be employed as an under-labourer in clearing ground a little, and removing some of the rubbish that lies in the way to knowledge. . . .' (58). Both Spinoza and Leibniz (like Descartes) set their sights much higher; though they certainly would have agreed with Locke when he went on to say that knowledge would be 'very much more advanced in the world, if the endeavours of ingenious and industrious men had not been much encumbered with the learned but frivolous use of uncouth, affected, or unintelligible terms, introduced into the sciences, and there made an art of . . .' (58–9). Locke no doubt was thinking of philosophical rationalists when he said this, as well as philosophers in the medieval tradition; but Leibniz and Spinoza would have countered that Locke, far from 'removing some of the rubbish that lies in the way to knowledge,' in fact introduced a new impediment to knowledge by his dogmatic assertion that all of our meaningful ideas are nothing but compounds of simple impressions of external and internal sense.

Locke was not a professional philosopher; and, like Leibniz, much of his time and energy throughout his adult life were spent in involvement in public affairs. But, unlike Leibniz, he did not write great numbers of short essays, each expressing some particular idea he was developing at the time. Rather, he spent years working off and on on a small number of lengthy comprehensive and systematic studies. But this was simply his methodical English way of proceeding. Unlike Descartes, Leibniz and Spinoza, he was not motivated to write the *Essay* by the desire to develop an all-embracing metaphysical system, in which everything from God to man to the world would be dealt with systematically, and within the context of which a reconstruction of the foundations of the sciences on the model of mathematics could be effected. Rather, his interests were primarily epistemological. 'My purpose,' he says, '[is] to inquire into the original, certainty, and extent of *human knowledge*, together with the grounds and degrees of belief, opinion, and assent' (I: I: 12). For, as he remarks in the 'Epistle,' it seemed to him that 'before we set ourselves upon inquiries of [a metaphysical] nature, it [is] necessary to examine our own abilities, and see what objects our understandings [are], or [are] not, fitted to deal with' (56).

In point of fact, Locke does ultimately have a good deal to say about the things which make up the world, the human mind and man's nature, and even the existence of God. But for him, the scope and extent of possible human knowledge are much more problematical than they are for the philosophers discussed; and it is because he feels that possible human knowledge is limited in ways they did not recognize that he is so much more restrained in his metaphysical claims than they are. In this way, he began a tradition of distrust toward metaphysics, and of emphasis upon epistemological considerations, which has characterized subsequent English-language philosophy up to the present day. And surely his basic point is sound: we must determine the scope and limits of our cognitive abilities before we proceed to try to discover the natures of things. Otherwise our reach will exceed our grasp; and the results we achieve will not be genuine knowledge at all, but rather merely groundless and very likely misguided speculation. The other side of the coin, however, is that if we take our cognitive abilities to be more limited than they really are, and thereby impose undue restrictions upon ourselves, we will be depriving ourselves of knowledge which it is in fact within our power to achieve. And this, according to critics of Locke in the rationalist tradition (beginning with Leibniz), is just what Locke did.

Program and method

Locke could content himself with his relatively unambitious program (metaphysically speaking), because he did not take nearly so much to depend upon the attainment of metaphysical knowledge as the rationalists did. In particular, it did not seem to him that a degree of certainty comparable to that achieved in mathematics needed to be introduced into the foundations of the sciences, in order to set them apart from mere belief, and to render them worthy of the name of knowledge. And he did not share Spinoza's feeling that enduring happiness was to be found only in the knowledge of imperishable and eternal truths, and therefore only in metaphysical knowledge. With regard to the latter: the kind of passion Spinoza had for the absolute, and for that profound happiness which unity with it alone can afford, is something which Locke either never felt or learned early to suppress. Moreover, he had Christian revelation to fall back upon – a short-cut to ultimate truth which Spinoza rejected.

It is with regard to the former consideration, however, that Locke breaks most decisively with the program of rationalism. The rationalists had been dominated in their thinking by the model of mathematics. For them, mathematics provided both an example of how philosophical arguments ought to be constructed, and a criterion of knowledge which was held to be generally applicable. Geometrical proofs were taken to be the model for philosophical arguments; and logical certainty was taken to be the criterion of all genuine knowledge. Locke, on the other hand, was much more impressed with the newly developing physical sciences. To his mind, they had their own standards of truth, and stood in no danger of collapsing into mere belief. Geometry was fine for discovering the properties of geometrical figures; but it was the physicists who were making more and more discoveries about the world. He concluded that if it was knowledge of the world one wanted, one would do better to emulate the physicist, with his emphasis upon empirical data as his starting point and criterion of verification, rather than the geometer, with his non-empirical definitions and axioms as his starting point, and his disregard of empirical data. Locke therefore took the empirical analysis and inductive reasoning of the physicist as the model for his philosophical arguments; and he took the criterion of genuine knowledge, where matters of fact are concerned, to be that which he supposed the empirical scientist employs as he goes about his business; namely, the accordance of theories or ideas with observable data. Descartes attempted to free philosophy from the external restrictions imposed upon it by Christian theology; Locke attempted to free it from what he took to be the alien standards of mathematics.

One might ask, however, whether in doing so he did not simply exchange one set of alien standards for another; or, as a rationalist would argue, whether he did not abandon the standards truly appropriate for metaphysics in favor of those appropriate merely for physics. Leibniz and Spinoza, after all, had not questioned the practical appropriateness of the empirical method in physics. Their contention, however, was that metaphysics and physics deal with differing sorts of questions, which can be answered only by employing the methods appropriate to each, and to which answers different sorts of criteria are applicable. *Of course*, they would say, metaphysical questions are questions which transcend the limits of empirical knowledge. That is why they are called *meta-physical*. What the issue comes down to, therefore, is whether Locke is right in claiming (as he does go on to claim) that empirical knowledge is the only sort of knowledge that is possible for creatures of our kind.

Locke suggests that the kind of inquiry he undertakes in his *Essay* has the twofold justification that it is both pleasant and useful. It is pleasant, in his view, because it does result in the attainment of knowledge, even if that knowledge is knowledge merely of the extent of our own cognitive powers; and because the attainment of knowledge of any sort is something he finds pleasant for its own sake. 'The Understanding,' he says, 'as it is the most elevated faculty of the soul. . . , is employed with a greater and more constant delight than of any other' (55). The usefulness he sees in his inquiry, however, consists largely in putting an end to what he regards as idle, empty speculation about matters beyond our comprehension. He writes:

> I suppose it may be of use to prevail with the busy mind of man to be more cautious in meddling with things exceeding its comprehension; to stop when it is at the utmost extent of its tether; and to sit down in a quiet ignorance of those things which, upon examination, are found to be beyond the reach of our capacities. (I: I: 4)

He does see at least some positive advantage deriving from this, however; for if men can be brought to stop spending their time disputing about matters which cannot be resolved, then once it is established within what limits we *can* achieve knowledge, we can set about to expand our knowledge as far as it can be expanded. And Locke does feel that there is enough we can come to know both to keep us quite busy and to meet our practical needs. 'Our business,' he says,

> is not to know all things, but those which concern our conduct. If we can find out those measures, whereby a rational creature, put in that state which man is in this world, can and ought to govern his opinions, and actions depending thereon, we need not to be troubled that some other things escape our knowledge. (I: I: 6)

The method he proposes to follow, in determining the nature, extent, and limits of human knowledge, is (as he says in the first chapter of Book I) to 'inquire into the original of those *ideas* . . . which a man observes, and is conscious to himself he has in his mind; and the ways whereby the understanding comes to be furnished with them' (I: I: 3). Locke, like all of the philosophers considered, simply takes it to be given that we think, or are conscious of a variety of things. And he uses the term 'ideas' to refer to whatever the contents of our consciousness might be, whenever we are conscious at all. He says: ' "Idea" . . . being that term which . . . serves best to stand for whatsoever is the object to the understanding when a man thinks, I have used it to express whatever . . . it is which the mind can be employed about in thinking.' He continues: 'I presume it will be easily granted that there are such ideas in men's minds; everyone is conscious of them in himself. . . . Our first inquiry then shall be how they come into the mind' (I: I: 8).

This would seem a reasonable enough beginning. For all of the knowledge anyone could suggest we have must obviously consist in certain ideas we have, given that 'ideas' is understood to comprehend everything whatever of which we may be conscious. To know something is to have certain ideas, or to have certain ideas come to mind under the appropriate circumstances. And it should be obvious what Locke's strategy will be, given his stated intention of inquiring 'how they come into the mind' in the first place. For if he can show that all of our ideas are derived ultimately from experience, then he will suggest that it follows that experience alone can be the source of any knowledge it is possible for us to have, and that therefore empirical knowledge is the only kind of knowledge possible for man. Locke is thus taking the question of how we originally acquire the ideas we have to be decisive for the question of what the extent and limits of our knowledge are. As one reads him, therefore, one ought to ask oneself: Is our knowledge in fact confined to combinations of ideas which are derived directly from experience? Or is it possible for our knowledge somehow to extend beyond these limits? Do some of our ideas have a significant meaning or a content which cannot be completely analysed in terms of our impressions of external and internal sense? Or can all of our ideas either be completely analysed in this way, or be shown to be devoid of all meaningful content?

Because Locke approaches this question in terms of 'how our ideas come into the mind,' there seem to him to be only two possibilities: either they all come into the mind through experience (which for him means through the senses or through our introspective observation of the workings of our minds), or some of them are *innate*: that is, 'as it were, stamped upon the mind of men, which the soul receives in its very first being, and brings into the world with it' (I: II: 1). He seems to think that if he can show that there are no innate ideas – no ideas which the mind brings with it into the world at birth – then it will follow that all of our ideas must come into our minds in the course of our development, through experience.

The first book of his *Essay* is thus devoted to an attack on this notion of innate ideas. His procedure is indicated at the outset of Chapter II: 'It would be sufficient to convince unprejudiced readers of the falseness of this supposition,' he asserts, 'if I should only show . . . how men, barely by the use of their natural faculties, may attain to all the knowledge they have, without the help of any innate impressions' (I: II: 1). At the end of the first book, however, he admits that matters are not quite this simple: 'since the arguments which are against [innate ideas] do, some of them, rise from common received opinions, I have been forced to take several things for granted; which is hardly avoidable to anyone whose task it is to show the falsehood or improbability of any tenet' (I: IV: 26). Now it may be that the things he takes for granted are things one would not be inclined to dispute. And it may be that few people find the notion of innate ideas at all appealing. But any time things are taken for granted, deriving from 'common received opinions,' it should be recognized that this leaves the door open for the defenders of a view under attack, if there should turn out to be good reasons for denying some of those things that are commonly taken for granted.

Where his argument against innate ideas is concerned, however, this is not a serious matter; for, with the exception of Descartes's contention that the idea of God must be considered to have been implanted in the mind by God himself, and therefore to be in some sense innate, it would not seem that the views of any of the writers I have been considering necessarily entail a commitment to the doctrine of innate ideas, or innate propositions. The two principal candidates for the status of innate propositions which Locke considers are, first, 'What is, is,' and second, 'It is impossible for the same thing to be and not to be.' But while these two propositions (which might be regarded as statements of the principle of self-identity and the principle of non-contradiction) are assumed by Leibniz and Spinoza from the outset, they do not assert them to be innate, but rather consider them basic principles of all rational thought. And while Leibniz and Spinoza do assume their validity, Locke himself is not at all disposed to deny them. On the contrary, he holds that they may be intuitively seen to be valid as soon as one understands the meanings of the terms involved. So it would not appear that there is anything really at issue here between him and Leibniz and Spinoza. It would not even seem that they would take issue with Locke when he asserts, with regard to these propositions, that 'It is false that Reason discovers them,' and goes on to support this claim in the following way:

> Reason . . . is nothing else but the faculty of deducing unknown propositions from principles or propositions that are already known. . . . So that to make reason discover those truths thus imprinted, is to say that the use of reason discovers to a man what he knew before . . ., [which] is in effect to say, that men know and know them not at the same time. (I: II: 9)

Leibniz and Spinoza were not so naive as to claim that reason can be used to establish the validity of the fundamental principles upon which reason itself depends. Those against whom Locke is arguing in the first book were either writers of lesser intelligence than they were, or else crude caricatures of them.

Locke's main arguments against innate principles do not require much discussion; for the arguments they are designed to counter are not very substantial ones. Against the contention that some principles must be innate because they are universally consented to, he observes, first, that 'Universal consent proves nothing innate ..., if there can be any other way shown how men may come to that universal agreement in the things they do consent in,' as there surely can be (I: II: 3). Second, and more importantly, he observes that such universal consent to the propositions is a myth, since 'there are a great part of mankind to whom they are not so much as known' (I: II: 4). He comments, rather humorously, that 'Such kind of general propositions [as, "It is impossible for the same thing to be and not to be"] are seldom mentioned in the huts of Indians' (I: II: 27). And he goes on to reject the modification of the universal consent view to the effect that 'all men know and assent to them, when they come to the use of reason, and that this is enough to prove them innate.' For he observes, first, that this is empirically false; and second, that even if it were true that men came to assent to them *at the time* that they come to the use of reason, it would not follow that they were innate. For men's assent to them could with greater plausibility be explained simply in terms of the fact that at that time they become capable of recognizing that the truth of the propositions simply follows from the meanings of the terms involved. (Locke considers the claim in question to be empirically false only because he holds that it is only some time *after* men come to the use of reason that they become capable of recognizing this.)

Finally, he rejects the view that the fact that men assent to these propositions 'as soon as [they are] proposed and understood, proves them ... innate.' For, as he observes, 'Even natural philosophy, and all the other sciences, afford propositions which are sure to be met with assent as soon as they are understood' – for example, 'That "two bodies cannot be in the same place" ..., that "white is not black," that "a square is not a circle," that "yellowness is not sweetness" ' (I: II: 18). Yet no one would claim these propositions to be innate. What makes them true, and what gains our assent to them, is our understanding of the meanings of the terms involved. And since many of the ideas mentioned are clearly derived from experience, and therefore are not innate, he suggests that there is no good reason to regard as innate other propositions whose obviousness may be explained in a similar way.

Locke quite rightly observes that 'Principles [cannot be] innate, unless their ideas be innate'; ideas being, in his words, 'the parts out of which those propositions are made' (I: IV: 1). And he argues, quite plausibly, that 'Ideas, especially those belonging to [abstract] principles, [are] not born with children.' For, as he observes, 'There is not the least appearance of any settled ideas at all in [new-born children].' Yet when he goes on to elaborate upon this point, he would seem to go beyond the legitimate conclusion that therefore no ideas may be considered innate, and to assert a stronger thesis. For he continues: 'One may perceive how, by degrees, afterwards, ideas come into their minds, and that they get no more, nor no other, than what experience, and the observation of things that come in their way, furnish them with' (I: IV: 2). And by the end of this chapter, he feels able to draw a conclusion from his discussion which clearly goes beyond saying that none of our ideas are innate. He writes:

> Whatever idea was never perceived by the mind was never in the mind. Whatever idea is in the mind is either an actual perception or else, having been an actual perception, is so in the mind that by the memory it can be made an actual perception again. . . . Whether this be not so I appeal to everyone's observation. (I: IV: 21)

Now this claim is rather tricky. In one sense, it is quite innocuous; for if 'perceived by the mind' is construed in the sense of 'conscious,' then this is only the denial that there can be ideas in our minds of which we are not conscious. (This involves a rejection of the notion of a subconscious; but I will let that pass.) In another sense, however, this assertion is far from self-evident; for if 'perceived' is construed in terms of *sensation*, then this is a denial that there can be any ideas in our minds which do not derive from external or internal sense-experience. Locke would not seem to be aware of the ambiguity; he would seem to mean the statement in both ways. Construed in the latter sense, however, this is not a claim to which everyone would agree – at least, not someone who is not already committed to empiricism. If *this* is one of the 'common received opinions' he is taking for granted, then his argument to the effect that, if no ideas are innate, all are derived from sense experience, is certainly less than conclusive.

Ideas

For Locke, it is simply an obvious fact that we think. He further takes it for granted that to think is to have *ideas* of one sort or another. And, following conventional as well as philosophical usage, he terms that part of us which thinks (and has ideas) our *minds*. What our minds do is think, in the broad Cartesian sense of that term; and what happens when our minds think is that ideas occur in them. But Locke takes himself to have established, in Book I of the *Essay*, that our minds do not bring any of the ideas we have into the world with them. The mind thus is held to be initially quite literally blank. It may by its very nature be capable of performing a variety of operations, such as contemplating, remembering, distinguishing, comparing, and abstracting; but it can only perform these operations when it has some materials on which to perform them – some ideas to distinguish, compare, and so forth. And on Locke's view it is completely devoid of these at the outset. He uses a number of metaphors to characterize it in this initial state – referring to it, for example, as 'the yet empty cabinet' (I: II: 15); and as 'white paper [i.e., a blank sheet of paper], devoid of all characters' (II: I: 2). Elsewhere he uses the expression '*tabula rasa*,' or 'blank slate.' All of these expressions have overtones of passivity; a cabinet just sits there until someone puts something into it – it does not create its own contents. A blank slate or sheet of paper likewise does not come to have things written on it of its own accord; something else must do this. And the same is true of the mind, according to Locke; in its acquisition of its initial simple ideas, and of all subsequent simple ideas as well, he contends, 'the understanding is for the most part passive.' He continues: 'As the bodies that surround us do diversely affect our organs, the mind is forced to receive the impressions, and cannot avoid the perception of those ideas that are annexed to them' (II: I: 25).

Since the ideas we have in our minds are not innate, Locke asks how the mind comes to be furnished with them, and says: 'To this I answer, in one word, from *experience*. In that all our knowledge is founded, and from that it ultimately derives itself' (II: I: 2). And he further holds that there are only two sorts of sources of experience: 'external and internal sensation,' or the bodily senses and reflection upon the workings of the mind upon the ideas deriving from the bodily senses. In a very striking passage, he writes:

... external and internal sensation ... alone, as far as I can discover, are the windows by which light is let into this *dark room* [i.e., the mind]. For, methinks, the understanding is not much unlike a closet wholly shut from light, with only some little openings left, to let in external visible resemblances, or ideas of things without. ... (II: XI: 17)

Here again, Locke avails himself of a vivid metaphor to characterize the mind. His only reason for not claiming the analogy to be exact would appear to be that he supposes the mind to have the ability to actively arrange and combine the contents which it passively receives; whereas a dark room or a closet or a cabinet has no such capacity with reference to the contents which it passively receives.

My concern at the moment is not with Locke's concept of the mind, however, but rather with his theory of knowledge, and in particular, with his analysis of our ideas. And in that passage, as in the first chapters of Book II, he is claiming that we do and can have no ideas which do not derive ultimately either from sense-experience or from reflection on the workings of our own minds. He simply takes it for granted that we are surrounded by a variety of physical objects, which impinge upon our various sense organs, and thereby give rise to sensations. He considers it to be evident from introspection that our minds perform the operations I have mentioned, and others beside. And he further maintains that these are the *only* sources of our ideas. 'These two,' he says, 'external material things, as the objects of *sensation*, and the operations of our minds within, as the objects of *reflection* are to me the only originals from whence all our ideas take their beginnings' (II: I: 4). Indeed, he contends that 'These, when we have taken a full survey of them. . . , we shall find to contain *our whole stock* of ideas; and ... we have nothing in our minds which did not come in one of these two ways' (II: I: 5).

In support of this contention, Locke does not simply refer to his purported refutation of innate ideas. Rather, he issues the following challenge: 'Let anyone examine his own thoughts . . . ; and then let him tell me whether of all the original ideas he has there are any other than of the objects of his senses, or of the operations of his mind. . .' (II: I: 5). This challenge is issued again, in an even stronger form, several chapters later: 'I . . . desire anyone to assign any simple idea which is not received from one of those inlets before mentioned, or any complex idea not made out of those simple ones' (II: VII: 10). Locke is here basing his thesis on his belief that there is no idea one could cite which cannot be shown to derive from one of the two mentioned sources. It follows, of course, that this thesis would have to be abandoned if one *could* come up with an idea, with some clear meaning and some significant content, for which a derivation of this sort could not be given. But Locke is confident that there are no such ideas:

> All those sublime thoughts, which tower above the clouds. . . , take their rise and footing here; in all that great extent wherein the mind wanders. . . , it stirs not one jot beyond those ideas which *sense* or *reflection* have offered for its consideration. (II: I: 24)

I will return shortly to the question of whether this is really so. For the moment I would simply point out that Locke's conclusion rests more on his confidence that his challenge cannot be met than it does on any *argument* against the possibility of any other sort of ideas. Before pursuing the matter any further, however, there are several points that have been touched on briefly which should be considered in more detail.

First of all, Locke considers it important to distinguish between our ideas and things. It is the action of things upon our sense-organs which he takes to give rise to our ideas of things and their qualities. But he contends that we must distinguish 'ideas or perceptions in our minds' from 'modifications of matter in the bodies that cause such perceptions in us' (II: VIII: 7). We commonly say that what we see or touch is some particular thing. Locke contends, however, that what really happens in perception is that we are conscious of a certain idea, which he terms 'the *immediate* object of perception, thought, or understanding.' It may be *produced* by an actual physical object, and may in various ways *resemble* that actual physical object; but it is not that object itself. Our knowledge of the nature of a given physical object is a function of the ideas we have as the result of its action upon our senses; but that still does not mean that what we are conscious of when it acts upon our senses is the very thing itself. *Things* are not in our minds; *ideas* are – even though they may be there because things have affected our bodily senses in various ways. Locke is quite explicit about this: there is 'the immediate object of perception,' which is 'whatsoever the mind perceives in itself,' and then there is the external physical object, which has various qualities, and various 'powers to produce . . . ideas in our minds' (II: VIII: 8).

Locke therefore is not only a *realist*, or one who maintains the reality of physical objects independent of our minds, but also a proponent of the *causal theory of perception.* For the causal theory of perception is precisely the view I have been describing – the view that our sense-perceptions are the mental effects of the actions upon our bodily senses of physical objects which are their causes. Our sense-perceptions and physical objects are 'two very different things. . . , it being one thing to perceive and know the idea of white or black, and quite another to examine what kind of particles they must be, and how [arranged] . . . , to make any object appear [to us to be] white or black' (II: VIII: 2). Having distinguished between them, he says: 'The next thing to be considered is, how they cause us to have the ideas they do;' and his explanation is very clearly a causal one:

> external objects [being] not united to our minds when they
> produce ideas therein. . . , it is evident that some motion must
> be thence continued by our nerves, or animal spirits, by some
> parts of our bodies, to the brains or seat of sensation, there
> to produce in our minds the particular ideas we have of
> them. . . . (II: VIII: 12)

Since he is concerned with the theory of perception, rather than the mind-body relation, Locke does not attempt to explain how it is that bodily processes give rise to mental impressions or ideas; he is content simply to state that they do so, and to leave open the question of how they manage to do it. I should observe, however, that since he would not appear to adopt Spinoza's solution of regarding thought and extension as but two different attributes of one and the same thing, this would seem to be a problem for him. (I will consider his views on mind and body subsequently.)

Next: Locke holds, with regard to our ideas, that 'some of them are *simple* and some *complex*' (II: II: 1). He takes this to be important, not merely because there are some physical objects which are simple and some which are complex, but rather because this distinction enables him to distinguish cases in which our minds are *passive* and cases in which they are *active*. This distinction figures importantly both in his account of how our knowledge of things develops, and in his account of the origin of fictitious and erroneous ideas. It is *simple* ideas, in his view, and simple ideas alone, with which our senses provide us. Our senses provide us with a great variety of particular ideas of various colors, tastes, smells, and the like. All of these are ideas which he suggests 'come into our minds by one sense only.' But there are other ideas, which he also considers simple ideas, which are said to 'convey themselves into the mind by more senses than one' (II: III: 1). He writes: 'The ideas we get by more than one sense are of space or extension, figure, rest and motion. For these make perceivable impressions both on the eyes and touch' (II: V). And there are other ideas which are said both to be simple and to be derived from *all* of our senses: namely, existence, unity, power and succession (II: III: 7 – 9).

It may seem rather odd of Locke to term the ideas in these last two categories 'simple' ideas. His reason for doing so would appear to be that each of them is an idea which cannot be analysed or broken down into other, simple ideas, and which we have not in virtue of combining any others, but rather through direct experience. They are all ideas, he holds, which the mind merely passively acquires, as the result of various impressions it receives. *Complex* ideas, on the other hand, are ideas we come to have by joining together a variety of these simple ideas, either as they occur together in experience, or according to our fancy. To use one of Locke's examples, take the idea of *lead*. The idea of lead is a complex idea; for it may be broken down into a variety of simple components. 'If to substance be joined the simple idea of a certain dull whitish colour, with certain degrees of weight, hardness, ductility, and fusibility, we have the idea of lead' (II: XII: 6). More generally, he states:

> When the understanding is once stored with these simple ideas, it has the power to repeat, compare, and unite them, even to an almost infinite variety, and so can make at pleasure a new complex idea. But it is not in [its] power . . . to *invent* . . . one new simple idea in the mind. . . .' (II: II: 2)

Locke is not merely asserting that the simple ideas he mentions are *logically* prior to complex ideas – that the ideas of qualities, for example, are logically prior to the ideas of physical objects, since the objects are defined and conceived in terms of their various qualities. He is further taking the position that simple ideas are *psychologically* prior to complex ideas; and that even though a complex thing may exist as a unity, we do not perceive it as a unity, but rather immediately perceive only a great number of simple ideas, and out of them construct a complex idea which may more or less accurately correspond to the object. So he says:

Though the qualities that affect our senses are, in things themselves, so united and blended that there is no separation, no distance between them, yet it is plain, the ideas they produce in the mind enter by the senses simple and unmixed. . . . The simple ideas thus united in the same [complex idea of an] object are as perfectly distinct as those that come in by different senses. (II: II: 1)

Now this is a contention with which a Gestalt psychologist would take issue; and it would not seem to be a logical consequence of Locke's causal theory of perception. For even if we have the ideas we do as the result of the action of objects on our senses, it is still true that it usually takes a good deal of effort to sort out the various 'simple' ideas which make up a single complex perception. Locke cannot reply that we really do have all of the simple ideas which go together to make it up, distinct in our minds, only we are not explicitly aware of them as such; for in his polemic against innate ideas, he himself takes the position that it is meaningless to speak of having an idea without being aware of it. This does not mean that his thesis that some of our ideas are simple and some complex must be rejected; but it does raise questions about the view that, as ideas first enter the mind, they are 'simple and unmixed,' and that all of our compound ideas are the result of an active operation of 'composition' on the part of the mind, 'whereby it puts together several of those simple ones it has received from sensation and reflection, and combines them into complex ones' (II: XI: 6).

The thesis that complex ideas presuppose and are dependent upon simple ideas might be defended on logical grounds (though in recent years some philosophers have *disputed* it on logical grounds). If it were strictly a logical point, however, it would have little to do with the theory of perception. If there is some intuitive plausibility in Locke's insistence upon this distinction in his theory of perception, it would seem to derive from the fact that we do have the idea of the color red, and not just the ideas of red things; and the idea of sweet, and not just the ideas of particular sweet things, and so on. But it would seem questionable whether this is enough to establish his thesis that what we are immediately conscious of in external and internal sensation is simple ideas, and that a further operation of composition is required before we have complex ideas. This thesis might be rendered more plausible if it were modified in such a way that these 'simple ideas' were treated as something which we are generally not conscious of as such at all; and that the combination of them into a complex perception for the most part takes place quite unconsciously. But however this may be, it is not decisive with regard to the tenability of the causal theory of perception, or to the validity of Locke's thesis, that we have no ideas which do not derive either from sensation or the observation of the workings of our minds.

The next point to be observed is that, for Locke as for the other philosophers discussed, not all of our simple and complex ideas are on the same footing. A further distinction is to be made, which cuts across his division of our ideas into those which are simple and those which are complex: 'some are *clear* and others *obscure*; some *distinct* and others *confused*' (II: XXIX: 1). Locke's ways of distinguishing distinct ideas from confused ideas is similar to Leibniz's: 'A *distinct* idea is that wherein the mind perceives a difference from all others; and a *confused* idea is such an one as is not sufficiently distinguishable from another, from which it ought to be different' (II: XXIX: 4).

His distinction between clear and obscure ideas, however, is rather different; and the way in which he draws this distinction has important consequences. 'Our simple ideas are clear,' he says, 'when they are such as the objects themselves from whence they were taken did or might, in a well-ordered sensation or perception, present them. . . . So far as they . . . want anything of that original exactness. . . , so far are they obscure' (II: XXIX: 2). Or, somewhat more simply stated: 'A clear idea is that whereof the mind has such a full and evident perception as it does receive from an outward object operating duly on a well-disposed organ' (II: XXIX: 4). And as for complex ideas, they are clear when each of their component simple ideas is clear; while they are obscure if any or all of their component simple ideas are obscure.

This way of distinguishing between clear and obscure ideas obviously is cast in terms of Locke's causal theory of perception. But this is less important in itself than are the implications of defining clear ideas in this way. For if an idea may be said to be clear only if it is either a perception resulting from the action of an object on a 'well-disposed organ' or a recollection of such a perception which is as exact as the original, then it will follow that all ideas which are *not* of this nature are automatically to be considered obscure – and if obscure, then to that extent devoid of significant content.

The consequences of this move should be obvious. Locke has based his contention, that our ideas are all either simple ideas (of sensation or reflection upon the workings of our minds) or complexes of such simple ideas, on a challenge to anyone who would dispute this claim to come up with some idea which cannot be analysed in this way. But, given his criterion of a clear idea, he has ruled out the possibility of coming up with any counterexamples; for any counterexample, as an idea which does not derive directly from sensation or reflection, will by definition be a confused idea and not a clear one, and therefore will not be a legitimate counterexample. 'For surely,' he would say, 'when I issued my challenge, it was a challenge to come up with a counterexample that is a *clear* idea, and not a confused one.' This seems innocent enough, until one realizes that on his criterion of a clear idea, no counterexample is in principle even possible. So, for example, Spinoza might attempt to meet Locke's challenge by citing his idea of a substance, which he takes to be well-defined and therefore very clear; but Locke would deny that this idea is a valid counterexample to this thesis, since the idea of a substance is not one which satisfies his criterion of a clear idea. It is only a confused idea, because it is not an idea 'whereof the mind has such a full and evident *perception* as it does receive from an outward object operating duly on a well-disposed organ.' Thus Locke explicitly says, of the idea of substance:

> since, by those ways whereby other ideas are brought into our minds, this is not, we have no such *clear idea* at all; and therefore signify nothing by the word 'substance' but only an uncertain supposition of we know not what, i.e. of something whereof we have no particular distinct positive idea, which we take to be the substratum, or support, of those ideas we do know. (I: IV: 19)

The idea of substance has a rather curious position in Locke's discussion. It is an idea he himself finds it necessary to make use of, since he does not see how we can get along without the notion of a substratum in all existing things in which all of their particular qualities inhere. But he refuses to grant it the status of a clear idea (and a legitimate counterexample to his general thesis about the origin and status of our ideas), because we never have any direct experience of substance as such, either in sensation or reflection.

Now there is clearly something dubious both about this way of dealing with the idea of substance (that is, making use of it without allowing it to be a genuine idea) and about the way in which Locke precludes the possibility of counterexamples or replies to his challenge in general. He does not worry very much about this, because he feels he is able to account for most if not all of the other ideas which might be cited as counterexamples by showing how we derive them from various direct experiences. But perhaps he should have worried more. For his way of dealing with the idea of substance is troublesome; and it is also questionable whether his explanation of the origin of a number of our other ideas is satisfactory. I refer in particular to our ideas of space, motion, existence, unity, power, and cause and effect. I shall not discuss all of them, or even any of them in much detail; but I will say something about a few of them.

That we have these ideas is not disputed by Locke; on the contrary, he readily allows that we do have them. The issue is whether we come to have them in the fashion he indicates – whether they are really to be deemed empirical ideas. Consider space, for example. We have, Locke grants, an idea of 'pure space.' And he says: 'We get the idea of space, by both our sight and touch' (II: XIII: 2). But we never *perceive* pure space; the idea of space is not an idea we get by the action of some object or objects upon our organs of either sight or touch. All we perceive by sight or touch are certain objects of varying sizes in varying degrees of proximity to each other. But surely it is a far cry from this to our idea of pure space. Can this idea really be accounted for, as Locke contends, by reference simply to perceptions such as these, together with the mental operation of abstraction?

Or consider the idea of existence. Existence, Locke says, is an idea

> suggested to the understanding by every object without, and every idea within. When ideas are in our minds, we consider them as being actually there, as well as we consider things to be actually without us; which is, that they exist, or have existence. (II: VII: 7)

But surely existence is not a feature of ideas or things which we observe along with color, shape, and the rest, through either external or internal sensation. We have the idea of existence; but do we acquire it in anything like the way in which we get the idea of 'red' or 'square' or 'rock' or 'dog'? Do we really get the idea of existence simply from having ideas of this sort, or seeing things of this sort?

Finally, consider the idea of causality, or cause and effect. Locke writes:

> In the notice that our senses take of the constant vicissitude of things we cannot but observe that several particulars, both qualities and substances, begin to exist, and that they receive this their existence from the due application and operation of some other being. From this observation we get our ideas of *cause* and *effect*. (II: XXVI: 1)

But do we really *observe* anything corresponding to these ideas? We have these ideas; but do we observe things or qualities 'receiving their existence from the . . . operation of some other being?' Or do we simply observe something in some state, and then that thing in another state, in the presence, perhaps, of something else? Doesn't our idea of causation go beyond anything we actually observe with our senses? For the time being, at least, these must be left open questions. They do raise doubts, however, about whether Locke's account is adequate. And the point to keep in mind is that if it is not, then we are either going to have to deny these ideas the status of clear ideas with meaningful content, or we must reconsider the thesis that all such ideas derive from sensation or introspection.

Knowledge

Locke holds that all of the ideas we have are derived from experience. But this does not mean that all of our ideas are derived solely from sensation. Some of our ideas are not simply ideas of sensible qualities; for experience affords us also a number of ideas of the operations of our minds *upon* the ideas we derive from sensation. We have, for example, the idea of *perception*; and this is not simply the idea of this or that thing which we perceive, but rather the idea of a mental process or operation, which may have all sorts of sensible things as its objects. In other words, we are (or can be) aware not only of various sensible things, but also of the fact that our minds are engaged in a certain kind of activity when we are seeing or hearing or touching something.

There are a number of activities of this sort – a number of operations of the mind, or mental faculties, as Locke often calls them – of which we find ourselves to be capable through experience. He takes perception to be the most basic of these; for it is through perception, on his view, that we acquire the various ideas of sense which provide the materials for our other mental operations. He regards it simply as that operation whereby we acquire particular simple ideas. 'Perception', he says, 'is only when the mind receives the impression' (II: IX: 2). He observes that in perception our sensations are often colored by our judgments, so that our perceptions to this extent are not strictly identical with our sensations. Unfortunately, however, he does not do much with this interesting observation, which becomes so important for Kant. For the most part he tends to regard perception as the passive reception of simple ideas, and commonly uses the terms 'perception' and 'sensation' synonymously.

It is interesting to observe that, unlike Descartes, though like Leibniz and Spinoza, Locke does not consider perception to be something distinctively human. He remarks: 'Perception, I believe, is, in some degree, in all sorts of animals' (II: IX: 12). He does, however, take it to be 'that which puts the distinction betwixt the animal kingdom and the inferior parts of nature. . . , [which lack] any sensation in the subject, or the having or receiving of any ideas' (II: IX: 11). Locke does not hesitate to grant animals ideas, since they are capable of sensation, and therefore of perception. But while they perceive, it does not follow for him that they are capable of knowledge. For while he holds that perception is 'the first step and degree towards knowledge, and the inlet of all the materials of it' (II: IX: 15), it does not of itself actually constitute knowledge, at least of any very interesting sort. Knowledge is attained only through the operation of a number of other faculties upon the simple ideas derived from it.

The first of these further faculties or mental operations Locke calls 'retention,' which subsumes both our power of 'contemplation' and our power of 'memory' (II: X: 1, 2). But these, according to him, are simply the powers of keeping in mind or recalling to mind some idea acquired through perception; and these operations are held not to transform the original idea itself in any significant way, but rather only to add to it the 'perception' that it was perceived previously. And this faculty too, according to Locke, is one which 'several other animals seem to have to a great degree, as well as man' (II: X: 10).

The next faculty or operation he cites is that of 'discerning and distinguishing between' our various simple ideas – in other words, being able to notice that one simple idea differs from another, and what its character is. This operation too leaves our simple ideas essentially as they were when we first perceived them, as does the next operation he mentions; namely, that of 'the *comparing* them one with another in respect of extent, degrees, time, place, or any other circumstances' (II: XI: 4). Both of these, moreover, are also operations which he takes to be found in other animals as well as men; though he does suggest that man discerns, distinguishes and compares *better* than other animals do.

Beyond these, there are only two further mental operations of which Locke holds us to be capable. Since those already mentioned do not in themselves result in any sort of knowledge, either of general propositions or propositions about particular things, all such knowledge, in his view, is the result of these further two kinds of mental operations. 'The next operation we may observe in the mind about its ideas,' he says, 'is *composition*, whereby it puts together several of those simple ones it has received . . . , and combines them into complex ones' (II: XI: 6). It is through this operation of composition, and only through it, according to Locke, that we arrive at our ideas of particular things, which involve a variety of simple characteristics. Animals are said to be capable of performing this operation too, though not as well as we do.

It is only with respect to the final operation Locke mentions – that of *abstraction* – that he sees a qualitative difference between our mental faculties and those of animals. He traces this difference to the fact that abstraction involves the use of *words*; and that animals 'have no use of words, or any other general signs' (II: XI: 10). But here again, even in this most distinctive operation of the human mind, as Locke conceives it, he holds that the mind is limited to a kind of modification of its simple and complex ideas of sense, and does not really generate any radically new ones. He describes the development leading up to abstraction as follows:

> When children have, by repeated sensations, got ideas fixed in their memories, they begin by degrees to learn the use of signs . . . [and] to make use of words, to signify their ideas to others. . . . The use of words then being to stand as outward marks of our internal ideas, and those ideas being taken from particular things, if every particular idea that we take in should have a distinct name, names must be endless. To prevent this, the mind makes the particular ideas received from particular objects to become general; which is done by considering them as they are in the mind such appearances,

separate from all other existences, and the circumstances of
real existence. . . . This is called *abstraction*, whereby ideas
taken from particular beings become general representatives of
all of the same kind. (II: XI: 8, 9)

Locke here is advancing the thesis that all of our abstract or
general ideas are simply abstractions from various particular ideas
we have acquired through perception. The support he gives here
for this thesis is a rather simple-minded theory about the way in
which language is acquired. If this theory were to be questioned,
however, he would no doubt fall back on the challenge mentioned
previously, for anyone who would dispute this thesis to come up
with a counterexample of a clear idea whose content cannot be
explicated in this way. But the problem associated with this challenge remains, and is a serious one.

This completes Locke's inventory of the mental operations which
the mind is capable of performing upon the ideas acquired through
experience. All of our knowledge, therefore, must on his view be
analysable in terms of one or more of these operations. Before
turning to his discussion of knowledge (in Book Four), however,
mention should be made of several distinctions he makes between
different classes of our ideas. I have already noted his distinction
between clear and obscure ideas, and between distinct and confused
ideas. In addition to this, he suggests that our ideas 'come under
a threefold distinction' with reference to 'things from whence they
are taken, or which they may be supposed to represent.' First, in
his words, they are 'either real or fantastical; Secondly, [either]
adequate or inadequate; Thirdly [either] true or false' (II: XXX:
1). Since, as he himself suggests, it is more appropriate to speak
of 'truth' and 'falsity' in connection with *propositions* than it is in
connection with *ideas*, and since the distinction he draws between
true and false ideas seems to boil down to his distinction between
real and fantastical ones, I will only consider the first two
distinctions he mentions. And there is really very little that needs
to be said about them, other than simply to take note of them.
First, with regard to the distinction between 'real' and 'fantastical'
ideas, Locke says:

By *real ideas*, I mean such as have a foundation in nature; such
as have a conformity with the real being and existence of
things, or with their arch-types. *Fantastical* . . . I call such as
have no foundation in nature, nor have any conformity with

that reality of being to which they are tacitly referred.
(II: XXX: 1)

In other words, a real idea is an idea of something that really exists; and a 'fantastical' or imaginary or false idea is an idea of something that does not really exist. The only point of interest here is that this way of drawing the distinction presupposes both that there is a world existing independently of our thoughts, and that it is meaningful to speak of whether our ideas conform to it. But while others might wish to question these presuppositions, Locke is committed to them, for reasons to be considered below.

Next, with regard to adequate and inadequate ideas, he says:

> Of our real ideas, some are adequate, and some are inadequate.
> Those I call adequate which perfectly represent those
> archetypes which the mind supposes them taken from, which
> it intends them to stand for. . . . Inadequate ideas are such
> which are but a partial or incomplete representation of those
> archetypes to which they are referred. (II: XXXI: 1)

The main use to which Locke puts these distinctions is to mark off simple ideas as a class from complex ideas of particular things. Since he takes the mind to be completely passive in its reception of simple ideas, he holds that simple ideas in general are both real and adequate. The matter is otherwise, however, with complex ideas of particular things or kinds of things. He maintains, first, that 'Complex ideas are voluntary combinations. . . . For those being combinations of simple ideas, put together, and united under one name, it is plain that the mind of man uses some kind of liberty in forming these complex ideas' (II: XXX: 3). And from this it follows that our complex ideas may or may not be *real* ideas.

Second, Locke holds that *none* of our complex ideas of particular things can be known to be adequate. For adequacy is defined in terms of 'perfect representation'; and we cannot suppose that any complex idea we may have of a particular thing completely captures all of its features. 'Those qualities and powers of substances,' he writes, 'whereof we make their complex ideas, are so many and various that no man's complex idea contains them all' (II: XXXI: 8). And what Locke says about our complex ideas of particular things is surely right, given his assumption that the criterion of reality and adequacy of our ideas is their correspondence to things existing independently of our thoughts; not even the rationalists would dispute his point. On the contrary, it is precisely for this reason that they attached little importance to our ideas of particular existing things which are derived from experience. Where they differed from him was in thinking it is possible to achieve a knowledge of the fundamental natures of things generally, otherwise than through perceptual experience; namely, through rational argument from self-evidence premises. If anything is questionable in what Locke says about real and adequate ideas, given his presupposed realism, it is his contention that all of our simple ideas are both real and adequate; for this contention assumes that the mind is completely passive with regard to them – and this is an assumption that might be challenged.

Now knowledge obviously must have to do with our ideas. Knowledge is inseparable from thought – indeed, it is nowhere to be found except as thought – and thought is an activity of the mind, whose only contents are ideas. This leads Locke to say:

> Knowledge . . . [is] nothing but the perception of the connexion and agreement, or disagreement and repugnancy, of any of our ideas. In this alone it consists. Where this perception is, there is knowledge, and where it is not, there . . . we always come short of knowledge. (IV: I: 2)

At first glance this might seem to imply that knowledge is strictly a matter of the 'connexion and agreement' of some of our ideas with *other ideas*. But this is not what Locke intends. He does maintain that the greater part of our knowledge is simply a matter of observing the connection and agreement of some ideas with others. If there were no more to our knowledge than this, however, then none of our knowledge would be knowledge of anything independent of our thoughts; and so we would have no knowledge of things in the world, let alone of the world in general. But Locke does hold that at least some knowledge of this sort is possible; and when he speaks of the 'connexion and agreement' of our ideas, he has in mind not only their 'connexion and agreement' with other ideas, but also with actually existing things. Accordingly, the 'four sorts' of such 'agreement' he distinguishes are: '1. Identity, or diversity. 2. Relation. 3. Co-existence, or necessary connection. 4. Real existence' (IV: I: 3).

When Locke speaks of 'identity or diversity,' what he has in mind is simply our awareness of the nature of our various ideas and of their difference from each other. Knowledge here is simply knowing 'each idea to agree with itself, and be what it is, and all distinct ideas to disagree.' (IV: I: 4). In other words, it is simply knowledge of what each of our ideas as such (e.g., white, black, triangle, square, table, tree) involves, and of their differences (e.g., that white is not black, that a triangle is not a square, that a table is not a tree).

In speaking of 'relation,' Locke is thinking of the fact that some of our ideas are associated with others in various ways. White and black, for example, are related to each other in a way in which triangles and trees are not related to them; and a tree and a table are related to each other in a way in which a triangle and a rainbow are not. While the names of purportedly real objects may be used here, however, it is not the objects themselves, but rather the relations between the ideas involved that is in question. Such knowledge is simply a matter of the 'connexion and agreement, or disagreement and repugnancy of [various of] our ideas.'

Similarly, it is the connection of various ideas that Locke has in mind when he speaks of 'Co-existence, or necessary connection.' For here he is thinking of the fact that a complex idea – for example, the idea of a chair – consists of the conjunction of a number of simple ideas, which we think of together when we think of a chair. Or, to use his example, one may think of 'that particular sort of yellowness, weight, fusibility, malleableness, and solubility in aqua regia, which make our complex idea signified by the word "gold" ' (IV: I: 6). The sort of knowledge in question here is knowledge of what simple ideas are inseparable parts of a given complex idea; or, to use his word, it is knowledge of what simple ideas necessarily 'co-exist' in a given complex one.

It is only when he comes to his fourth category, of 'real existence', that he speaks of knowledge in connection with anything other than the relations of ideas to themselves and to each other. The first three sorts of knowledge are purely conceptual rather than existential (that is, pertaining to existing things). This sort of knowledge, in Locke's words, is knowledge 'of the actual real existence agreeing to any idea.' To use his example, he says that the proposition ' "God is" is of real existence' (IV: I: 7). Only propositions of the form 'X exists,' or 'there are X's in the world,' or propositions implicitly presupposing some such assertion, pertain to real existence, rather than simply to the connection of one idea with another.

Locke takes these to be the four kinds of knowledge it is possible for us to have; and he argues that there are three different ways in which we may come to have them: through *intuition*, through *demonstration* and through *sensation*. It might seem that, in mentioning intuition and demonstration, he is here extending his list of mental operations discussed earlier; but in fact, these are only different complexes of the operations already mentioned. This becomes clear when one sees what he means by each of them. First of all, he speaks of 'intuitive knowledge' in those cases in which 'the mind perceives the agreement or disagreement of two ideas immediately by themselves, without the intervention of any other.' His examples are 'that white is not black, that a circle is not a triangle' (IV: II: 1). This involves nothing but the perception of the ideas involved (together, no doubt, with the operation of abstraction) and their comparison.

As for 'demonstration': on Locke's account, it does not differ essentially from 'intuition.' The only difference is that the connection of one idea with another is not made directly, but rather by means of the intervention of a number of other intermediary ideas – each of which, however, is intuitively connected with the previous one. 'Each step,' he says, 'must have intuitive evidence' (IV: II: 7). And if each step in a demonstration is itself a matter of intuited agreement, then the operations involved in a demonstration are simply those involved in intuition. This is Locke's analysis of 'that which we call reasoning,' and of what is involved in rational 'proofs' (IV: II: 2, 3). His examples are drawn primarily from geometry, as the paradigm case of reasoning, proof, or demonstration. And he goes on to claim that all of our knowledge of general truths – all of our knowledge, in other words, which is not simply knowledge of the existence of some particular things – is obtained in one or the other of these two ways: 'These two,' he says, 'intuition and demonstration, are the degrees of our knowledge: whatever comes short of one of these, with what assurance soever embraced, is but faith or opinion, but not knowledge, at least in all general truths' (IV: II: 14).

Except for the matter of knowledge of the existence of particular things through sensation, therefore – a kind of knowledge to which he himself assigns a rather inferior position – Locke's account of what counts as knowledge, and of the procedures by which it is acquired, sounds very much like that of the rationalists. For him as well as for them nothing is to be counted as knowledge if it is not completely certain, and if it is not arrived at either through intuition or demonstration. The principal difference is that he restricts the ideas upon which intuition and demonstration may be brought to bear to those which derive ultimately from particular perceptions. But for him as for them, disciplines such as mathematics provide the greatest part of our knowledge; while most of the propositions of natural science cannot be said truly to constitute knowledge. For our ideas of the entities with which the sciences are concerned fall short of adequacy; and the propositions of natural science are neither intuitively nor demonstrably certain.

When Locke comes to consider how far our knowledge extends, insofar as it is attained either through intuition or demonstration, he comes up with results which are much narrower than those of the rationalists, because of the restrictions he places upon the ideas we have to work with. With regard to 'identity or diversity,' he holds that we have an intuitive knowledge of the identity of all of our clear ideas and of the differences between them (IV: III: 8). With regard to 'relation,' he contends that while this is 'the largest field of our knowledge' (IV: III: 18), it is confined to the demonstration of relations of ideas which they have in virtue of their conceptual interconnections and implications. These truths consist largely of the truths of mathematics and other propositions which we today would call analytically true – true by virtue of the meanings of the terms involved. But since these truths merely concern relations between our ideas, they do not constitute knowledge of anything which exists independently of our ideas.

As for 'co-existence or the necessary connection of ideas,' Locke says that 'in this our knowledge is very short' (IV: III: 9). We may observe that a variety of simple ideas occur together, and our idea of a certain kind of complex thing may involve a collection of certain simple ideas; but for the most part we cannot know whether these ideas are necessarily connected with each other, or simply happen to occur together. Locke says: 'The simple ideas whereof our complex ideas of substances are made up are, for the most part, such as carry with them, in their own nature, no visible necessary connexion or inconsistency with other simple ideas' (IV: III: 10). Neither by intuition nor by demonstration, therefore, can we go very far in determining the necessary connection of ideas with each other. And since most of the general propositions of the sciences purport to relate different ideas to each other, this means that to the extent that these propositions are not simply reports of particular experiences, they fall short of being genuine general knowledge. For the ideas they relate for the most part can neither be intuitively grasped, nor be demonstrated to be necessarily connected.

Finally, with regard to real existence, Locke holds that intuition and demonstration together assure us of the existence of only two things: ourselves, and God (IV: III: 21). He does not stop here; for he maintains that we also have knowledge of another kind – 'sensible' knowledge, or knowledge by sensation – of 'objects present to our senses.' But this knowledge does not reach very far. For, first, he contends that knowledge of this sort does not extend to objects which are *not* now present to our senses. And second, he holds that while we can have knowledge *that* these objects exist, we can know relatively little of their true natures.

Thus for Locke the scope of our knowledge is quite restricted, since he supposes (a) that all that we are directly aware of is ideas rather than things themselves, (b) that all of our ideas either derive from perception or are devoid of significant content and (c) that a general proposition cannot be said to constitute *knowledge* unless it is either intuitively or demonstrably certain. Locke is an empiricist, and manifests an attitude similar to that of the empirical scientist in the importance he attaches to experience, and in his unwillingness to accept a logical system deduced from non-empirical principles as a description of reality. Because he holds that what we have before our minds are not things themselves, however, but rather ideas whose exact relation to things is beyond our understanding, and because of his high standard of certainty in determining what does and does not count as knowledge, he winds up – very much like the rationalists – denying that most of scientific and empirical knowledge is really knowledge at all. Only, unlike the rationalists, for him there is no other path to any other kind of knowledge of the natures of things.

God, man, things

Given Locke's view of the nature and origin of our ideas, and of the nature, extent and limits of our knowledge, the question then arises: What can we know concerning the existence and natures of whatever there really is? Here we move from his epistemology to his metaphysics – or at least, to his views concerning God, ourselves, and the world of things. And he does feel that we can achieve a certain amount of knowledge in these matters, despite the limits upon our knowledge he indicates. Since knowledge is a matter of ideas, however, we obviously can have no knowledge of anything of which we have no ideas; and according to him, 'We have the ideas but of three sorts of substances: (a) God; (b) finite intelligences; (c) bodies' (II: XXVII: 2). Even in principle, therefore, we can only have existential knowledge of these three sorts of things.

It is Locke's further contention that we do (or at least can) have genuine knowledge that all three of these things in fact exist. 'I say,' he writes, 'that we have the knowledge of *our own existence* by intuition; of the *existence of God* by demonstration; and of *other things* by sensation' (IV: IX: 2). But it is one thing to know *that* we, God, and other things exist; it is another to know what their natures are. So there are two questions to be considered: How, according to Locke, may the existence of these entities be established? And what, if anything, can we know concerning their natures? I will begin with what he has to say on the matter of our own existence.

It would not really be accurate to say that he provides an *argument* for our own existence; for it is his contention that we have an immediate knowledge of our own existence, and do not infer it from anything else. On his view, nothing is more certain than our own existence – not even that we think or have various perceptions. He writes:

> As for our own existence, we perceive it so plainly and so certainly that it neither needs nor is capable of any proof. For nothing can be more evident to us than our own existence. I think, I reason, I feel pleasure and pain: can any of these be more evident to me than my own existence? . . . If I know I doubt, I have as certain perception of the existence of the thing doubting as of that thought which I call doubt. Experience then convinces us that we have an intuitive knowledge of our own existence, and an internal infallible perception that we are. (IV: IX: 3)

The first thing to be observed here is that Locke is not reasoning as Descartes does. Descartes had argued that my existence is necessarily established by the fact that I think; but my existence is asserted as the conclusion of an argument: 'I think; *therefore* I exist.' For Locke, on the other hand, my existence is not something I *infer* from the fact that I think; rather, it is something I *perceive* (he uses this term a number of times in the passage in question); and it is something I perceive as directly and immediately as I perceive that I think or reason or doubt.

This is the way Locke speaks. Yet one might ask: Just what is it that I am said to perceive? I do not simply perceive 'existence' as such, for there is no such thing as 'existence'; rather, there can only be things which exist. Locke would seem to have to say that what I perceive is *myself* existing. But do I actually *perceive* anything which can be called 'myself'? Do I perceive, in addition to a variety of thoughts and simple and complex ideas, a 'self' which is *having* these thoughts and ideas? Locke says that 'I have as certain perception of the existence of *the thing doubting* as of that thought which I call doubt'; but do I *perceive* a 'thing doubting' as well as the 'thought which I call doubt,' even if this term is construed very loosely?

Presumably the 'self' Locke has in mind is something like Descartes's 'thinking substance'; Locke himself, in Book II, uses the expression 'spiritual substance.' This, if anything, would seem to have to be that the existence of which Locke says that I perceive (or discern). But in Book II, in his discussion of 'spiritual substance,' he explicitly *denies* that we actually perceive any substance at all, 'spiritual substance' included. He writes:

> If anyone will examine himself concerning his notion of pure
> substance in general, he will find he has no other idea of it
> at all, but only a *supposition* of he knows not what *support*
> of such qualities which are capable of producing simple ideas
> in us, which qualities are commonly called accidents.
> (II: XXIII: 2)

He is here speaking about what he calls 'corporeal substance'; but he goes on to say:

> The same thing happens concerning the operations of the mind,
> viz. thinking, reasoning, fearing, etc., which we concluding
> not to subsist of themselves, nor apprehending how they can
> belong to body, or be produced by it, we are apt to think
> these the actions of some other substance, which we call *spirit*
> ...; [this] being supposed to be (without knowing what it
> is) the substratum to those ... operations we [experience]
> within ourselves. (II: XXIII: 5)

Now this obviously creates a problem with regard to what Locke says about our knowledge of our own existence. For if the 'self' is not something we actually perceive, but rather is merely a substratum we are led to *suppose* exists in order to 'support' the various mental processes we perceive within ourselves, then it is hard to see how we can be said to have a direct and intuitive knowledge of its existence. If it is something the idea of which is only inferred, then it would seem that its *existence* is something which we can only infer at best. In short, if what Locke says about the status of our idea of 'spiritual substance' is right, then it is not clear what (if anything) his remarks about our knowledge of our own existence establish.

The existence of God, on the other hand, is something Locke holds may be established by *demonstration*. His proof of the existence of God is not a form of the 'ontological argument,' however, but rather is a version of the 'cosmological argument.' In brief, he argues that the existence of God can be established, along with a number of his characteristics, given only that we ourselves exist, and are capable of perception and knowledge. He takes the existence of an 'eternal Being' to follow from the fact that we ourselves exist. For 'Man knows,' he says, 'by an intuitive certainty, that bare nothing can [not] produce any real being. . . . If, therefore, we know there is some real being [as we do – namely, ourselves] . . . , it is an evident demonstration, that from eternity there has been something' (IV: X: 3).

So far, however, nothing has been said of the *nature* of this 'something' which must have existed from eternity. For all that has been said so far, this 'something' might simply be mere matter. But now, Locke observes, 'a man finds in himself perception and knowledge' (IV: X: 5). And he claims that 'it is evident that what has its being and beginning from another must also have all that which is in and belongs to its being from another' (IV: X: 4). And from this, he says, it follows that 'there has been . . . a knowing being from eternity . . . ; it being impossible that things wholly devoid of knowledge. . . and without perception, should produce a knowing being. . . . For it is . . . repugnant to the idea of senseless matter that it should put into itself sense, perception, and knowledge' (IV: X: 5).

Locke thus holds that there are two radically different 'sorts of beings in the world. . . : First, such as are purely material, without sense, perception, or thought. . . . Secondly, [there are] sensible, thinking, perceiving beings, such as we find ourselves to be.' He calls the second sort 'cogitative,' and the first sort 'incogitative' (IV: X: 9). And because he supposes that something produced by something else cannot have any features which that which produces it does not have, he concludes from the fact that there are 'cogitative' beings (namely, ourselves) that that which produced us must itself be 'cogitative.'

If, then, there must be something eternal . . . , it is very obvious to reason that it must necessarily be a cogitative being. For it is as impossible to conceive that even bare incogitative matter should produce a thinking intelligent being, as that nothing should of itself produce matter. . . . Whatsoever is the first eternal being must necessarily contain in it, and actually have, at least, all the perfections that can ever after exist. (IV: X: 10)

In this way, Locke arrives at the 'certain and evident truth, that there is an eternal, most powerful, and most knowing Being. . . ; and from this idea duly considered, will easily be deduced all those other attributes, which we ought to ascribe to this eternal being' (IV: X: 6). This Being is that which has traditionally been called 'God'; and it turns out to have the very attributes traditionally predicated of God.

The general pattern of this argument should be familiar by now; though Locke does give it a few special twists. I will only make two remarks about it. First, it should be obvious that his argument goes through if, but *only* if, one assumes that things cannot by themselves come into existence out of nothing, *and* that an effect can have no perfection or attribute which its cause does not have. In short, the argument depends upon the validity of a strong version of the principle of sufficient reason. And second, it should be obvious that this creates a problem for Locke. For, given his views about the nature and origin of our ideas, and the nature and limits of our knowledge, it is not easy to see how he can justify his reliance upon this principle. Locke warns time and again against reasoning from abstract principles which are not derived from and established by experience; but it would certainly seem that he is doing just that in his argument concerning the nature and existence of God. A rationalist might say that where Locke goes wrong is not in making use of this principle, but rather in setting forth a theory of knowledge in which the use of such principles is disallowed. But given Locke's theory of knowledge, it certainly would seem that his argument concerning the existence and nature of God is open to objection.

With regard to things other than ourselves and God, Locke holds that their existence can be established neither by simple intuition, nor by logical reasoning or demonstration. But he does feel that a knowledge of their existence is possible in another way – namely, to use his word, through 'sensation.' He is willing to allow that the existence of objects not immediately present to our senses may be doubted, and so cannot be said to be *known*. But, he says, when they *are* immediately present to our senses, 'We are provided with an evidence that puts us past doubting' (IV: II: 14). When he first argues this point, he does so by maintaining that there is an undeniable difference between ideas which we merely remember or imagine, and ideas 'actually coming into our minds by our senses.' 'I ask anyone,' he says, 'whether he be not invincibly conscious to himself of a *different perception* when he looks on the sun by day, and thinks on it by night; when he actually tastes wormwood, or smells a rose, or only thinks on that savour or odour.' And from this he concludes that

> we may add to the two former sorts of knowledge this also, of the existence of particular external objects, by that perception and consciousness we have of the actual entrance of ideas from them. (IV: II: 14)

He subsequently recurs to this argument, contending that a 'man can know the existence of [an] other being . . . when, by actually operating on him, it makes itself perceived by him' (IV: XI: 1). 'It is . . . the actual receiving of ideas from without,' he says,

> that gives us notice of the existence of other things, and makes us know that something doth exist at that time without us, which causes that idea in us, though perhaps we neither know nor consider how it does it. For it takes not from the certainty of our senses . . . , that we know not the manner wherein [our ideas] are produced. . . . This, though not so certain as demonstration, yet may be called knowledge, and proves the existence of things without us. . . . (IV: XI: 2, 3)

But *does* this really 'prove the existence of things without us'? First of all, even if one grants that there is a difference between the ideas we have when we are engaged in the activities we call 'seeing the sun' or 'tasting wormwood' or 'smelling a rose,' and the ideas we have when we are engaged in the activities we call remembering or imagining the way the sun looks, or wormwood tastes, or a rose smells, this *difference* by itself does not establish that in the first set of cases there really are objects independent of us which are causing us to have those ideas. There is a *difference*; but in both cases, according to Locke's own account of the matter, all that we directly perceive are certain ideas. He *says* that in the first cases it is the action of some object upon our senses which produced the ideas we have; this is his causal theory of perception. But how do we *know* that there are objects independent of these ideas which are producing them, since all we perceive – on his own account – are the ideas, which he quite emphatically distinguishes from the things?

This leads into a second point. Locke speaks as though we actually observe the objects acting on us, which action produces the ideas we have of those objects. But we do not have two perceptions simultaneously – one of the idea which is produced by the action of the object, and another of the object which produces the idea. There is only one perception, and it is either the perception of an object, or the perception of an idea which is somehow produced in us. Locke explicitly states, however, that it is always and only *ideas* which we directly perceive. But if this is so, then we do not perceive anything other than these ideas thus producing them. As has been observed, he says: 'It takes not from the certainty of our senses . . . that we know not the manner wherein [our ideas] are produced.' And this is true, where the *content* of our ideas is concerned. But it very definitely *does* make a difference, where the *origin* of our ideas is concerned. If we never experience anything other than our ideas, then sensation itself can tell us nothing what-soever of the origin of our ideas. And the fact that we perceive colors, sounds, tastes, and smells does not by itself 'prove the existence of things without us.' Locke might respond by saying: 'But if *things* do *not* produce these ideas within us, then what does?' To which the only legitimate response, given Locke's theory of knowledge, must be: That's a hard question.

To be sure, it might still be *true* that there *are* objects which exist independently of us, and which produce the ideas we have; but Locke has not *shown* that this is so, and therefore cannot be said to *know* that this is so. Descartes, when he found himself in a similar predicament, came up with the proof to be found in his Sixth Meditation. Locke would seem to be rather contemptuous of this proof, and doesn't think such a proof is needed anyhow. But in point of fact, it would seem that his general position is such that he *does* need one, if knowledge of the existence of things other than ourselves and God is to be achieved. And he doesn't have one. This is a difficulty of which Berkeley and Hume will make much.

If it is assumed that things other than God and ourselves exist, however, the question then arises of what their natures are. And here Locke quite consistently holds that whatever their inner essences may be, our knowledge of their natures is restricted to the ideas we have of them which our senses render us capable of having. He writes:

> Whatever ... be the secret and abstract nature of substance in general, all the ideas we have of particular distinct sorts of substances are nothing but several combinations of simple ideas, co-existing in such, though unknown, cause of their union, as makes the whole subsist of itself. It is by such combinations of simple ideas, and nothing else, that we represent particular sorts of substances to ourselves.
> (II: XXIII: 6)

Locke feels sure that the ideas we have of them are in some way produced by their action on our senses. But for the most part, at least, we are incapable of discovering what it is about these things which makes them produce the particular sets of simple ideas in us which they do produce. Our lack of any knowledge of the essential natures of things is indicated by the fact that, if we *did* have such knowledge, we could logically deduce what all of their properties are, without having to resort to experience; whereas in fact, it is only through experience that we put together our ideas of what properties they have. And, for all we know, if we had more senses than we do, we might well have other ideas of them. All of this goes to show that we do *not* know what their essential natures are, in virtue of which they affect us as they do; but rather, we only have certain ideas of them in virtue of the fact that they happen to affect us as they do. And this means that our ideas of them, and therefore our knowledge of them, fall far short of adequacy.

Among those collections of simple ideas which make up the ideas of substances that we *do* have, Locke distinguishes two classes. First, there are those ideas which correspond to what he terms *primary* qualities of things; and second, there are those which correspond to what he terms their *secondary* qualities. Some of the qualities we attribute to things are qualities the things actually do have, pretty much as we picture them in our ideas of them; these are the *primary* qualities. But we also have simple ideas which are not resemblances of qualities actually in the things themselves. They rather are produced in us by what Locke calls 'powers' in things themselves (actually configurations of primary qualities which escape our apprehension); these he calls *secondary* qualities. So he says:

Qualities thus considered in bodies are, First, such as are utterly inseparable from [them] . . . , [e.g.] solidity, extension, figure, and mobility. These I call original or primary qualities of body, which I think we may observe to produce ideas in us. . . .

Secondly, such qualities which in truth are nothing in the objects themselves but *powers* to produce various sensations in us by their primary qualities, i.e. by the bulk, figure, texture, and motion of their insensible parts, as colours, sounds, tastes, etc. These I call secondary qualities. (II: VIII: 9, 10)

While we may not be able to achieve an adequate knowledge of the natures of material things, therefore, Locke holds that, to the extent that our ideas of them include ideas of their primary qualities, we know at least *some* of their real properties. For, he says, 'The ideas of primary qualities of bodies are resemblances of them, and their patterns do really exist in the bodies themselves' (II: VIII: 15). Thus for Locke there are in the world not only 'spiritual substances' (ourselves) and God, but also extended substances, or bodies, whose properties at least include those various primary qualities he mentions. And since he takes our ideas of these qualities to be 'resemblances' of them, we may at least have some knowledge of what these objects are like, both in general and in particular.

It should be observed, however, that if there is a problem with Locke's argument for the *existence* of such things, there is also a problem of a similar nature which arises here. For it might be asked: if we never directly perceive these objects, but rather only ideas which it is *presumed* originate from their action on our senses, how can we *know* that those of our ideas which Locke calls ideas of primary qualities actually do resemble features of these objects? It may be that extension, figure, motion, number and the like, are inseparable from *our idea* of body or corporeal substance; but how can we establish that that which actually produces our idea *is really* something answering to our idea of body or corporeal substance? In short, as subsequent philosophers were to notice, Locke's contention that ideas are all we ever directly perceive raises doubts not only about his contention that we can know that physical objects exist, but also about his distinction between primary and secondary qualities, and his contention that we can know anything at all about the properties of the objects which supposedly produce ideas of things in us. He does insist that the knowledge we can have of things other than ourselves and God is quite limited; but he believes at least *some* such knowledge is possible. His own epistemology would seem to have the consequence, however, that such knowledge is not possible at all. And this is not because he embraces a standard of complete certainty which cannot in fact be met where physical objects are concerned. Rather, it is because he contends that we never directly perceive anything other than ideas, and that only those ideas which derive from sense-perception and the operations of our own minds have any significant content.

In conclusion, a few words should be said about Locke's view of our human nature. I have already pointed out, in discussing his enumeration of the various operations of our minds, that the only qualitative difference he sees between ourselves and other animals is that we alone are capable of performing the operation of *abstraction*, and therefore are capable of certain kinds of knowledge of which lower animals are not. Locke would appear to accept the Cartesian dualism of material and spiritual substances, with Leibniz's modification. But since he holds that sensation and perception, no less than abstract reasoning, are marks of a 'cogitative' being, it would seem to follow that animals no less than we ourselves are 'cogitative' beings, and therefore 'spiritual' as well as 'material' substances, rather than the latter entirely. Locke does not pretend, however, to have a very clear understanding of the essential nature of a 'spiritual' or 'cogitative' substance, any more than he does of 'material' or 'incogitative' substances. He contents himself simply with taking note of the various operations of which such substances show themselves to be capable. And he also does not pretend to have a solution to the problem of how mind and body are capable of interacting; though he takes it to be an obvious fact that they do. This is something, in his view, which simply surpasses human understanding. He winds up merely saying that 'we can attribute their connexion to nothing else but the arbitrary determination of that all-wise Agent who has made them to be, and to operate as they do' (IV: III: 28). This is hardly more satisfactory than the strange hypotheses of Descartes and Leibniz.

There is much else that is of more interest, however, in Locke's very suggestive discussion of our nature. His main point is that discussions of this matter commonly suffer from a failure to distinguish between the ideas of a thinking or spiritual substance, a person, and a man. The idea of a thinking substance makes no reference to a body; whereas that of a man makes reference both to a thinking substance and to an extended or material substance. And the idea of a thinking substance differs from that of a person, in that the former is completely impersonal, whereas the latter contains the notion of individuality (II: XXVII).

The interest of what he has to say along these lines notwithstanding, however, the soundness and upshot of the arguments he advances with respect to the main issues here (and his formulation of them as well) are problematical at best. In this respect his discussion of them is like his treatments of most of the other matters with which he deals in the *Essay*. Intelligent and commonsensical though his handling of them may be (or at least seem), serious questions and difficulties come to light as soon as one begins to scrutinize the accounts and arguments he gives. It was this discovery that led his successors (Berkeley, Hume, and ultimately Kant) to depart from him and take the differing positions they developed, which in their own ways are no less remarkable than are those of the rationalists.

CHAPTER V

BERKELEY

George Berkeley was born in 1685, eight years after Spinoza's death. Locke was then 53, and Leibniz 41; and both of them were still alive when Berkeley entered college, at the age of 15. He was 19 when Locke died, and 31 when Leibniz died. Thus when he was receiving his philosophical education, and forming his philosophical views, the philosophical scenes in Great Britain and on the Continent reflected their influence. Hume was born when Berkeley was 26, and Kant when he was 39; and when he died, in 1753, Hume was 42, and Kant was 29. Chronologically as well as philosophically, therefore, Berkeley is a transitional figure between the first post-Cartesian philosophical generation and the last two philosophers to be considered.

Berkeley was born and raised in Ireland, and lived much of his life there; but he was of English descent, and always identified more closely with the English than with the Irish. Unlike Locke and Kant, but like Leibniz and Hume, he worked out his basic philosophical position when he was quite young. It was first set forth in his *Principles of Human Knowledge*, which was published in 1710, when he was only 25; and he did not greatly modify his views in his later writings. After this book, his other most influential philosophical work was his *Three Dialogues* – a statement of his views in a more popularizing form, which he also published before he was 30. He continued to do some philosophical writing in his later years; but he became increasingly involved in other activities, perhaps feeling that there was little more to be said about philosophical problems than he had already said, and that there were many matters of a more practical nature which demanded his attention. Among other things, he became quite interested in the New World; and he was also very much concerned to stem the tide of religious unbelief and atheism, and to defend traditional Christianity against it.

In view of his articulateness on behalf of religious orthodoxy, it is not at all surprising that he was made Bishop of the Anglican

Church in 1734. He was Bishop of Cloyne, in Ireland, from then until his death some twenty years later. And he was a very good bishop, devoting a great deal of time and effort to the cause of improving the lot of the poor, with regard to their economic situation, their education and their health. In fact, his interest in matters of health led him to investigate various inexpensive remedies for various ailments, one of which, he concluded, is tar-water. He even published a little book entitled *A Chain of Philosophical Reflexions and Inquiries Concerning the Virtues of Tar-Water*. His judgment concerning the medicinal value of tar-water may not have been sound; but that matters less than his humanitarianism. He was very popular with the people in his bishopric on this account; and it is said that to this day he is revered by the people in the district of Cloyne, who continued to refer to him simply as 'the Bishop,' even though he died over two hundred years ago.

His interest in the education of Blacks and Indians in the New World also consumed a good deal of his time. In fact he spent a number of years in Rhode Island in this connection. When it became clear that the British government was not going to provide any funds for his cause, he returned home. But he left a part of his library and some money to Yale, where one of the residential colleges bears his name.

Program and method

Berkeley's program, in his philosophical writings, is suggested quite clearly by the subtitles of the two main works mentioned and to be considered. On the title page of the *Principles* we read: 'A Treatise concerning the Principles of Human Knowledge, wherein the chief causes of error, and difficulty in the sciences, with the grounds of skepticism, atheism, and irreligion, are inquired into.' And on the title page of the *Dialogues* we read:

> *Three Dialogues between Hylas and Philonous*, the design of which is plainly to demonstrate the reality and perfection of *human knowledge*, the incorporeal nature of the *soul*, and the immediate providence of a *Deity*, in opposition to sceptics and atheists; also to open a method for rendering the sciences more easy, useful, and compendious.

This program, as Berkeley states it here, is very reminiscent of that of Descartes; even if the procedure he adopts in carrying it out, and the arguments he uses in his attempt to do so, are rather different. The more general part of his program is concerned with an analysis of the nature and scope of human knowledge, with a view to providing knowledge with a firm foundation, and to defending the claim that we can have knowledge of the existence and natures of the things against the counter-claims of skeptics. But his more specific interest, like that of Descartes, is to demonstrate conclusively the two points most central to traditional religious thought – namely, that there is a God, and that we have immortal souls.

Like Descartes, Berkeley was not content to fall back on revelation to assure men of the truth of these points. He felt that it was necessary to provide rational proofs of their truth, in order to stem the tide of skepticism and atheism – and further, he was convinced that it is possible to construct such proofs. To work out an adequate theory of knowledge, and to 'render the sciences more easy, useful, and compendious,' is all well and good; for this is both satisfying intellectually and of some practical utility. But Berkeley held it to be of much greater importance that men should not abandon what he regarded as true religion; for, given that there is a God and that the soul is immortal (as he believed), the consequences of denying or failing to recognize these truths are much more fateful for the individual than an inadequate theory of knowledge or an unsatisfactory foundation of the sciences could ever be.

This concern might seem to make Berkeley primarily a theologian (or bishop), and only secondarily a philosopher. But the same might be said of Descartes; and it would be wrong for the same reason. It would be right if Berkeley and Descartes had rested their views about God and the soul on mere faith or revelation. But it is wrong because they do not. Their discussions of God and the soul are philosophically relevant because they base their claims about God and the soul on rational argument. And if arguments about God and the soul are based on reason and direct common experience, rather than on appeals to faith or personal revelation, then they are not merely theological, but philosophical; and a philosopher must take them seriously. Berkeley says, in his Preface to the *Dialogues*:

> It has been my endeavor strictly to observe the most rigid laws of reasoning. And, to an impartial reader, I hope it will be manifest that the sublime notion of a God, and the comfortable expectation of Immortality, do naturally arise from a close and methodical application of thought. (D 221)

Here Berkeley poses the issue squarely; and it is a philosophical one. He holds that the existence of God and the immortality of the soul are rationally demonstrable, and not merely matters of faith. And so, future bishop or not, his discussion is a philosophical one; for he submits his discussion to judgment before the bar of rational analysis and criticism.

His grand design, however, was broader than this, as I have already indicated. He was not content *simply* to argue these points. He was also concerned, as Locke had been, to put an end to what he regarded as the meaningless nonsense so many metaphysicians have uttered on topics which are accessible neither to sense nor to reason – or, in his words, 'to divert the busy mind of man from vain researches' (D 219). (This recalls Locke's assertion (*Essay*, I: I: 4) that he would 'prevail with the busy mind of man to be more cautious in meddling with things exceeding its comprehension.') Both are sharply critical of speculative metaphysics. And this requires not merely the demonstration of the existence of God and the immortality of the soul, but also the presentation of epistemological arguments and principles which undercut *both* groundless metaphysical speculation *and* skepticism about the nature of reality. Both, according to Berkeley, require to be laid to rest; and he has both in mind when he says with a great flourish, in the Preface to the *Dialogues*:

> If the Principles which I here endeavor to propagate are admitted for true, the consequences which . . . evidently flow from thence are, that Atheism and Scepticism will be utterly destroyed, many intricate parts made plain, great difficulties solved, several useless parts of science retrenched, speculation referred to practice, and men reduced from paradoxes to common sense. (D 220)

After a passage like this, no one could accuse Berkeley of being overly modest. It invites comparison with Leibniz, and contrasts vividly with Locke's extreme modesty in his characterization of his efforts in his *Essay*. But then, Locke was 57 when he published his *Essay*; while Berkeley was only 28 when he wrote these lines. And just as young writers today who hit upon an idea which they regard as new and profound tend to have a very high estimate of their importance, while older writers in general tend to be more modest, so it was then; the more things change, the more they remain the same.

Berkeley thus was concerned to put an end *both* to non-empirical speculation about the inner, unexperienceable natures of things, *and* to skepticism with regard to the true natures of things. Both of these viewpoints, though they seem to be diametrically opposed to each other, share an assumption which he rejects; namely, that things *have* inner natures of some sort which we do not directly perceive with our senses. He attempts to undercut both non-empirical speculation and skepticism by arguing that it is meaningless and even self-contradictory to suppose that there is anything more to the things which make up the world than what we experience of them. With the rationalists, he holds that there are no good grounds for metaphysical skepticism, and that we can know all there is to know about the natures of things. But with Locke, he holds that we can have no knowledge of things except that with which our senses provide us.

In short, he contends that we can know all there is to know about things; only there is nothing more to know about things than we already know by the simple use of our senses. Philosophy in his view neither provides us with knowledge we did not have before about the natures of things, nor shows us that the knowledge we ordinarily think we have of them is not worthy of the name. It leaves us just where we were before we began our philosophical reflections – the only difference being that at the end we come to see that there is nothing we are missing. 'And,' Berkeley says, in his Preface to the *Dialogues*,

> although it may, perhaps, seem an uneasy reflexion to some, that when they have taken a circuit through so many refined and unvulgar notions, they should at last come to think like other men; yet, methinks, this return to the simple dictates of nature, after having wandered through the wild mazes of philosophy, is not unpleasant. It is like coming home from a long voyage. . . . (D 220–1)

Berkeley, like Locke, is an empiricist, in that he holds that we can have no knowledge of things which does not derive from the ideas we have through sense-perception or direct experience. But he rejects Locke's conclusion that we must therefore 'sit down in a quiet ignorance of those things which, upon examination, are found to be beyond the reach of our capacities' (*Essay*, I: I: 4). With this very passage apparently in mind, he writes, in the Introduction to the *Principles*, that it is an objectionable consequence of earlier empiricism that in the end it leads one to 'sit down in a forlorn Scepticism' (P: Intro: 1). 'The cause of this,' he says, obviously thinking of Locke,

> is thought to be the obscurity of things, or the natural weakness and imperfection of our understanding. It is said that the faculties we have are few, and those designed by nature for the support and pleasure of life, and not to penetrate into the inward essence and constitution of things. . . . (P: Intro: 2)

This is just what Locke says. But against this view, Berkeley suggests that

> those lets and difficulties, which stay and embarrass the mind in its search after truth, do not spring from any darkness and intricacy in the objects, or natural defect in the understanding, so much as from false Principles which have been insisted on, and might have been avoided. (P: Intro: 4)

In other words, Berkeley is suggesting that skepticism arises only by the acceptance of certain assumptions about the natures of things which place them beyond our comprehension; and that these assumptions are not sound. Or, as he says, in a famous line: 'We have first raised a dust, and then complain we cannot see' (P: Intro: 3). His initial project, therefore, is to show what the assumptions are which lead to Locke's predicament, and to argue for their untenability – 'to try,' he says, 'to discover what those Principles are which have introduced all that doubtfulness and uncertainty, those absurdities and contradictions, into the several sects of philosophy' (P: Intro: 4). In the words of Wittgenstein, his aim is therefore 'to help the fly escape from the fly-bottle' – by showing him how he got into it in the first place. That is, he proposes to deal with a set of philosophical problems associated with knowledge of the natures of things, not by *solving* them, but by *dissolving* them: by showing that these problems only arose from the acceptance of principles which ought never to have been accepted in the first place.

Berkeley therefore might seem to be a champion of common-sense, against the seemingly formidable philosophical proponents of both speculation and skepticism. And this is how he presents himself, particularly in the *Dialogues*. Yet it is not without reason that he feels constrained to urge his readers, at the outset of both the *Dialogues* and the *Principles*, to read them through before forming any judgment concerning them; and to say, in his Preface to the *Principles*:

He must be either very weak, or very little acquainted with the
sciences, who shall reject a truth that is capable of
demonstration, for no other reason but because it is newly
known, and contrary to the prejudices of mankind.
(P: Pref: 102–3)

He says these things because he realizes that his central thesis,
on which both his rejection of skepticism and speculation and his
so-called defense of common sense depends, will strike most people
as incredible: namely, his thesis that all so-called material things
or physical objects are nothing more than ideas in our minds; and
that the whole of reality consists solely of spiritual beings which
perceive and the ideas which are perceived by them. He is able to
undercut skepticism only by denying that there are material things,
existing independently of the ideas we have of them, which cause
us to have the ideas we do, and which have natures in themselves
that we do not directly experience. He does not adopt this position,
however, simply in order to be able to avoid skepticism; rather,
he is able to avoid skepticism because he holds there are compelling
reasons for taking this position. And one's final judgment about the
soundness of his position should be based solely on an evaluation of
his arguments for it, as he himself argues. If he *is* providing a
defense of common sense, however, it is a very unusual one, which
involves the rejection of one of the most fundamental tenets of the
commonsense view of the world; namely, that the world consists
largely of things whose existence and natures are independent of
any consciousness of them.

In conclusion, a few remarks are in order concerning the method
Berkeley employs. The matter is somewhat complicated by the fact
that one of the pair of his works to be dealt with is rather like
Locke's *Essay* in its form, while the other is written in the form of
a dialogue. The use of the dialogue has a long history in philosophy; it was used extensively not only by Plato, but also by late
ancient and Renaissance philosophers. And it continued to be used,
though less frequently, by philosophers after Berkeley; Hume, for
example, wrote *Dialogues Concerning Natural Religion*.

The dialogue form has both strengths and weaknesses. Among
its strengths is the fact that a philosopher who writes a dialogue
– and Berkeley is no exception – usually goes to much greater pains
to state his views in language that is more readily comprehensible to
the lay-reader than he does otherwise. This is partly because more
technical and complex language would sound silly in what is

144

purportedly a spoken dialogue between several people; and it is partly because a philosopher who uses the dialogue form is usually trying to reach a wider audience than he is in his other writings. (Thus Berkeley wrote his *Dialogues* expressly in the hope of popularizing the basic views he had put forth in his *Principles*.)

The dialogue form has the further advantage, from the standpoint of the writer, that it allows him to use a variety of rhetorical devices which he might not otherwise feel he can permit himself. And this means that he is often able to be more persuasive than he might be in straight exposition. He can develop his points in a way calculated for its dramatic effect; and he can deal with objections to his views in a manner calculated to deprive them of their plausibility.

Yet all of these factors, which are strengths considered from the standpoint of rhetorical persuasiveness, are weaknesses when considered from the standpoint of philosophical rigor. If a writer is skillful, he may be able to persuade his readers of points by rhetorical means, of which he could not persuade them by means of straightforward arguments. And he can have objections raised in a form in which he can most easily handle them, giving the impression that his views are less vulnerable to criticism than in fact they may be. In short, the dialogue form is useful for getting people interested in the problems with which one is concerned, and for rendering one's position popularly more comprehensible than it might otherwise be; but before one reaches any final conclusions, it is a good idea at least to try to see what the arguments for them look like when set out more prosaically.

For this reason, it is fortunate that we are able to consider Berkeley's *Principles* together with his *Dialogues*. For in his *Principles*, he attempts to develop his arguments point by point. He does not, however, present them in the geometrical fashion Spinoza adopts in his *Ethics*; nor are they are rigorously formulated as are Descartes's proofs, or Leibniz's *Monadology*. Berkeley professes to 'observe the most rigid laws of reasoning'; but it is more accurate to describe his procedure as he goes on to speak of it, in terms of 'a close and methodical application of thought.' And this for the most part consists in laying down criteria for the meaningfulness of terms, and pointing out certain things which it is suggested are obviously true, and then going on to suggest what it does and does not make sense to say, given that these things are true, and given the suggested criteria for the meaningfulness of terms.

This is the kind of *informal* reasoning which Locke employed before Berkeley, and Hume and most subsequent English-speaking philosophers after him. And it may be the only practical way to proceed in dealing with most philosophical problems. The trouble is, first, that the various steps in the argument do not always follow strictly from previous ones; second, that a great deal comes to hinge upon claims about what is or is not *conceivable* – which is something weaker and less precise than the notions of logical consistency and self-contradiction; and third, that it is easy for hidden assumptions with important consequences to creep into one's statements of the seemingly obvious and the criteria of meaningfulness. We have already seen an example of the kind of problem of the latter sort that can arise, in the case of Locke. It remains to be seen whether there are any problems of a similar nature in what Berkeley does.

Ideas and immaterialism

Before getting into Berkeley's arguments against the existence of material things independently of the mind, it is necessary to say something about his use of the term 'idea,' and his views concerning the nature of our ideas. He follows Locke in holding that all we ever directly or immediately perceive are *ideas*, as opposed to whatever it is which causes us to have the ideas we do; that none of our ideas is innate, and that rather all of our ideas derive from perceptual experience; and that, since our knowledge must be a function of the ideas we have, all of our knowledge pertains to or derives from the ideas we come to have through experience. In the first section of the First Part of the *Principles* he says, in a manner very reminiscent of Locke:

It is evident to any one who takes a survey of the *objects of human knowledge*, that they are either ideas actually imprinted on the senses; or else such as are perceived by attending to the passions and operations of the mind; or lastly, ideas formed by help of memory and imagination – either compounding, dividing, or barely representing those originally perceived in the aforesaid ways. (P: I)

Berkeley does not hesitate to draw the consequence that since I never have any direct perceptual experience of my *mind* or *myself*, but rather only of various particular perceptual qualities or operations of the mind, I cannot be said to have any *idea* of my mind or myself. But he does not conclude from this that it is utterly meaningless even to speak of the 'mind' or the 'self'; though he does not go so far as to speak of it as a 'spiritual' or 'mental' or 'thinking' *substance*, as earlier philosophers had done. Rather, he uses the rather noncommittal term 'being' in referring to it; and he claims that it is not meaningless to speak of it because, though we have no *idea* of it, 'we have,' he says, 'some *notion* of soul, spirit, and the operations of the mind, such as willing, loving, hating – inasmuch as we know or understand the meaning of these words.' It is not at all clear that he is justified in taking this position, given his treatment of other terms whose meanings we think we understand, but which do not correspond to any ideas we directly experience. 'Such is the nature of Spirit,' he says, 'that it cannot be of itself perceived, but only by the effects which it produceth' (P: 27). He generally holds that, if we have no *idea* – no direct perceptual experience – of something, it makes no sense to speak of it; but here he seems to make an exception. And so he claims that,

> besides that endless variety of ideas or objects of knowledge, there is likewise Something which knows or perceives them; and exercises divers operations as willing, imagining, remembering, about them. This perceiving, active being is what I call *mind, spirit, soul, or myself*. By which words I do not denote any one of my ideas, but a thing entirely distinct from them, wherein they exist, or, which is the same thing, whereby they are perceived. (P: 2)

Berkeley may have been led to make this exception to his general rule because he could not conceive of ideas being perceived, willed, imagined, remembered, and so forth, without there being *something doing* the perceiving, willing, imagining, and remembering. But with this single exception, he holds that we are incapable of forming any conception with significant content, except through the direct perceptual experience of certain ideas. And, setting aside those ideas which are ideas of operations of the mind, it is quite clear that by 'ideas' he means something on the order of perceptual *images*, which are either original sensations of various qualities, or else copies of them remembered or imagined. To have an idea, as he uses the term, is not to think of a verbal definition; rather, it is either to experience certain sensible qualities with one or more of the five senses, or to remember or imagine certain of these qualities either separately or in combination.

Berkeley is quite insistent upon distinguishing between *ideas* and *words*. Words can be used without any definite ideas being associated with them; and this he regards as the source of a great deal of meaningless talk. To have certain words in mind is not necessarily to have any real ideas. It is only if our words correspond to definite ideas, in his sense of the term, that our words are meaningful and significant. For this reason, he is very suspicious of words. 'So long as I confine my thoughts to my own ideas, divested of words,' he says, 'I do not see how I can easily be mistaken' (P: Intro: 22). But he thinks that the moment one allows one's attention to stray from direct experience, and begins to use words independently of directly experienced ideas (as, no doubt, he would accuse Leibniz and Spinoza of doing), one's reflections cease to have any real meaning, and become simply so much nonsense. He therefore states:

> Since . . . words are so apt to impose on the understanding, I am resolved in my inquiries to make as little use of them as I possibly can; whatever ideas I consider, I shall endeavour to take them bare and naked into my view. . . . (P: Intro: 21)

It may seem odd for someone writing a book to vow to make as little use of words as he possibly can; but Berkeley's point is not that he really should not be writing at all. Rather, it is that, in philosophical inquiry, we should not direct our attention to words themselves, their definitions and conceptual implications and interrelations, but rather to the concrete phenomena of direct experience, the description of which is the only valid philosophical functions of words. The view that it is *possible*, in Berkeley's phrase, to 'draw the curtain of words,' and to gain access to a level of pre-linguistic experience unsullied by any language, is a view which many recent philosophers no longer consider tenable. But for him this *is* possible, and is desirable as well; and it is this determination to get back to the analysis of pure experience, and to rely on it alone, that was the distinguishing feature of traditional empiricism.

In what has been said so far, Berkeley is in basic agreement with Locke. But he parts company with Locke quite emphatically over the issue of *abstract ideas*. Locke rejected the view that any of our abstract ideas are *innate*; but he did not question the view that we *have* some. In fact, our ability to form abstract ideas was for Locke the only mental faculty we have that animals lack; and so, for him, the faculty of abstraction occupies a rather special position.

Berkeley, however, not only denies that we have any *innate* abstract ideas, but also denies that we have *any* abstract ideas at all. 'Whether others have this wonderful faculty of abstracting their ideas,' he says, 'they best can tell. For myself, I dare be confident I have it not' (P: Intro: 10). He readily agrees with Locke that animals are incapable of abstraction; but he suggests that if this capacity is what distinguishes men from animals, then there are precious few men in the world, and many more brutes than we suppose. And even this is an understatement; for Berkeley's contention is not simply that abstraction is something of which few are capable, but rather that no one is capable of it.

But what is it that he is denying? He is not denying that we have *general* ideas, or ideas which stand for numbers of particular ideas of the same sort. He also is not denying that we have abstract *terms* in our vocabulary, such as 'motion,' 'extension,' and 'triangle.' What he *is* denying is the possibility of our ideas ever being anything other than *particular* in their content. A *general* idea, on his view, is simply a particular idea which by convention is made to stand for a variety of similar particular ideas; it is not abstract, in the sense of being indefinite. Abstract terms, on the other hand, are indefinite; but Berkeley denies that we have any abstract ideas corresponding to them, of an equally indefinite nature.

The reason Berkeley takes this view is rather simple, and it derives from his conception of what an idea is. 'Ideas,' as he understands them, are not verbal *concepts*, but rather perceptual *images*, rather like pictures. And just as you cannot draw a picture of a horse or a triangle without making the horse some definite size and color, and without making the triangle have some definite form, so also (he claims) you cannot have an *idea* of a horse or a triangle without picturing some definite horse or triangle in your mind. You can use the *words* 'horse' and 'triangle' without doing so; but then you are using them loosely, and without having any clear idea associated with your use of them. The same is true in the cases of 'motion' and 'extension.' One can use the words without thinking of any particular extended thing, or any particular thing moving quickly or slowly; but one has no *idea* associated with one's use of the words unless one forms such an image in one's mind. And such an image must by its very nature have determinate features; otherwise it is no image at all. In short, there can be no abstract ideas because, as Berkeley understands 'idea,' an idea must be determinate and particular if it is to be an idea at all; and therefore an *abstract* idea is a contradiction in terms.

One might be inclined to take little notice of this, and to let it pass as a mere terminological idiosyncrasy of little consequence. But while many terminological idiosyncrasies *are* of little consequence, and may be allowed to pass for that reason, *this* one has very important consequences. For Berkeley, words are employed meaningfully only when used in connection with ideas. If no ideas correspond to the words we use, then we are uttering meaningless sounds when we use them. And if 'ideas' are construed as he construes them, and consist solely of sensible qualities (in specific combinations, as in sense-perception), then no term may be considered meaningful or significant which does not correspond to something like a particular sense-perception. This is a move similar in its effect to the one Locke makes when he defines a distinct idea. As has already been observed, Berkeley makes an exception of the term 'spirit' and the related terms 'mind,' 'soul,' 'self,' and also 'God'; but he makes no other such exceptions. In particular, he makes no such exception in the case of 'matter' or 'material substance,' as Locke does. This leads directly to his rejection of the view that there is such a thing as 'matter' or a material substratum underlying and giving rise to our various perceptions; and this brings us to his doctrine of 'immaterialism.'

While Berkeley himself used the term 'immaterialism' to characterize his position, the term more commonly used to refer to it is *idealism*. The reason for the use of the term 'idealism' is that it conveys the fact that for Berkeley *things* exist only as complexes of *ideas* in the minds of spiritual beings who perceive them. It is somewhat misleading, however, not only because this term is also used to characterize those who are enamoured of lofty *ideals*, but also because it suggests that nothing exists but *ideas*. Berkeley himself is partly responsible for this, owing to his use of the slogan: '*esse est percipi*' – 'to *be* is to be perceived'; that is, they exist only in perception, and only insofar as their component ideas are perceived. But he holds that, in addition to these ideas which are perceived, there are and must be beings which *perceive* them. More completely stated, therefore, to *be* is either to *be perceived* or to *be a perceiver*. Reality consists not only of ideas, but also of the spiritual beings who perceive them. Both, according to Berkeley, are *immaterial* entities; neither are material things. And it is for this reason that the term 'immaterialism' is a more appropriate one; for it better conveys the idea that there are no material things in the world – no unthinking substances or inert matter, as the materialists hold there to be – and that everything that really does exist is immaterial in nature.

Up to a point, Berkeley is agreeing with Locke, when Locke says that our ideas of things consist simply of collections of simple ideas or sensible qualities, and that our knowledge of them consists solely in the ideas we have of them, which are in our minds. Locke presumably could go along with him when he says:

> And as several of these [simple ideas] are observed to accompany each other, they come to be marked by one name, and so to be reputed as one *thing*. Thus, for example, a certain colour, taste, smell, figure, and consistence having been observed to go together, are accounted one distinct thing, signified by the name apple. . . . (P: 1)

Where Locke and Berkeley part company is, first, that Berkeley denies that any different account is to be given of those ideas which Locke terms ideas of *primary* qualities, from the account which is to be given of those ideas which Locke terms ideas of *secondary* qualities; and, second, that he denies that we have any reason (given that all of these ideas are in our minds) to assume that there is anything existing independently of our minds which corresponds to the ideas in our minds – and indeed, that it is even meaningful to speak of such things. However strange this may sound at first, he feels that anyone who thinks the matter through must agree that it is true:

> Some truths there are so near and obvious to the mind that a man need only open his eyes to see them. Such I take this important one to be, viz., that all . . . those bodies which compose the mighty frame of the world, have not any subsistence without the mind; that their *being* is to be perceived or known. (P: 6)

Berkeley allows that, however obvious to the mind this truth should be, most people have not yet opened their eyes and seen it; though he at least professes to find this rather odd. He writes:

> It is indeed an opinion strangely prevailing amongst men, that houses, mountains . . . , and in a word all sensible objects, have an existence, natural or real, distinct from their being perceived by the understanding. But . . . , if I mistake not, [this] involves a manifest contradiction. For, what are the forementioned objects but the things we perceive by sense?

And what do we perceive besides our own ideas or sensations?
And is it not plainly repugnant that any one of these, or any
combination of them should exist unperceived? (P: 4)

Here his argument is presented in a nutshell. Houses and moun-
tains and the rest are things we perceive by our senses. We in fact
perceive nothing by our senses except our own ideas or sensations.
Our ideas or sensations can exist nowhere except in our minds.
Therefore whatever we perceive by our senses is in our minds.
Therefore houses, mountains and the rest exist only in our minds.

Now there seem to me to be only two points in this argument
at which objections might be raised; for I think everyone will grant
Berkeley that ideas and sensations cannot exist except in the act
of perception. First, it might be questioned whether we do in fact
perceive houses or mountains; that is, whether what we perceive
is in fact *the house* or *the mountain*. This undoubtedly is the
objection Locke would raise. Locke might argue that we never
perceive the house *itself*, but rather only certain ideas which arise
in our minds owing to the action of the house itself upon our senses,
through some medium. This objection, however, presupposes not
only that the only thing we ever directly perceive is our own ideas
or sensations (which is fine with Berkeley), but also that *the house
itself* is not identical with our ideas, but rather stands to them as
cause to effect. This would *not* be fine with Berkeley; and he would
be quick to point out that it begs the question at issue, by in effect
assuming the falsity of his conclusion. Berkeley would ask Locke:
'*Setting aside* your version of the causal theory of perception, which
begs the issue, what reason can you give for holding that what we
perceive is something other than the house itself? That, after all,
is what we ordinarily *take* ourselves to perceive. What reason can
you give for saying that the house is anything other than that
which we perceive?' And it would seem to be rather difficult for
Locke to give a satisfactory answer.

Second, it might be questioned whether we perceive nothing by
our senses except our own ideas or sensations. The questioning of
this premise is usually accompanied by an acceptance of the first,
since few would maintain *both* that we do not perceive houses,
mountains and the like by our senses, *and* that what we perceive
is not our own ideas or sensations either. To question this second
premise is to question a basic supposition of Locke's *and* Berkeley's, and of most other modern philosophers from Descartes
onward as well; and it is only very recently that some philosophers

have begun to do this. If this premise is questioned, of course, the argument does not go through. But Berkeley, and many other philosophers before and after him, would regard this as a move of desperation, which ignores the persuasive support for this contention that derives from the many considerations they bring up to show the implausibility of attributing colors, tastes, smells and sounds, *as we perceive them*, to things outside our minds.

Rather than trying to refute Berkeley's argument by attacking one or the other of his major premises, many philosophers have been content simply to grant his premises, which are epistemological ones, and to refrain from drawing his ontological conclusion. That is, they have been willing to grant that his point against Locke is sound: given that we have no experience of anything other than our own ideas or sensations, there is nothing in our experience to justify the supposition that our ideas or sensations are produced by the action of independently existing material things upon our senses. But they have stopped short of asserting that nothing exists except ideas and spirits; and that there is nothing more to the things we perceive than the ideas we have of them in our minds. Our knowledge of them is limited to our ideas of them; but whether or not there is anything more to them than the ideas we have of them, and what their source might be, are topics on which they remain silent.

Berkeley would have regarded this reticence as a sign that those who adopt this course lack the courage of their convictions. It amounts to 'sitting down in a forlorn skepticism,' when all that is necessary is to draw the necessary implications to put an end to this skepticism. But is it really a necessary implication, given that we perceive nothing but our own ideas, that therefore nothing exists except perceivers and the ideas they perceive? Berkeley may be right to maintain that the thought of ideas existing independently of any perception of them is self-contradictory; and he may also be right to maintain that, if we are never conscious of anything other than ideas, we can never form any positive or meaningful conception of anything other than ideas. But it still does not logically follow that there *cannot be* anything other than spirits and ideas; and so his conclusion that 'to be is to be perceived or to be a perceiver' is not strictly implied by his argument.

Against Locke's contention that, despite the restriction of our immediate experience to our ideas, we can have knowledge of the real existence of particular things independent of the mind, however, Berkeley's counter-argument is quite persuasive. And his argument against Locke's distinction between secondary qualities (which do not exist in things themselves) and primary qualities (which do) is also quite persuasive. For he points out, first, that we cannot imagine what things would be like which had primary qualities, but lacked secondary ones.

> It is not in my power to frame an idea of a body extended and moving, but I must withal give it some colour or other sensible quality, which is acknowledged to exist only in the mind. In short, extension, figure, and motion, abstracted from all other qualities, are inconceivable. Where, therefore, the other sensible qualities are, there must these be also, to wit, in the mind and nowhere else. (P: 10)

Second, and more decisively, Berkeley points out that our ideas of extension, figure, motion, and the rest, are *ideas* no less than our ideas of colors, sounds and tastes; and that if it is true, as Locke allows, that we never directly experience anything other than our own ideas, then in neither case are we justified in holding that our ideas of these qualities correspond to actual qualities of things existing independently of our minds.

With this collapse of the distinction between primary and secondary qualities, Berkeley feels that the only remaining reason to hold to the existence of matter independently of the mind is removed. So he observes:

> It [once] was thought that colour, figure, motion and the rest of the sensible qualities or accidents, did really exist without the mind; and for this reason it seemed needful to suppose some unthinking *substratum* or substance wherein they did exist, since they could not be conceived to exist by themselves. Afterwards, in the process of time, men being convinced that colours, sounds, and the rest of the sensible secondary qualities had no existence without the mind, they stripped this *substratum* or material substance of *those* qualities, leaving only the primary ones, figure, motion, and such-like; which they still conceived to exist without the mind, and consequently to stand in need of a material support. But, it having been shewn that none even of these can possibly exist otherwise than in a Spirit or Mind which perceives them, it follows that we have no longer any reason to suppose the being of Matter . . . ; so long as that word is taken to denote an *unthinking*

substratum of qualities or accidents, wherein they exist without the mind. (P: 73)

This is a fairly accurate description of the actual historical development in philosophy proceeding from the unqualified realism of scholasticism, through its modification by Descartes and Locke, to Berkeley himself. And it certainly seems like a logical development. If you are not prepared to accept Berkeley's conclusion, therefore, where do you get off before the end of the line? And how do you justify doing so?

Ideas and things

Berkeley's main argument for the thesis of immaterialism, as was suggested above, is that our own ideas are all we ever directly perceive; that, while they have a *real* existence in our minds, not even the materialists hold that they have an *absolute* existence independent of any mind whatsoever; that we never directly perceive the Matter or material substance which the materialists hold exists absolutely, independently of all minds – again, as the materialists themselves can be forced to admit; and that no reason can be given for assuming the existence of Matter conceived as existing by itself, since its existence is neither logically implied nor logically required by anything that we *do* directly perceive. These last points require further discussion. But first, a little more needs to be said about what conclusion would follow from this argument, assuming it to be valid.

Berkeley seems to equivocate between asserting that it follows that it is *impossible* that anything other than ideas and spirits could exist, and that it follows that it is *meaningless* for us to speak of anything existing other than ideas and spirits. And the latter claim would seem to be a good deal weaker than the former. For while it might be *meaningless* for us to speak of anything of which we can know nothing either by experience or by reason, it would not seem to follow logically that there *can be* nothing of which we have no knowledge through either experience or reason.

Berkeley's seeming equivocation on this point can be seen to be merely apparent, at least to some extent, by observing that he is addressing himself here to two conceptions of matter. When he talks of the impossibility of the existence of matter, or of the self-contradictory nature of the notion of matter, he has in mind a concept of matter or material substance cast in terms of Locke's 'primary qualities.' Here his point is that, to the extent that material substance is both held to exist independently of any mind and to have the properties of extension, figure, motion and solidity, it involves a contradiction; since these are all terms for sensible qualities, no less than color, sound, taste and smell; since, as sensible qualities, these are all ideas, which by their very nature cannot exist absolutely or independently of any mind; and since to regard something which cannot exist independently of any mind and existing independently of any mind is to contradict oneself. The point here is that one can avoid self-contradiction only by not attributing any qualities to matter which are sensible qualities in our perceptions; and this means not attributing any qualities to matter of which we have ever had any experience.

Now it certainly would seem self-contradictory to speak of ideas existing in themselves, independently of any mind or any act of perception whatsoever. But one still might be inclined to think, as Locke did, that things could exist independently of any mind which have qualities *resembling* our ideas of primary qualities. In that case one would not be saying that certain ideas exist independently of any mind, but rather that things with qualities *conforming* to certain of our ideas exist independently of any mind. And this would seem to avoid self-contradiction.

To this Berkeley replies that 'an idea can be like nothing but another idea; a colour or figure can be like nothing but another colour or figure' (P: 8). This might seem to be rather dogmatic, for it goes beyond saying simply that we cannot *know* whether our ideas resemble qualities of things, since we never have the opportunity to compare them (our experience being confined to our ideas themselves). To say *this* would seem quite reasonable, given that we never directly perceive anything but our own ideas. But Berkeley goes further; and there is at least something to be said for the position he takes. He says:

> I ask whether those supposed originals, or external things, of which our ideas are [supposed to be] the pictures or representations, be themselves perceptible or no? . . . If you [grant] they are not, I appeal to anyone whether it be [reasonable] to assert a colour is like something which is invisible; hard or soft, like something which is intangible; and so of the rest. (P: 8)

His point is that one cannot coherently speak of a resemblance between our ideas and the qualities of independently existing things, when there is a very great difference between them *in principle*, in virtue of the fact that one is perceptible while the other by its very nature is conceived not to be. We know what it means for one perceptible quality to resemble another; but what could it possibly mean to talk about resemblance outside of this context? Before one rejects Berkeley's claim that nothing but an idea can resemble another idea, and his conclusion that therefore it is self-contradictory to attribute the kinds of qualities we experience to things existing independently of any mind, one is obliged to show that some sense can be made of this.

It is in connection with a conception of matter which does not involve any attribution of specific positive qualities to it, on the other hand, that Berkeley tends to speak of the *meaninglessness* of such a notion, rather than of self-contradiction. And, after all, if one cannot say anything definite about matter except that it is an unknown Something that exists independently of any mind, one has said so little about it that one scarcely leaves oneself open to the possibility of self-contradiction. When a notion of matter of this sort is suggested, Berkeley shifts his argument. Of such a notion, he says that matter so conceived neither is *required* to explain any single fact of experience, nor even provides an *easier* and *simpler* explanation of any fact of experience than can be given in purely immaterialist terms. Thus he issues the following challenge: 'I challenge you to shew me a thing in nature which needs Matter to explain or account for it' (D 292).

Berkeley's point here is surely sound; for if matter is construed in a completely indeterminate and negative manner, with no characteristics whatsoever being attributed to it, then it can perform no explanatory function whatsoever. In short, if matter is so conceived (in an attempt to avoid the self-contradiction involved in attributing experiential qualities to it), the notion becomes an empty one with no explanatory power. It becomes a useless hypothesis, which as such is very vulnerable to Occam's Razor. This leads to Berkeley's next point, which is that under these circumstances the notion of matter or independently existing material substance loses all practical and theoretical interest:

If what you mean by *Matter* be only the unknown support of unknown qualities, it is no matter whether there is such a thing or no, since it in no way concerns us. And I do not see the advantage there is in disputing about we know not *what*, and we know not *why*. (P: 77)

But this would still seem to leave open the possibility that there *is* something in the world other than ideas and spirits; and as long as this remains a possibility, Berkeley's thesis of immaterialism still has not been conclusively established. At this point, therefore, he attempts to establish his thesis by contending that this possibility is not a *real* possibility, because it is not a *meaningful* one to which any real sense can be attached. A purely negative notion of matter, he argues, is utterly meaningless:

> where there is not so much as the most inadequate or faint idea pretended to – I will not indeed thence conclude against the reality of any notion, or existence of anything; but my inference shall be, that you *mean* nothing at all; that you employ words to no manner of purpose, without any design or signification whatsoever. (D 291)

If in fact a term is employed in such a way that nothing is meant by it at all, then it would seem rather odd of someone to keep insisting that, still, it is possible that there *is* some such thing as it purports to name. So Berkeley concludes, at the end of the Second Dialogue, that 'If this be not sufficient to prove the impossibility of a thing, I desire you will let me know what is' (D 295). Yet while the inability to attach any definite meaning to the idea of something which is neither an idea nor a spirit may create a strong presumption against anyone who maintains that there might be some such thing, it would seem to fall short of 'proving the impossibility' of such a thing. Thus Berkeley would appear to overstate his case against someone who wishes to maintain the bare logical possibility of *something* existing other than ideas and spirits.

Even if he is only able to show that this is the strongest opposing claim that can rationally be maintained, however, he will have established a great deal; for traditional materialism maintains not only that material substance does in fact exist, but moreover that a good deal can be said about it. If we can in fact only have knowledge of the existence of ideas and spirits; if we can meaningfully speak only of them; if the existence of anything else is only a bare logical possibility; and if that 'something else' could in no way resemble anything of which we have any experience even if it should exist; then, at least for all practical purposes, traditional materialism would in fact be undermined, and the notion of material substance would lose all philosophical interest.

Berkeley finds it quite incomprehensible that anyone should be disturbed at this result. For he argues quite persuasively that this would not make the slightest bit of practical difference, where either science or ordinary experience is concerned. Science may continue with its business just as before – its business being to investigate which phenomena are associated with which other phenomena. It may continue, in other words, to investigate the laws of nature, under no handicap whatsoever. The only difference would be in its understanding of what these laws are laws *of*. And in this matter, Berkeley has a very modern understanding of the enterprise of science. For, like modern practitioners and philosophers of science, he regards the laws of nature which the scientist discovers, not as utterly independent of human experience, sitting there waiting to be discovered, but rather as descriptions of patterns of phenomena occurring in human experience. 'My aim,' he has Philonous say, 'is only to know what ideas are connected together; and the more a man knows of the connexion of ideas, the more he is said to know of the nature of things' (D 320). Science is not concerned with anything which might be the case or might exist independently of the phenomena of which we are or may be conscious, but rather only with the description of regularities among observed phenomena. The scientist as such does not concern himself with the question of whether anything might be said to exist above and beyond these phenomena, which we never experience. And the scientist would not think of denying that what he achieves is knowledge of the natures of things, simply because what he discovers are *only* regularities of phenomena we actually experience, and because it is logically possible that there is some sort of material substance underlying these phenomena, which lies beyond our experience, and whose essential or inner nature we therefore cannot know.

In fact, Berkeley is the first philosopher considered to argue that empirical knowledge – the knowledge of things we acquire through experience – is in fact genuine knowledge in its own right, quite independently of any recourse to arguments about God. He quite rightly observes that skepticism with regard to the true natures of things, and the tendency to regard empirical knowledge of things as something less than genuine knowledge, is a direct consequence of the view that there is something more to things than we do or ever can experience. If one holds that all we ever directly experience is our own ideas, *and* that things have an existence independently of our minds, then skepticism with regard to their true natures is inescapable, as Locke himself admits; and the so-called empirical knowledge of science and ordinary experience can never in principle be said to constitute genuine knowledge of the natures of things. It is only if one holds that things have no features which are inaccessible to our experience, that one can also hold empirical knowledge to be genuine knowledge of them. So if Berkeley is right in maintaining that we never directly experience anything other than our own ideas, then he is also right in maintaining that it is only if one holds that things are nothing more than complexes of our ideas, that one can avoid skepticism and regard empirical knowledge as genuine knowledge.

Berkeley is also quite right in maintaining, against Locke, that if we never directly experience anything other than our own ideas, then we not only can never know the true natures of things, but also, we can never even know *that* particular things exist. It is a consequence of *his* position, on the other hand, that we *can* know that they exist. For if 'to be is to be perceived,' where things are concerned, then where things are concerned it is also true that 'to be perceived is to be.' For on this view, if we perceive something, we do not have to satisfy ourselves that there is something independent of our perception but corresponding to it (an impossible task) before concluding that it exists.

Of course, Berkeley is not saying that everything which passes before our minds is on an equal footing. Like everyone else, he too wants to distinguish between *real* existence on the one hand, and things merely dreamed or imagined or hallucinated on the other. He holds that to be perceived is to be, but not that to be dreamed or imagined or hallucinated is *also* to be. And he believes that it is just as possible to make out this distinction on his view as it is on any other. He has Philonous say: 'By whatever method you distinguish *things* from *chimeras* on your scheme, the same . . . will also hold upon mine' (D 306). He argues that we ordinarily distinguish those perceptions we call 'real' from others by some combination of three criteria: (a) their vividness and clearness, (b) the fact that they are involuntary rather than voluntarily brought to mind, and (c) their coherence with the rest of our experience. And he quite rightly observes that he can consistently employ these criteria as well as anyone else. There will of course be problem-cases, such as certain kinds of hallucinations and visual deceptions and very vivid dreams; but they are no more problems for him than they are for anyone else; and his ultimate judgment about them is made in the same way as any one else's.

In short, while Berkeley denies the *absolute* existence of things (that is, their existence independent of any mind), he does retain the distinction between the *real* existence of things and the mere imagination, hallucination, or dreaming of things. Only he does not draw this distinction in terms of their absolute existence versus their existence merely in our minds, but rather makes it out in terms of qualitative and other differences between some ideas in our minds and others. And he even goes so far as to retain the use of the expression 'external' things, provided that it is understood simply to designate those complexes of ideas driving from involuntary sensation, rather than from imagination or dreams.

Berkeley recognizes that one objection to his view will be that it makes it impossible to say that two people can perceive the *same thing*. And he grants that, if one means the 'same' numerically and not simply qualitatively, this does follow. But he quite rightly points out that no one can hold this is an objection to his view, who takes the position that we never directly perceive anything but our own ideas. For the same result follows on Locke's view, or on the view of anyone else who takes that position, even if he holds that the causes of our ideas are independently existing material things. The only way of avoiding this problem is to hold that we directly perceive independently existing material things; and Berkeley, like Locke, considers that an absurdity. Moreover, he does not think this is really a very serious problem anyhow. For it is quite possible, in his view, to speak of two people perceiving the same thing in the qualitative sense of 'same'; and one does not have to suppose that there is some independently existing material substance that is causing both of them to have the ideas they do, in order to account for both of them having these qualitatively similar ideas at the same time. One can account for this in the same way that Berkeley accounts for each of us having all of the perceptions we do; and this brings us to his account of the origin of our perceptions.

Berkeley rejects Locke's version of the causal theory of perception, in part for very obvious reasons. For Locke's version of this theory presupposes that material substances exist independently of our minds, and cause us to have the ideas we do by acting physically upon our senses; and Berkeley rejects the very notion of such independently existing material substances. But he also has another argument against Locke's view, designed to show that even if there is some sort of material substance, it cannot be the cause of our ideas. The argument is as follows: A material substance would not be the cause of our ideas unless it were *active*; for if it were completely inactive, it would not be the cause of anything. If it were to be physically active, however, it would have to have the characteristics of motion, extension, and solidity. But to conceive of material substance existing completely independently of the mind as extended, solid, and in motion, is to conceive of it in just the sort of way which was earlier argued to be self-contradictory; for motion, extension and solidity are all qualities we directly experience, or ideas in the mind. Therefore matter must either be conceived in such a way that it is incapable of being a cause of anything (and thus as inactive), or it must be so conceived that its very conception is self-contradictory; and so in neither case is the doctrine coherent that matter or material substance is the cause of our ideas.

To this interesting argument, Berkeley adds another (also used by Leibniz), that it is incomprehensible that any amount of movement of anything merely extended and solid could ever produce a thought or idea. Locke himself had admitted that this is incomprehensible, but had taken it simply to be a fact that this happens. Berkeley, like Leibniz, regards this blithe acceptance of something inconceivable as completely unwarranted. And to this, he adds the further argument that, since we never experience independently existing material things producing ideas in us – since we never experience independently existing material things at all – we have no right to apply the concept of causality beyond the limits within which we have observed it to apply, even if some sort of unknown material substance *is* granted to be logically possible.

But Berkeley does not conclude, from all of this, that the causal theory of perception is completely wrong. On the contrary, he himself adopts another version of it. Particularly in view of the fact that our perceptions of sense are not voluntary, he is in complete agreement with Locke that there must be *some* cause of them outside of ourselves. Where he differs is in what he takes the nature of this cause to be. So he has Philonous say: 'I do by no means find fault with your reasoning, in that you collect *a* cause from the *phenomena*: but I deny that *the* cause deductible by reason can properly be termed Matter' (D 282).

In place of Matter, Berkeley proposes that the cause of our ideas is God. He thus advances a version of the causal theory of perception, with God rather than matter as the cause. For if matter is ruled out (for the reasons already mentioned), and if my ideas cannot be their own causes or the cause of each other – a suggestion he perhaps quite rightly regards as absurd – and if I myself am not the cause of them (as I certainly would not seem to be, in perception), it would seem only logical to conclude, as Berkeley says, that 'There is therefore some other Will or Spirit that produces them' (P: 29). He does not even bother to consider the possibility that the 'other Will or Spirit' that produces all of our involuntary ideas or perceptions might be another being like himself (another person); no one would seriously maintain *that*. If my perceptions are to have a cause at all, therefore, there is only one remaining candidate: God.

It might be objected that this suggestion that God is the cause of our perceptions is just as arbitrary as the suggestion that matter causes them, in that we never experience God producing our perceptions either. But Berkeley does have a reply to this objection. For he observes that we *do* have the experience of spiritual beings producing ideas – namely, we ourselves, when we imagine various things at will. And if we know it to be within our power as spiritual beings to produce ideas in ourselves, then this provides at least some basis in experience for the notion of another spiritual being producing ideas within us.

Berkeley thus reasons as follows: The only time we ever actually experience the causing of ideas is when we cause them in ourselves. The only active being of which we have any experience is ourselves. When it comes to assigning a cause for those of our ideas we do not ourselves cause, therefore, the only kind of being we are warranted by experience in inferring as their cause is another being similar to ourselves, that is, another spiritual being. And who could that being be but God? Given Berkeley's immaterialism – or even given the possibility of the sort of matter he does not strictly rule out – and given that our perceptions must have *some* cause, this argument is actually a pretty strong one.

This is not the only important function God performs in Berkeley's view. He also serves to enable Berkeley to make some sense of one of our most fundamental convictions regarding the existence of things: namely, that things exist when we ourselves are not perceiving them, and existed before there were any beings such as we are in existence, and would continue to exist even if we were to cease to do so. Berkeley by no means is willing to accept the seemingly absurd idea that things are constantly blinking into and out of existence, as we first perceive them, and then cease to do so, and then do so again. He grants that continuousness of existence is one of the most basic elements of our conception of what it is for something really to exist. And he is able to include this element of our ordinary conception in his own, by making reference to God.

Where things are concerned, in short, to be is to be perceived – but not only by men, and not just by all of us. Things may be said *to be* even when they are not perceived by any of us, since even when they are not perceived by any of us, they are still perceived by God. They are in God's mind, even when they are not yet or are no longer in our own. In this way, Berkeley avoids having to hold that things are constantly coming into and going out of existence, avoids having to suppose the independent existence of material things after all, and also avoids having to grant ideas the power to continue in existence without anyone perceiving them. How he *knows* that things exist continuously is something of a problem; for he obviously does not know they do from experience, and he does not use God's existence to prove it. In fact, he cannot do this, as will be seen. But he is quite convinced of it, as all of us are; and by including God among the perceivers, he is able to avoid having to abandon this conviction. Yet what would one be left with, if one accepted his critical arguments against materialism, but dropped God out of the picture? This problem is indeed a vexing one.

Mind and God

It was observed in the first section of this chapter that Berkeley denies that we do or can have any *idea* of ourselves, or any other spiritual being, in his usual sense of the term 'idea.' We never perceive spiritual beings – either ourselves or any others – with any of our senses; and we therefore can have no 'idea' of them. But Berkeley does not conclude from this that the notion of a spiritual being is meaningless, as he takes the notion of matter to be. '*I know what I mean*,' he has Philonous say, 'when I affirm that there is a spiritual substance or support of ideas' (D 304). Locke had argued that the notions of spiritual substance and material substance stand or fall together, since we have no direct perception of either one, and since our notions of both are equally obscure; but rather than rejecting both for this reason, he accepted both notions, since he did not see how we could do without them. Berkeley, on the other hand, holds that we can get along perfectly well without the notion of material substance, but not without the notion of spiritual substance; for he too supposes that there must be *some* substance for ideas to inhere in – some being for them to be perceived by. And he denies that the notion of a spiritual substance is altogether meaningless, since he can say what he means by it: namely, 'that which thinks, wills, and perceives' (P: 138). 'A spirit,' he says, 'is an active being, whose existence consists, not in being perceived, but in perceiving ideas and thinking' (P: 139).

If in fact we have some sort of meaningful notion of ourselves as spiritual beings, however, then it would seem possible for us to have a meaningful notion of God as well, provided that he likewise is construed as a spiritual being (as he traditionally has been). Berkeley's account of how we come to form the notion of God thus is basically the same as Locke's: 'In a large sense,' Philonous says,

> my soul may be said to furnish me with an idea, that is, an image or likeness of God – though indeed extremely inadequate. For, all the notion I have of God is obtained by reflecting on my own soul, heightening its power, and removing its imperfections. (D 302)

This much at least one can grant to Berkeley: if the notion of a spiritual being is meaningful in our own case, a notion of God formed in this way can be meaningful as well. If it is meaningful to speak of the self as he does, then it is also meaningful to speak of God as he does – though *only* if it is meaningful to speak of the self as he does, and *only* if God is conceived in an analogous way. Spinoza, of course, would not be satisfied with this sort of conception of God; it is precisely the sort of conception that he attacks in his Appendix to the first book of his *Ethics*. But Berkeley holds that it is *only* if God is conceived in this way that the notion of God is meaningful. He would regard the notion of God which Spinoza himself adopts as being as meaningless as the notion of matter.

But it is one thing to construe the notion of God as Berkeley does, and another to know that a being answering to that description exists. And Berkeley holds that the existence of such a being can be demonstrated. His argument for the existence of God, however, is neither a version of the ontological argument, nor the same as the versions of the cosmological argument which Leibniz and Locke give. That is, he does not argue either that the existence of God is presupposed by the existence of the world, or that the existence of God is presupposed by his own existence as a thinking and perceiving being. He actually gives two arguments, one in the *Principles*, and one in the *Dialogues*. The one he gives in the *Principles* is a different version of the cosmological argument. He says:

nothing can be more evident to any one that is capable of the least reflexion than the existence of God, or a Spirit who is intimately present to our minds, producing in them all that variety of ideas or sensations which continually affect us. (P: 149)

The reason he supposes this to be so evident is that he takes it for granted that the perceptions we have which are not produced voluntarily by ourselves must have *some* cause outside of ourselves; that the great majority of these cannot plausibly be attributed to the actions of other human beings; and that, since this cause cannot be some independently existing material substance, it must be some other sort of spiritual being. So he writes:

it is evident to everyone that those things which are called the Works of Nature, that is, the far greater part of the ideas or sensations perceived by us, are *not* produced by, or dependent on the wills of *men*. There is therefore some other Spirit that causes them; since it is repugnant that they should subsist by themselves. (P: 146)

This, Berkeley feels, suffices to establish the *existence* of a God of some sort, although it would remain a problem whether the evidence from our perceptions supports the conclusion that this God has the characteristics traditionally attributed to God. For the moment, however, I would merely observe that this argument depends upon the validity of two premises: *first*, that our perceptions must have some cause which transcends both them and our own minds; and *second*, that this cause cannot possibly be some sort of independently existing material substance.

The argument Berkeley gives in the *Dialogues* is rather different; and it is one of the most astonishing arguments for the existence of God in the history of modern philosophy. (The only other one which even rivals it in this respect is Kant's.) Here the fact which Berkeley takes to presuppose the existence of a God is not the involuntary occurrence of perceptions in my mind, but rather the existence of *things* independently of my mind and of all human minds, which nevertheless can only be said to exist insofar as they are perceived in *some* mind. To Hylas's great atonishment, Philonous says:

Men commonly believe that all things are known or perceived by God, because they believe in the being of a God; whereas I, on the other side, immediately and necessarily conclude the being of a God, because all sensible things must be perceived by him. (D 276)

Hylas thinks he has come up with a devastating objection to Philonous's contention that, for things, 'to be is to be perceived'; namely, that it is part of what we *mean* when we talk about something really existing that it exists when no one is around to perceive it; and that to deny that things exist when we do not perceive them would be absurd. But Philonous responds by agreeing with him completely; and it is his acceptance of this point that real things (as opposed to merely imaginary ones) *do* exist when *we* do not perceive them, *together with* his insistence that, for things, 'to be is to be perceived,' which leads him to the conclusion that there must exist some spiritual being other than ourselves who perceives things even when we do not, and therefore accounts for their continuous existence: namely, God. 'Supposing you were annihilated,' Hylas says, 'cannot you conceive it possible that things perceivable by sense may still exist?' And Philonous replies:

I can; but then it must be in another mind. . . . It is plain [that sensible things] *have* an existence exterior to my mind. . . .
There is therefore some other mind wherein they exist, during the intervals between the times of my perceiving them: as likewise they did before my birth, and would do after my supposed annihilation. And, as the same is true with regard to all other finite created spirits, it necessarily follows there is an *omnipresent eternal Mind*, which knows and comprehends all things. (D 300)

This argument is not a version of the cosmological argument, because it does not involve arguing that God's existence must be presupposed in order to provide a cause for something we know through experience to exist, such as the material world, or ourselves, or our perceptions. It is an argument without any established name. And it is a very curious one. It would seem to be logically sound if the premises are valid; but the premises are, first, that for things, to be is to be perceived; and second, that things have an existence which is continuous and independent of their being perceived by us.

Let us grant the first premise, at least for the present. It is the second which is the curious one. It does agree with common sense, and does express part of what we mean when we speak of the existence of things. But neither consideration establishes that this premise is *true*. Its truth also is not established by the fact that I do not produce my sense-perceptions by an act of my own will. So what justification does Berkeley have for assuming it to be true? Without running afoul of his own theory of knowledge, it would seem impossible to establish the truth of this premise, either by experience or by reason. If this is so, then it cannot be an established fact for him, but rather a mere belief or assumption for which no empirical or rational justification is to be found. But a proof which has as one of its premises an unjustifiable belief is no proof at all. And so, however interesting Berkeley's line of thinking may be, it would not seem to give us a sound proof of the existence of God.

But even if this proof does not work, there is still the proof in the *Principles*; and that proof does not rest upon the same unjustifiable assumption. So it is still worth asking: if that proof is supposed to establish the existence of a spiritual being other than ourselves as the cause of our sense-perceptions, what can be said about the *nature* of that spiritual being? Does its nature as indicated by our experience correspond to God's nature as traditionally conceived? It must be a spiritual being, by previous argument; but of what sort? Berkeley's answer to this question is pretty much the same in both the *Principles* and the *Dialogues*. He says:

> if we attentively consider the constant regularity, order and concatenation of natural things, the surprising magnificence, beauty, and perfection of the larger, and the exquisite contrivance of the smaller parts of creation, together with the exact harmony and correspondence of the whole . . . ; – I say if we consider all these things, and at the same time attend to the meaning and import of the attributes One, Eternal, Infinitely Wise, Good, and Perfect, we shall clearly perceive that they belong to the . . . Spirit [in question]. (P. 146)

In short, by what has come to be known as an *argument from design* – an argument, that is, based on the design and order and beauty of what we experience – Berkeley concludes, with respect to the spiritual being he supposes to be the cause of the things we perceive, that it has all those attributes traditionally predicated of God. So he says that when he speaks of the existence of God,

> I do not mean an obscure general Cause of things, whereof we have no conception, but God, in the strict and proper sense of the word. A Being whose spirituality, omnipresence,

providence, omniscience, infinite power and goodness, are as conspicuous as the existence of sensible things, and of which . . . there is no more reason to doubt than of our own being. (D 335)

It is worth stressing that Berkeley does not use the argument from design to try to establish the *existence* of God, as some have. Rather, he uses it to establish the *nature* of that non-human spiritual being whose existence he attempts to establish by a form of the cosmological argument, on the one hand, and by his argument from the persistence and independence of sensible things, on the other. In light of his use of this argument for this purpose, it may seem rather odd when he then remarks:

God is a Being of transcendent and unlimited perfections: His nature, therefore, is incomprehensible to finite spirits. It is not, therefore, to be expected, that any man . . . should have exactly just notions of the Deity, His attributes, and ways of operation. (D 331)

However, his point is simply that we cannot have a very precise and adequate understanding of God's nature and various attributes, but rather only a general one – which, nonetheless, is enough to give one a pretty good idea of what he is like. Since Hume has a good deal to say about what one can and cannot conclude by any such argument from design, I will not go into Berkeley's argument any further now. I will only suggest two questions: Does the evidence of one's experience in fact warrant the inference of the attributes Berkeley infers? And even if it does, is there any justification for going beyond this and saying, as he does in the passage just mentioned, that 'God is a Being of transcendent and unlimited perfections,' whose 'nature . . . is [therefore] incomprehensible to finite spirits'?

I suggested earlier that, on Berkeley's own admission, the very meaningfulness of the notion of God is dependent upon the meaningfulness of the notion of a spiritual substance as this notion is applied to ourselves. But now it is perhaps time to raise the question of whether he is warranted in holding the notion of a spiritual substance or spirit to be meaningful at all, even in our own case. If it is assumed that we do not directly perceive anything corresponding to abstract terms and to the expression 'material substance,' and if this is taken to imply that we therefore really mean nothing at all when we speak of them, and that we have no right even to hypothesize that something might really exist corresponding to them, then it is difficult to see why an exception should be made in the case of 'spiritual substance' or 'spirit' or the 'self', which Berkeley grants we do not directly perceive either.

The justification Berkeley gives for using these expressions is that he feels he knows what he means by them; and the justification he gives for supposing that at least one such 'spiritual substance' exists (namely, himself) is that he cannot conceive of perceptions and volitions and thoughts occurring without their being some subject – some spiritual substance – whose acts they are. But Spinoza and Locke can say *they* know what they mean when they employ the expressions 'substance' and 'material substance' too; and Berkeley's statement of what he means by 'spirit' is not so very much more informative than theirs. And while his reason for concluding that at least one such spirit does in fact exist may be persuasive, it is not a reason warranted by the strict empiricist principles he professes.

In short, since there appears to be no good reason for proceeding differently in the case of 'spirit' than in other cases, it would seem to be necessary – if one is to be consistent – either to stick to Berkeley's strict empiricist criterion of meaningfulness and knowledge, in which case 'spirit' goes the way of 'matter' at his hands; or to abandon his strict empiricist criterion, and in doing so open the door to abstract ideas and independently existing material substance once again. Berkeley wants to have his cake and eat it too; but it is not clear that he can, without being inconsistent. One might ask: why be consistent? The answer to this is, first, that to be inconsistent is to be irrational, and to be irrational is to give up doing philosophy; and second, that if one indulges in an inconsistency to get the conclusions one wants, what is to prevent someone else who wants to reach different conclusions from doing the same?

But let us grant that it *is* meaningful to speak of a 'self' – *myself* – which is the subject of my perceptions, volitions and thoughts. What is its nature? To this question, Berkeley answers: 'What I am *myself*, that which I denote by the term *I*, is the same with what is meant by *soul*, or *spiritual substance*. . . . A *soul* or *spirit* is an active being, whose existence consists, not in being perceived but in perceiving ideas and thinking [and willing]' (P: 139). In other words, I am not the ideas I have through perception – all or any of them. Rather, I am that which *has* these ideas, and that alone. And this means that I do not have a *dual* nature, of spirit and body; rather, I have a single, spiritual nature. For if the two categories of 'spirit' and 'idea' exhaust all of reality, then what is that which I call 'my body' except a certain set of ideas, which I have, but which, as nothing but a set of ideas I *have*, is not *me*.

For Berkeley, therefore, there are none of the problems to worry about which are so difficult for dualists. There is no body distinct from the mind; and so there is no problem of how they can interact, and how they can be united. His is not even a two-aspect theory, like Spinoza's; so there is no problem of conceiving how one and the same substance could have two different aspects, one of extension and one of thought. I am solely a spiritual being, not a being one part or aspect of which is material, and another spiritual. Yet it does not follow, for Berkeley, that I am 'Pure Spirit,' in the sense that God is 'Pure Spirit.' Using language which sounds much more ordinary (and dualistic), he says that, unlike God,

> We are chained to a body: that is to say, our perceptions are connected with corporeal motions. By the law of our nature, we are affected upon every alteration in the nervous parts of our sensible body. . . . (D 313)

But he goes on to explain that this admission does not really commit him to dualism, and that this circumstance can be explained solely in immaterialist terms:

> [Our] sensible body, rightly considered, is nothing but a complexion of such qualities or ideas as have no existence distinct from being perceived by a mind. So that this connexion of sensations with corporeal motions means no more than a correspondence in the order of nature, between two sets of ideas, or things immediately perceivable. (D 314)

In other words, what our 'being chained to a body' amounts to is the fact that in our case, our perceptions of what we call external objects are linked to another set of ideas which we do not ordinarily perceive or take notice of – those which go together to make up that thing which we call 'our body'; whereas in the case of God this is not so. This account certainly is consistent with Berkeley's general position, and is not incoherent; and in fact it is the only position he could take on the matter within the framework of his immaterialism.

Berkeley's argument for the immortality of the soul, or self, follows quite logically from his conception of its nature. He says:

The Mind, Spirit, or Soul is that indivisible unextended thing which thinks, acts, and perceives. I say *indivisible*, because unextended; and *unextended*, because extended, figured, moveable things are ideas; and that which perceives ideas . . . is plainly itself no idea, nor like an idea. (D 301)

[It] is consequently incorruptible. Nothing can be plainer than that the motions, changes, decays, and dissolutions which we hourly see befall natural bodies . . . cannot possibly affect an active, simple, uncompounded substance; such a being therefore is indissoluble by the force of nature; that is to say, the soul of man is naturally immortal. (P: 141)

There is nothing faulty in Berkeley's reasoning here. If his conclusion is invalid, this can only be because he is mistaken in holding that there is no material substance existing independently of any mind, that the human mind is an 'indivisible unextended thing which thinks, acts, and perceives,' and that all of reality consists solely of spirits and the ideas they perceive.

I shall conclude by drawing attention to an issue which would seem to raise a rather serious problem for Berkeley, within the context of his own general views. The issue is that of how we know, not that there is a God, or that I myself exist and have the nature he describes, but in addition that there are other beings like myself. This is the issue of our knowledge of the existence of other minds, which continues to concern philosophers today. That it is *possible* that there should be other minds is conceivable enough. And Berkeley says: 'My own mind and my own ideas I have an immediate knowledge of; and, by the help of these, [I] do mediately apprehend the possibility of the existence of other spirits and ideas' (D 302). But how can I know that there *are* other minds or spirits like myself? Berkeley quite consistently admits that 'A human spirit or person is not perceived by sense, as not being an idea' (P: 148). Since the existence of other minds is not directly established by perception, therefore, it can only be established (if at all) by reasoning. Berkeley thinks it *can* be established by an argument which has come to be known as the *argument by analogy*. 'It is plain,' he contends, that

we do not see a man, if by *man* is meant, that which lives, moves, perceives, and thinks as we do: but only such a certain collection of ideas, as directs us to think there is a distinct principle of thought and motion, like unto ourselves, accompanying and representing it (P: 148).

I perceive several motions, changes, and combinations of ideas, that inform me there are certain particular agents, like myself, which accompany them, and concur in their production. Hence, the knowledge I have of other spirits is not immediate, as is the knowledge of my ideas, but depending on the intervention of ideas, by me referred to agents or spirits distinct from myself, as effects or concomitant signs. (P: 145)

In other words, I know there to be other spiritual beings or minds like myself by a kind of inductive inference. My mind is associated with a set of perceptible ideas which I call my body and its actions; I perceive other similar sets of ideas; and I may therefore infer that a mind similar in nature to my own is likewise associated with them. Now there are problems with this argument, even when it is presented in connection with an ontology which affirms the existence of material substances, and a theory of perception which holds that we directly perceive them. But greater problems are raised by Berkeley's contention that I never directly perceive anything other than my own ideas, that things are nothing but configurations of various ideas in some mind or other, and that my 'sensible body' is nothing more than a certain special set of ideas I have in my mind.

If these points are granted, then it is inconceivable how I could ever arrive at a knowledge of the existence of other minds. For it would seem to follow from these assumptions that we are all rather like Leibniz's monads, in that we are all radically isolated from each other, without windows through which we could ever observe anything outside of our own minds. We can only perceive our own ideas; and while some of these ideas are complex ideas similar to the complex idea which we call our own 'sensible body', this would not seem to warrant the kind of inference Berkeley draws. His general views thus would appear to entail a kind of epistemological solipsism – the position that I cannot know, or have any rational grounds for even supposing, that any mind exists other than my own. Berkeley refuses to draw this conclusion, perhaps feeling (quite rightly) that it is unacceptable; and that if it necessarily follows from a given set of premises, this would show that there is something wrong with them.

It is rather telling that at one point in the *Principles* Berkeley says of God: 'He alone it is who ... maintains that intercourse between spirits whereby they are able to perceive the existence of each other' (P: 147). Something on the order of divine intervention *would* seem to be required to enable us to know that other minds than our own exist, given Berkeley's general views. But to have to resort to God in this matter is a rather unsatisfactory way of dealing with an issue as important as this. We should be able to account for our knowledge of the existence of other minds – or other persons – without having to resort to such extreme measures. And the fact that Berkeley is impelled to do so suffices to raise serious doubts about his general position, even if one has been persuaded by the arguments he gives in support of it.

CHAPTER VI

HUME

Of all the philosophers dealt with here, David Hume may well have been the one it would have been the most enjoyable to know. Others may have had more powerful and creative minds; but Hume's combination of modesty, wit, sophistication, and humane erudition was and remains hard to beat. His short autobiographical essay 'My Own Life,' written shortly before his death in 1776, nicely conveys more about him than the events of the life it records. Born in Scotland in 1711, he was very much a man of his place and time; yet he transcended both, and seems in many ways more our contemporary than any of the others.

Like Berkeley, Hume arrived at his basic philosophical position very early; and he published the most systematic and comprehensive statement of his views – his *Treatise of Human Nature* (well over 600 pages) – at the age of 27. As he acknowledges, the publication of this work (which he completed during a long sojourn in France) aroused no interest whatsoever; and it was only after he had made a reputation for himself with his literary and political essays, and to a much lesser extent with his *Inquiry Concerning Human Understanding*, that even a few people began to read it seriously. (One of those who did see its significance, however, was Kant, whose own work it greatly influenced.) During his lifetime, Hume had to content himself largely with the reputation he acquired as a historian, literary critic, and social and political philosopher. In the course of the past two hundred years, of course, things have been very different; it is little exaggeration to say that mainstream English-language philosophy during this period, at least until Wittgenstein, was largely a series of footnotes to Hume. But even his *Inquiry*, written in the hope of gaining a wider hearing for a small selection of issues from his *Treatise*, did not attract much attention until after his death. And his masterpiece on the topic of religion – *Dialogues Concerning Natural Religion* – was not published until after his death; for he did not want to have to endure the polemics which he knew it would arouse from defenders of the kinds of arguments and views he attacks in it.

Hume remarks that he was 'seized very early with a passion for literature, which has been the ruling passion of my life and the great source of my enjoyments' (3). One fortunate consequence of this was that he developed his own literary skills to the point that few philosophers surpass or even equal him as a writer. The two books of his I will discuss are literary as well as philosophical masterpieces. None of the other works considered have any standing as literature. But Hume's works do, just as Gibbon's history of the Roman Empire does; and one should be able to enjoy him as well as understand him, whether or not one accepts what he says.

If there is any philosopher in the history of philosophy whose feelings about philosophy are the exact opposite of Spinoza's, it is Hume. He couldn't stand to work for very long on philosophical problems. This may partly account for the fact that, after his first long work, he confined himself largely to short essays (even in the *Inquiry*), dealing with a number of problems of limited scope. His use of examples involving billiard balls is no accident; for he found himself a great deal happier playing billiards than doing philosophy. When he has Nature deliver a little lecture to the philosopher in Section 1 of the *Inquiry*, it is his own experience to which he is giving expression. Nature says:

> Abstruse thought and profound researches I prohibit and will
> severely punish by the pensive melancholy which they
> introduce, by the endless uncertainty in which they involve
> you, and by the cold reception your pretended discoveries
> shall meet when communicated. (18)

A few hours at a time in his study was all Hume could take, before fleeing to the sanctuary of the billiards room, where he could revive his spirits. There is no use denying that this is how it was with Hume (as it no doubt is with most people). But it is also worth remembering Spinoza's very different experience, and the supreme happiness he found in philosophy, and there alone. The moral of the story is simply that different people have different temperaments, and that even great philosophers have not found philosophy satisfying to the same degree and in the same way. It is not surprising, however, given the kind of experience Hume reports, that he did not spend his life doing philosophy, but rather turned more and more to other matters in his later years. In the end, he spent much more time on his *History of England* than he ever did on his philosophical writings. But this does not detract from the importance of his philosophical writings, any more than it proves that philosophy can be no more personally satisfying than he himself found it.

Program and method

In light of his own experience, however, it is not at all surprising that Hume has a very different conception of the importance of philosophy – both the kind he does and the kind he does not do – than do most of the others dealt with. He does not consider philosophy to be of great significance because of the importance of a Cartesian reconstruction of knowledge, since he does not think that the kind of reconstruction of knowledge Descartes attempted is possible. And he does not accord significance to philosophy because of the importance or satisfaction of attaining a knowledge of reality – of the existence and natures of God, the soul and the world – since he does not think that metaphysical knowledge in these matters is possible. In this respect, Hume is even more skeptical than Locke, and feels compelled to 'sit down in a quiet ignorance' long before Locke does. He regards all metaphysical systems which profess to give knowledge of the true natures of things – whether those of the rationalists or Berkeley's – as disguises in which 'popular superstitions' (meaning, above all, the doctrines of traditional religion), 'which, being unable to defend themselves on fair ground, raise these entangling brambles to cover and protect their weakness' (20). The principal function of true philosophy, as he conceives of it, is to show these disguises for what they are, and to put an end to such speculations altogether.

> The only method of freeing learning at once from these abstruse questions is to inquire seriously into the nature of human understanding and show, from an exact analysis of its powers and capacity, that it is by no means fitted for such remote and abstruse subjects. . . . Accurate and just reasoning is the only catholic [i.e., universal] remedy fitted for all persons and all dispositions, and is alone able to subvert that abstruse philosophy and metaphysical jargon which, being mixed up with popular superstition, renders it in a manner impenetrable to careless reasoners and gives it the air of science and wisdom. (21)

It remains to be seen, of course, whether Hume is right in what he says about the status of the traditional sort of metaphysical inquiry and about the limits of our knowledge and our powers of understanding. But it is clear that he *thinks* that at least one of the most important functions of philosophy is this negative one, of criticizing the claims of the metaphysicians, and of showing the limits beyond which knowledge is impossible.

But there is more to philosophy as Hume conceives of it than this. It also has a positive function, and a positive contribution to make. This contribution lies in the area of exploring how the human mind works, and the nature and scope of human knowledge. 'It cannot be doubted,' he says, 'that the mind is endowed with several powers and faculties, that these powers are distinct from each other . . . , and, consequently, that there is a truth and falsehood [in these matters] which lie not beyond the compass of human understanding' (22). There are two parts of the kind of 'inquiry concerning the human understanding' which he proposes. The first part consists simply in a description of our various capacities; and the second consists in an explanation of how they operate in relation to each other. He says:

> It becomes . . . no inconsiderable part of science barely to know
> the different operations of the mind, to separate them from
> each other, to class them under their proper heads, and to
> correct all that seeming disorder in which they lie involved
> when made the object of reflection and inquiry. . . . And if we
> can go no further than this mental geography or delineation of
> the distinct parts and powers of the mind, it is at least a
> satisfaction to go so far. . . .
> But may we not hope that philosophy, if cultivated with
> care. . . , may carry its researches still further and discover, at
> least in some degree, the secret springs and principles by which
> the human mind is actuated in its operations? Astronomers
> had long contended themselves with proving, from the
> phenomena, the true motions, order, and magnitude of the
> heavenly bodies, till a philosopher [Newton] at last arose who
> seems, from the happiest of reasoning, to have determined
> the laws and forces by which the revolutions of the planets are
> governed and directed. . . . And there is no reason to despair
> of equal success in our inquiries concerning the mental powers
> and economy if prosecuted with equal capacity and caution.
> (24)

Hume thus aspired to be something like the Newton of epistemology and the philosophy of mind, and not simply a subverter of all previous metaphysics. It was this positive contribution he hoped to make which made him feel it was worthwhile to devote himself at least in part to philosophy. The importance he attached to his efforts in this area, however, even if they were to be successful, was only a modest one. He by no means thought that it would be the key to human happiness, or even that it would be attended by any great practical advantage. Life would go on just as before; and if people were able to find no true happiness in life without his philosophy, he did not think they would be any more able to find it with his philosophy. But just as the theoretical physicist may find personal satisfaction in the knowledge he achieves of natural phenomena, Hume felt that the kind of philosophy he advocated could yield knowledge of the mind which would also have a certain satisfaction for those who find knowledge satisfying for its own sake. 'Obscurity,' he says, 'is painful to the mind as well as to the eye, but to bring light from obscurity, by whatever labour, must needs be delightful and rejoicing' (20). If some do not find such knowledge pleasurable, well and good; but for those who do, Hume (who is one of them) will do what he can to increase it. At times, however, he seems to indicate that he finds as much satisfaction in undermining the new pseudo-philosophical props of 'popular superstition' as he does in this; and the source of this satisfaction would seem to be the conviction that people will be better off if they are disabused of false doctrines, and cease being fanatical about them, than if they remain captive to them. In fact, this was undoubtedly the primary motive which led him to write the *Dialogues Concerning Natural Religion*, the upshot of which is almost entirely critical and negative.

Hume feels that it is possible to arrive at some definite positive conclusions where the operations of the mind are concerned. He has no such hopes, however, in relation to anything else (outside of mathematics), and in particular, in relation to God, and to whatever else there may be in the world in addition to the human mind. On these matters, his philosophical position is one of complete skepticism. Starting from the assumption (shared by Locke and Berkeley) that we never directly perceive anything except our own ideas, he argues that we are in principle incapable of coming to *know* that things external to our own minds exist – or, on the other hand, that nothing else *does* exist. We can never prove that anything else exists; but we can never prove that *nothing* else exists either. So, while Hume accepts many of Berkeley's critical arguments against materialism, he stops short of concluding that Berkeley's immaterialism and his *denial* of the existence of anything other than minds and ideas are correct. He is a skeptic because, first, he rejects the commonsense view that in perception we perceive independently existing material things just as they are in themselves; and second, because he refuses to take sides between materialism and immaterialism, maintaining rather that they both are untenable positions, in that they both make claims about what does and does not really exist which they cannot adequately support. Thus he endorses not only a modified version of Descartes's methodological doubt, but also another kind of skepticism, which is not provisional and methodological but permanent.

> There is another species of skepticism, *consequent* to science and inquiry, when men are supposed to have discovered either the absolute fallaciousness of their mental faculties or their unfitness to reach any fixed determination in all those curious subjects of speculation about which they are commonly employed. (15)

These 'curious subjects' include most of the subjects of traditional metaphysics. Hume feels there are compelling reasons to adopt a position of complete skepticism with regard to most metaphysical issues. He for the most part does not conclude that it is meaningless even to *speak* of matters about which we can have no genuine knowledge, owing to the limitations upon our faculties. He seems willing to allow that we can speak of them, and have beliefs about them; and his only claim would seem to be that we are deceiving ourselves if we think we can have knowledge concerning them. For example, he speaks as though it is quite possible that there is a world of things existing independently of our ideas of them, and that it is governed by various laws. But he holds that we can never establish that it exists (or anything about it) either by direct experience or by rational argument; and that therefore we can have no knowledge of it. In his view, however, the problem lies less in our acceptance of false or meaningless principles (as Berkeley contends) than it does in the limitations upon our faculties, and in particular, our reason.

This leads to a related point. Hume differs radically from the rationalists, in that he sees no justification for assuming that reality is an essentially rational structure which is therefore, in principle at least, accessible to human reason. Leibniz and Spinoza argued that if this assumption is not made, rational inquiry into the natures of things is undercut before it even begins. Hume agrees; but rather than accordingly making this assumption, he feels obliged to refuse to make it, since he cannot justify it, and accepts the consequence, which to Leibniz and Spinoza was unacceptable. Hume is not a philosophical *irrationalist*; he does not claim that reality in fact is *not* a rational structure. He only claims that we cannot *know* whether it is, since we cannot base any claims to knowledge upon assumptions which we do not know to be valid.

In this way, Hume is led to take a far less exalted view of the power of our reason than does any other classical modern philosopher. He does not suppose that we have any other faculty which is better able to give us knowledge of the natures of things. He accepts the view that, where knowledge is concerned, reason is indispensable, and is the best faculty we have. But he holds that human reason is not powerful enough to give us the kind of metaphysical knowledge philosophers traditionally have sought. It cannot do the job – and nothing else can either; and he therefore concludes that skepticism is the only reasonable position to take.

Yet Hume does not regard this shortcoming as a very serious one. For he also has a much lower estimate of the *importance* of rational knowledge for life than most other philosophers from Descartes to Kant do. He observes that in our daily lives we get along perfectly well relying simply on what he terms our 'instincts' – tendencies we have by nature, which, though they are incapable of providing us with genuine knowledge, enable us to meet our practical needs quite adequately. (As he uses the term, 'instinct' must be construed quite broadly; for it includes the tendency to assume that past experience may be relied upon to anticipate what the future will be like – and so science itself, which rests upon this assumption, turns out to rest upon a non-rational tendency of thought or 'instinct.') However limited our rational knowledge may be in the last analysis, therefore, this is not a limitation which Hume feels is accompanied by any disastrous practical effect. Indeed, he contends that the adoption of the kind of skepticism he advocates, far from being harmful, cannot possibly have any real effect in the life of a person who adopts it. All the skeptic's arguments, he says, while quite valid,

are mere amusement, and can have no other tendency than to show the whimsical condition of mankind, who must act and reason and believe, though they are not able, by their diligent inquiry, to satisfy themselves concerning the foundation of those operations or to remove the objections which may be raised against them. (168–9)

For Hume it is as impossible to *live* in accordance with one's skeptical conclusions about the fundamental natures of things, as it is to avoid these conclusions in philosophical argument.

The great subverter of . . . the excessive principles of skepticism, is action, and employment, and the occupations of common life. These principles may flourish and triumph in the schools, where it is indeed difficult, if not impossible, to refute them. But as soon as they leave the shade, and by the presence of real objects which actuate our passions and sentiments are put in opposition to the more powerful principles of our nature, they vanish like smoke and leave the most determined skeptic in the same condition as other mortals. (107)

In short: of matters which transcend our immediate experience and the operations of our own minds, we can have no knowledge. We can know what we directly perceive; but what we directly perceive is only our own ideas. We can have no knowledge of matters of fact and existence which go beyond our own ideas; and therefore we can have no knowledge of the true natures of things (or even of their bare existence) independently of our ideas of them. We can continue to do empirical science; but however beneficial the practical effects of empirical science may be, and however compelling the demands and experiences of common life, the conclusions they lead us to adopt never attain the status of genuine knowledge. For these conclusions are founded solely on experience; and experience is incapable of providing us with genuine knowledge, since conclusions from experience could not possibly be considered genuine knowledge of the natures of things without several assumptions being made for which we have neither rational nor empirical justification. Knowledge is possible only where rational demonstration is possible; and rational demonstration is possible only in mathematics. Experimental reasoning, or empirical investigation, has a practical purpose, and so is legitimate; though it does not admit of rational demonstration, and therefore does not yield genuine knowledge. But nothing else – including, in particular, traditional metaphysical reasoning – has even this sort of practical justification. This leads Hume to say, in the famous last lines of the *Inquiry*:

> When we run over libraries, persuaded of these principles, what
> havoc must we make? If we take in our hand any volume –
> of divinity or school metaphysics, for instance – let us ask:
> Does it contain any abstract reasoning concerning quantity
> or number? No. Does it contain any experimental reasoning
> concerning matter of fact and existence? No. Commit it then
> to the flames, for it can contain nothing more than sophistry
> and illusion. (173)

It is clear that, rightly or wrongly, among the books he would commit to the flames would be most of the works of Descartes, Leibniz and Spinoza. But what about Locke and Berkeley? Here the matter is not quite so clear, even though Hume rejects both Locke's materialism and Berkeley's immaterialism. I will conclude this section with a word about his general attitude toward his two fellow 'empiricists.'

Hume seems to treat Locke rather harshly, in a footnote in which he refers to Locke's discussion of innate ideas. He seems to think that the whole dispute about innate ideas was rather silly, saying:

> To be ingenuous, I must own it to be my opinion that Locke
> was betrayed into this question by the schoolmen, who
> making use of undefined terms, draw out their disputes to a
> tedious length without ever touching the point in question. A
> like ambiguity and circumlocution seems to run through that
> philosopher's reasonings, on this as well as most other
> subjects. (30n. 1)

Yet he actually has a good deal of respect for Locke, referring to him in another footnote as 'really a great philosopher, and a just and modest reasoner' (17n.). The upshot of both of these passages would seem to be that Hume regards Locke as having had a number of important insights (particularly with regard to the nature of our knowledge) and as having seen at least *some* of their consequences with regard to the limits of our knowledge; although he rejects most of Locke's positive conclusions. He likes Locke's criticisms, as far as Locke carries them; the only trouble was that, in his view, Locke didn't carry them far enough.

Hume's treatment of Berkeley is quite different. He admires Berkeley, but for reasons which must have horrified Berkeley, who was still alive when the *Inquiry* was published. Hume observes that Berkeley 'professes . . . (and undoubtedly with great truth) to have composed his book [the *Principles*] against the skeptics as well as against the atheists and freethinkers'; but he says that in point of fact, 'most of the writings of that ingenious author form the best lessons of skepticism which are to be found among the ancient or modern philosophers' (163n.). Hume's reason for saying this should be obvious. Berkeley's criticisms of materialism are powerful; but in Hume's mind at least, his positive arguments, leading to his own doctrine of immaterialism, are without any force whatsoever. The result is that one doesn't know what to think; and this leads to a skepticism of the sort Hume advocates. And, in fact, one can arrive at a fairly accurate anticipation of Hume's own position if one asks oneself: What happens if one accepts Berkeley's criticisms, yet stops short of drawing his immaterialist conclusion, and then drops God out of the picture?

Ideas and experience

Hume simply takes for granted that we never directly perceive anything other than our own ideas. 'The slightest philosophy,' he says, 'teaches us that nothing can ever be present to the mind but an image or perception, and that the senses are the only inlets through which these ideas are conveyed' (160). He takes these points to have been amply demonstrated by Locke and Berkeley, and sees no need to go over the same ground again. His major concern in the main part of the *Inquiry* is to give an analysis of the different types of ideas we have, and to draw out certain implications of these basic points which Locke and Berkeley either had not seen or had not sufficiently emphasized.

He begins by observing that not all of our perceptions are on a par with each other. We commonly distinguish between sense-perceptions, on the one hand, and imagination, memory and thoughts on the other; and Hume wants to distinguish between them too. But since, like Berkeley, he holds that all of these are nothing but perceptions in our minds, he concludes that they are to be distinguished, not in terms of the presence or absence of some independently existing object, but rather in terms of some relative difference in their natures. And he takes this difference to consist simply in their different 'force or vivacity.' He says of memory and imagination: 'These faculties may mimic or copy the perceptions of the senses but they never can entirely reach the force and vivacity of the original [sensation]. . . . The most lively thought is still inferior to the dullest sensation' (26). He grants that an exception must be made if 'the mind be disordered by disease or madness'; but setting cases of that sort aside, he seems to think that this is a point which 'everyone will readily allow' if only we consider our own experience. And he proposes to make the relative difference in vivacity and forcefulness the defining features in distinguishing sense-perceptions, or 'impressions,' on the one hand, from the 'thoughts' or 'ideas' of memory and imagination, on the other.

> By the term 'impression' . . . , I mean all our more lively perceptions, when we hear, or see, or feel, or like or hate, or desire, or will. And impressions are distinguished from ideas, which are the less lively perceptions of which we are conscious when we reflect on any of those sensations [just] mentioned. (27)

Now this might seem quite reasonable. But there is a kind of circularity in Hume's procedure here. It is quite legitimate simply to *define* 'impressions' as 'all our more lively perceptions,' and to *define* 'ideas' as all of our 'less lively perceptions.' But these definitions are purely arbitrary, unless we have some independent way of verifying that all cases of seeing, hearing, and so on are in fact 'more lively' than all cases of remembering and imagining and thinking. And we have no such independent way of verifying this, unless it is assumed that we already know perfectly well which perceptions are sense-perceptions, and which are not. Hume seems to think that we do already know this; otherwise it would make no sense for him to say that, if we consider our sense-perceptions on the one hand and cases of remembering and imagining and thinking on the other, we *see* that the former are as a matter of fact more forceful and vivid than the latter. But if we are able to distinguish them prior to considering their relative forcefulness and vivacity, it must be by reference to some *other* criterion that we distinguish them.

In short: either their sole distinguishing feature is their relative forcefulness and vivacity – in which case it is a matter of definition rather than something we discover by experience that sense-impressions are more forceful and vivid than ideas; or they are distinguishable and definable in some other way – in which case Hume's claim that all that distinguishes them is their relative forcefulness and vivacity is falsified. There is no reason *a priori* why sense-perceptions must be more forceful and vivid than cases of remem-

bering, imagining and thinking, even if it is true that the latter are
nothing but copies of the former, as Hume also claims. He himself
would be the first to admit this, since he is quite insistent that
reasoning *a priori* can never demonstrate anything about matters
of fact and existence. So one does not really know quite what to
make of his initial discussion of the difference between impressions
and ideas.

But this only affects the matter of how we are to distinguish the
two. It does not affect his claim that all of our perceptions and
ideas are *either* sense-impressions *or* copies of them, remembered,
imagined, or thought of. It is this claim to which I now turn. It is
similar to claims made by both Locke and Berkeley. Hume holds
that all of our ideas are either derived directly from sense-perception, or else are the results of 'compounding, transposing, augmen-
ting, or diminishing the materials afforded us by the senses and
experience' (27). 'All the materials of thinking,' he says, 'are derived
either from our outward or inward sentiment . . .; all our ideas or
more feeble perceptions are copies of our impressions or more
lively ones' (28).

Hume recognizes that it would be dogmatic simply to assert this;
and that there are people – philosophers, at any rate – who would
wish to dispute or at least question this view. So he attempts to
'prove' it, in the following way. He says: 'When we analyze our
thoughts or ideas, however compounded or sublime, *we always
find* that they resolve themselves into such simple ideas as were
copied from a precedent feeling or sentiment' (28; emphasis added).
And he continues:

> Those who would assert that this position is not universally
> true, nor without exception, have only one . . . method of
> refuting it; by producing that idea which, in their opinion, is
> not derived from this source. It will then be incumbent on us
> . . . to produce the impression or lively perception which
> corresponds to it. (28)

This is Hume's version of Locke's challenge, by which Locke
attempted to defend essentially the same empiricist thesis about the
origin and content of all our ideas. And when Hume comes to
discuss the idea of causality, he does what he says here he must
do to defend this thesis: namely, he identifies an impression which
he takes to correspond to this idea, and which he therefore
concludes explains how we come to have this idea, and what its
precise meaning is. Yet if someone were to claim that our idea of

causality is not simply a copy of the impression Hume cites, or if someone were to come up with some other term or concept for which no corresponding impression is to be found at all, Hume is by no means actually prepared to abandon his thesis. On the contrary, he has no sooner issued his challenge as the main support for this thesis, than he makes use of this thesis to claim that a purported idea which is not copied from some sense-impression is devoid of all significant content, and that a term which corresponds to no such impression is meaningless. Only two pages after issuing his challenge, he says:

> When we entertain . . . any suspicion that a philosophical term is employed without any meaning (as is but too frequent), we need but inquire, *from what impression is that supposed idea derived*? And if it be impossible to assign any, this will serve to confirm our suspicion. (30)

At the end of Section VII, when he recapitulates his position, he asserts flatly: 'Every idea is copied from some preceding impression or sentiment; and where we cannot find any impression, we may be certain that there is no idea' (89). But what has happened to his challenge? We may be certain that there is no idea where there is no preceding sense-impression only if ideas are *defined* as copies of impressions. But to *define* an idea in this way is to rule out the very possibility of anyone meeting his challenge; and while this kind of procedure is a very easy way of dealing with counter-examples, it is also not a very satisfactory one. Unfortunately, the parallel with Locke goes farther than Hume's assertion of the empiricist thesis about our ideas and his support of it by issuing a challenge to anyone to come up with a counterexample. He can deal with 'metaphysical jargon' as he does only by begging the basic question at issue, and arbitrarily and dogmatically restricting the class of meaningful terms of ideas to the class of those which derive directly from sense-perception. The only way he can avoid begging the question is to allow that it is at least in principle possible for there to be ideas with significant content and meaningful terms which are *not* copies of our impressions. But to do this, he must abandon his quick and easy way of 'banishing all that jargon which has so long taken possession of metaphysical reasonings' (30).

Of course, it might turn out that Hume *would* be able to meet any response to his challenge to his thesis in the manner he indicates – by producing some impression or set of impressions adequately accounting for any idea or concept cited as a possible counter-example. But it is also conceivable that the kind of explication he would be able to give by proceeding in this way would *not* adequately account for that idea or concept (of causality, for example); and in that case, he would either be reduced to dogmatism, or be compelled to give up his empiricist thesis about the origin and content of our ideas. This problem is much more serious than the first one mentioned, concerning Hume's way of distinguishing and defining impressions as opposed to ideas; for it directly affects his discussion of causality, and his treatment of a number of other issues as well.

Empiricism has often been praised, and rationalism criticized, by saying that it is free from that dogmatism which is so characteristic of rationalism. But this simply is not true, at least where the philosophers discussed here are concerned; and the relative merits of the two are by no means so easily determined as this would seem to suggest. On the contrary, at least where the origin and content of our ideas are concerned, it might quite plausibly be argued that the rationalists are the more open-minded and truly empirical of the two. This helps explain why, on the Continent, at least, philosophers were by no means prepared to allow that Hume had the final word. His conclusion, that all books of philosophy not dealing with mathematics and experimental reasoning should be committed to the flames, may have been a bit hasty.

Section IV of the *Inquiry* begins with the famous and influential lines:

> All the objects of human reason or inquiry may naturally be divided into two kinds, to wit, 'Relations of Ideas,' and 'Matters of Fact.' Of the first kind are the sciences of Geometry, Algebra, and Arithmetic and in short, every affirmation which is either intuitively or demonstrably certain. . . . Propositions of this kind are discoverable by the mere operation of thought, without dependence on what is anywhere existent in the universe. . . . Matters of fact . . . [on the other hand] are not ascertained in the same manner, nor is our evidence of their truth, however great, of a like nature with the foregoing. The contrary of every matter of fact is still possible, because it can never imply a contradiction and is conceived by the mind with the same facility and distinctness, as if ever so conformable with reality. (40)

Most philosophers, including most rationalists, are willing to allow that mathematical propositions are discoverable by the mere operation of thought, without dependence on what exists anywhere in the universe; while, at least generally speaking, the truth of propositions concerning matters of fact cannot be demonstrated logically, since their contraries would not be self-contradictory. But one would like to know Hume's justification for asserting that 'the contrary of *every* matter of fact is still possible,' and that therefore no existential proposition can be certain. Consider, for example, the proposition 'I exist.' Descartes and Leibniz would certainly want to claim that when I utter this proposition, its truth is intuitively certain. Is its contrary even logically possible at the moment I utter it? Is it conceivable that, though I *think* I exist, I in fact do not?

Or consider a very different sort of proposition – Hume's own proposition, that 'nothing can ever be present to the mind but an image or perception' (160). Hume certainly would seem to regard this as indisputable and certain. Yet surely he would not hold that this proposition merely assets a 'relation of ideas,' which has no relation to or dependence upon 'what is anywhere existent in the universe.' On the contrary, he considers it to be a matter of fact. One could come up with a number of examples of this kind from Hume's own writings. Or think of the law of non-contradiction. Surely Hume would not regard that as merely a matter of the 'relation of ideas,' with no application to matters of fact. Yet he also would not seem to have any doubts about its validity. In short, even if it is true that there are only two kinds of objects of human inquiry, relations of ideas and matters of fact (a claim, by the way, for which Hume gives no argument or justification), it is not at all clear that only mathematical propositions, and propositions which are true by virtue of the meanings of the terms involved, are 'intuitively or demonstrably certain,' and that no factual claims can ever be certain.

But in speaking of 'matters of fact,' Hume has in mind primarily propositions pertaining to matters of fact and existence where particular things other than the mind itself are concerned. This is suggested, for example, when he defines the problem he wishes to discuss in the rest of this and the following several sections: 'It may . . . be a subject worthy of curiosity to inquire what is the nature of that evidence which assures us of any real existence or matter of fact beyond the present testimony of our senses or the records of our memory' (40–1). And this leads him directly to the matter of causality; for he holds that 'all reasonings concerning matter of fact seem to be founded on the relation of *cause* and *effect*. By means of that relation alone we can go beyond the evidence of our memory and senses' (41). It is his conclusions with regard to all reasoning employing or based on the concept of causality which lead him to his skepticism with regard to the natures and even the existence of things apart from our own minds and the particular sense-impressions we have. For we can explain neither the occurrence of our particular sense-impressions nor what we commonly call various natural phenomena without making use of the notion of causality. Hume asks: How do we arrive at our knowledge of cause and effect? And he answers:

I shall venture to affirm, as a general proposition which admits of no exception, that the knowledge of this relation is not, in any instance, attained by reasonings *a priori*, but arises entirely from experience, when we find that any particular objects are constantly conjoined with each other. . . . No object ever discovers, by the qualities which appear to the senses, either the causes which produced it or the effects which will arise from it; nor can our reason, unassisted by experience, ever draw any inference concerning real existence and matter of fact. (42)

The reason for this is that no particular event logically implies or excludes any other particular subsequent event. The law of non-contradiction is of no help here; and therefore logical demonstration is impossible. Only experience can show which events are associated with which other events. 'Every effect,' Hume says, 'is a distinct event from its cause' (44). And from this it follows that:

When we reason *a priori* and consider merely any object or cause as it appears to the mind, independent of all observation, it could never suggest to us the notion of any distinct object, such as its effect, much less show us the inseparable and inviolable connection between them. (46)

Having made this point, Hume next observes that even when we have had experience of the association of some events with others, this gives us no real knowledge of what causes what; for such experience only shows that, in the past, some events have been associated with others. But it shows us nothing which would warrant the general conclusion that events of one type are necessarily connected with events of another type. 'Past experience,' he says, can be allowed only to give *direct* and *certain* information of those precise objects only, and that precise period of time which fell under its cognizance. But why this experience should be extended to future times and to other objects which, for aught we know, may be only in appearance similar, this is the main question on which I would insist. . . . The consequence seems nowise necessary. (48)

The consequence would follow only if we either actually perceived the necessary connection between the types of events in question, or could show that the future must be like the past. But in fact we can do neither. For experience only shows us one event followed by another; we *perceive* no necessary connection between them with any of our senses. And no argument can show that the future must be like the past. For, first, it cannot be argued *a priori* that the future will be like the past, since the idea that the future might be *different* from the past is not self-contradictory. And, second, it cannot be argued that the future will be like the past on the basis of past experience; for any such argument can only show that the future has been like the past *in the past*. But it cannot show that the future will continue to be like the past *in the future*. To argue in this way, as Hume observes, 'must evidently be going in a circle, and taking that for granted which is the very point in question' (50). 'Let the course of things be allowed hitherto ever so regular, that alone, without some new argument or inference, proves not that for the future it will continue so' (52).

Hume is not arguing that the future *will not* resemble the past. He is not even arguing that we should stop *thinking* that the future will resemble the past. On the contrary, he grants that we do and must operate on this assumption in our ordinary lives; after all, we have nothing else to go on. His point is simply that there *is* an assumption being made here, which we cannot justify either rationally or by direct experience; and that therefore all of our conclusions based on this assumption – all our reasonings employing the category of causality, and therefore all our conclusions concerning matters of fact and existence in the world – fall short of being *knowledge*. They all involve a kind of leap of faith, and fall short of that certainty which is a necessary condition of genuine knowledge.

In Section V, Hume argues that, since we *do* form conclusions about causes and effects from past experience; since we *do* act on the assumption that the future will resemble the past; and since it is *not reason* which leads us to do so, it must be *some other principle* which is at work here. And 'this principle' he says, 'is *custom* or *habit*' (56). 'After the conjunction of two objects . . . , we are determined by custom alone to expect the one from the appearance of the other' (57).

Several remarks may be made with respect to this reasoning. First: Hume does not really give a positive argument for this conclusion. Rather, he arrives at it by a process of elimination. He assumes that custom is the only alternative conceivable to those he has considered and rejected, and therefore concludes that our employment of the category of causality is explainable only in terms of custom. But of course, if there are other alternatives which he has not considered, then his conclusion does not necessarily follow. Second: even if he is right in his contention that it is custom alone which leads us to 'expect one event from the appearance of another,' it does not necessarily follow that there is nothing more to our conception of causality than this. (More will be said about this subsequently.)

Third: if, as Hume says, 'custom . . . is the great guide of human life . . . , which renders our experience useful to us' (58), then this would certainly seem to be at least *some* reason for thinking that whatever the ultimate sources of our sense-perceptions may actually be, and however unknown to us they may necessarily be, they are governed by stable and uniform principles, which correspond reasonably closely to the order we discover among our perceptions through experience. For if this were not the case, it is hardly imaginable that the customary associations we form between our ideas would be of any use to us at all. Hume himself grants that here there would seem to be 'a kind of pre-established harmony between the course of nature and the succession of our ideas; and though the powers and forces by which the former is governed be wholly unknown to us, yet our thoughts and conceptions have still, we find, gone on in the same train with the other works of nature' (67–8). This fact of the usefulness of the customary associations of our ideas, while it may not suffice to yield knowledge of the nature of reality which passes the test of logical certainty, is certainly significant; and it would seem to warrant some suppositions about the nature of reality which are not merely empty and groundless speculations.

Now: what is to be made of our idea of causation, given that we never *perceive* any necessary connection between any two events which we observe to be constantly conjoined in our experience? For Hume grants that the notion of 'necessary connection' would *seem* to constitute an essential part of our idea of causation. When we speak of one thing being the *cause* of another, we at least *think* we mean more than simply that first one occurs, and then the other. Having abandoned his challenge, Hume would be quite ready to conclude that, if no impression can be found corresponding to the expression 'necessary connection,' this expression is 'absolutely without any meaning when employed either in philosophical reasonings or in common life' (85). And it would follow from this that we really have no idea of causation at all.

Hume does not draw this conclusion, because he hits upon an impression which he thinks is the one to which the expresson 'necessary connection' corresponds, namely, the *feeling* we have that two constantly conjoined events are connected, owing to the influence of custom. 'This connection,' he says, 'which we *feel* in the mind, this customary transition of the imagination from one object to its usual attendant, is the sentiment or impression from which we form the idea of power or necessary connection. Nothing further is the case' (86). So he concludes:

> When we say . . . that one object is connected with another,
> we mean only that they have acquired a connection in our
> thought and give rise to this inference by which they become
> proofs of each other's existence – a conclusion that is
> somewhat extraordinary, but which seems founded on
> sufficient evidence. (86)

Hume is quite right: this conclusion is 'somewhat extraordinary,' to say the least. For it involves regarding the notion of a necessary connection of two events as something purely subjective, deriving from a merely customary connection of our ideas of these events. And it would certainly seem that this is not *what we mean* when we speak of causation in connection with things; at most, it is all that we are *entitled* to mean, if Hume's conclusion is, as he claims, 'founded on sufficient evidence.' And if so, this would mean that our usual construal of the notion of causation would have to be quite fundamentally modified.

But *is* this conclusion 'founded on sufficient evidence'? It may be that Hume is right about how we come to regard some things as causes of others; and it may also be that he is right in maintaining that the impression he mentions is the only one to be found which bears the least resemblance to the notion of 'necessary connection.' But his conclusion follows only if we accept his contention that where there is no impression, there is no real idea at all; and that if an expression does not correspond to some impression, it is utterly meaningless.

But why should we accept this contention? Why should we not conclude, rather, that here we have a counterexample to this thesis; and that Hume's challenge has been accepted, and that he has not shown himself to be capable of providing a satisfactory explication on his model of an idea which we do have? If we are not prepared to grant that we mean only what Hume says when we speak of causation and if we are not willing to allow that our idea of causation is utterly devoid of significant content insofar as it goes beyond the characterization of it he gives, then we might be led to conclude that this is at least one idea we have which is not simply a copy of some sense-perception; and that a counterexample has been found to the empiricist thesis about the origin and content of our ideas. This was Kant's conclusion; and this was one of the considerations which led him to develop a quite different position.

Mind and reality

Let us now turn to a number of issues which arise in connection with Hume's discussion of the mind, the self, the body, things, and the external world generally. These issues are: what, according to him, can we *know* concerning the existence and natures of these things? What sense, if any, does it even make to speak of them? How does Hume construe the ideas of them which we have, or think we have? And to what extent do the things Hume himself says about our ideas of them lead beyond the empiricist thesis of the origin and content of our ideas, to which he is committed?

In a number of passages, Hume shows himself to be quite willing to speak of nature or the world as something independent of our ideas, governed by forces or principles other than those which govern the connections of our ideas with each other. For example, he speaks of the fact that there would seem to be 'a kind of pre-established harmony between the course of nature and the succession of our ideas; and though the powers and forces by which the former [i.e., nature] is governed be wholly unknown to us, yet our thoughts and conceptions have still, we find, gone on in the same train with the other works of nature' (67). Again: 'The scenes of the universe are continually shifting, and one object follows another in an uninterrupted succession; but the power or

force which actuates the whole machine [of nature] is entirely
concealed from us . . .' (75).

Here Hume seems to be granting that it is meaningful to speak
of the external world existing and operating independently of our
perceptions and ideas, even though asserting that, because we never
directly perceive anything other than our own perceptions or ideas,
we can never know anything of it. Otherwise, he could not speak
of there being some sort of 'correspondence' between our perceptions and the external world (68). Further, while he argues against
the attribution of either secondary or primary qualities to things
existing independently of our minds, he seems willing to allow that
it is both meaningful and reasonable to hold that our perceptions
have some sort of source which is independent of them. So he
writes:

> Bereave matter of all its intelligible qualities, both primary and
> secondary, you in a manner annihilate it and leave only a
> certain unknown, inexplicable *something* as the cause of our
> perceptions – a notion so imperfect that no skeptic will think
> it worth while to contend against it. (104)

The notion of an unknown something which causes us to have
the perceptions we do may be very 'imperfect'; but the fact that
Hume is willing to allow it shows that he does not consider it to
be utterly nonsensical. And he shows no inclination to identify this
'something' either with God (as Berkeley does), or with the mind
itself. On the contrary, his other remarks to which reference has
already been made seem to indicate that he would be inclined to
think of it as in some sense material rather than spiritual.

Hume also is willing to speak of both mind or soul and body;
and to speak of them as quite different, and also as being related
or connected – even though he also holds that their true natures
and the manner in which they are related are and must remain
unknown to us. Thus he asks: 'Is there any principle in all nature
more mysterious than the union of soul and body, by which a
supposed spiritual substance acquires such an influence over a
material one that the most refined thought is able to actuate the
grossest matter?' (76–7). 'We are ignorant,' he says, 'of the manner
in which bodies operate on each other'; and he suggests that we
are 'equally ignorant of the manner or force by which a mind . . .
operates, either on itself or on body' (83). But Hume would not
seem to conclude, from our ignorance about these matters, that it
is utterly meaningless to speak of them. In fact, he seems to embrace

a kind of dualism, in that he speaks of both mental events and physical ones, and regards them as quite different, and both quite real. 'We learn from anatomy,' he says,

> that the immediate object of power in voluntary motion is not the member itself which is moved, but certain muscles and nerves and animal spirits . . . , through which the motion is successively propagated ere it reach the member itself whose motion is the immediate object of volition. . . . Here the mind wills a certain event; immediately another event, unknown to ourselves and totally different from the one intended, is produced. . . . (77–8)

Now all of this is rather curious. Here is Hume, on the one hand holding that we never directly perceive anything other than our own impressions and ideas, and that all of our ideas are nothing but copies of one or more of our impressions; and, on the other hand, making use of such terms as 'mind,' 'self,' 'body,' 'things', and 'nature,' none of which – as he himself uses them – would seem to be terms for ideas which are merely copies of our impressions. It should be obvious why he holds that we can never have *knowledge* of the existence and actual natures of any of these things, given that we never directly perceive any of them, and given that nothing but experience can ever yield anything even resembling knowledge of matters of fact and existence. But perhaps this is something worth going into a little further, before turning to the question of Hume's account of these different notions we have.

In the *Inquiry*, most of his remarks on this issue are presented in Section XII. What he does here for the most part is simply to endorse many of Berkeley's critical arguments and negative conclusions. He begins by observing that men commonly 'suppose the very images presented by the senses to be external objects . . . , believed to exist independently of our perception and to be something external to our mind which perceives it' (160). This is the view, however, which he takes to be 'destroyed by the slightest philosophy, which teaches us that nothing can ever be present to the mind but an image or perception' (160). This, he says, is an 'obvious dictate of reason' – that is, of reflection on the implications of the dependence of all of the qualities we perceive upon our minds. Here he restates very briefly Berkeley's argument to the effect that this is no less true of primary qualities than of secondary ones (162–3). And the first conclusion he draws from this is that 'the existences which we consider when we say *this house* and *that tree* are nothing but perceptions in the mind' (161).

In this he is in complete agreement with Berkeley; and like Berkeley, he next proceeds to attack Locke's version of the causal theory of perception, which would explain the existence of the perceptions we have in terms of the action of external objects resembling our perceptions in various ways, upon our sense-organs. But Hume does not argue that Locke's theory is *false*, and even nonsensical, as Berkeley does. Rather, he confines himself simply to claiming that we have no grounds whatever for asserting it to be *true*:

> It is a question of fact whether the perceptions of the senses be produced by external objects resembling them. How shall this question be determined? By experience, surely, as all other questions of a like nature. But here experience is and must be entirely silent. The mind has never anything present to it but the perceptions, and cannot possibly reach any experience of their connection with objects. The supposition of such a connection is, therefore, without any foundation in reasoning. (161–2)

This conclusion is a very logical one, given that 'the mind has never anything present to it but perceptions.' But Hume does not go on to contend that the cause of our perceptions must be *spiritual* in nature, as Berkeley does, or even that the very notion of our perceptions having a cause (or the very notion of material things having some sort of natures in themselves) is meaningless. His own conclusion is the skeptical one, that because our experience is limited in our perceptions, we can form no rational conclusions about their sources.

Hume's willingness to allow the notion of 'a certain unknown, inexplicable *something* as the cause of our perceptions' seems to indicate that he is in principle willing to accept some version of the causal theory of perception. But he does not feel that it is possible for us to have any *knowledge* of what the cause of our perceptions might be. And in fact, he does not even regard the existence of our perceptions as sufficient to prove that something does really exist independently of them. We cannot have knowledge even of this. For while we may *suppose* that something causing our perceptions exists, its existence is not established by direct experience; and it cannot be established *a priori*, since the idea of perceptions occurring without any cause is not logically self-contradictory.

From this it follows that, although we may speak of the existence of things and the external world independently of our perceptions, and although we may speak of the existence of our bodies as things independent of our minds, we can never have any knowledge either of their independent existence or (if they do exist independently) of their natures in themselves. Nor, for that matter, according to Hume, can we have any knowledge either of the existence or nature of our minds, except insofar as we have some sort of direct experience of them. About all such matters, we must remain silent. Skepticism, rather than either materialism *or* immaterialism, is the only philosophically sound position; for any positive assertions on these matters go further than either experience or reason can take us.

So far as our knowledge is concerned, therefore, we are entitled to speak *neither* of material substances *nor* of spiritual substances. To speak of a *thing* – a chair, for example, or an apple – is to designate nothing more than a collection of qualities which occur together in our experience. We *experience* no substratum underlying these qualities and holding them together, but rather only the bundle of qualities themselves, which can plausibly be said to exist only in our minds. With respect to the status of things insofar as we have any knowledge of them, therefore, Hume agrees with Berkeley. But he departs from Berkeley in arguing that the same position must be taken with regard to the *self*. Here he in a sense agrees with Locke, who had held that the notion of a spiritual substance either stands or falls with the notion of material substance; only instead of concluding that they both stand, Hume concludes that where knowledge of both their existence and natures are concerned, they both fall. For we no more have any direct perceptual experience of the 'self' than we do of material substances. In his *Treatise of Human Nature*, he says:

> When I enter most intimately into what I call *myself*, I always
> stumble on some particular perception or other, of heat or
> cold, light or shade, love or hatred, pain or pleasure. I never
> can catch *myself* at any time without a perception, and never
> can observe any thing *but* the perception. (p. 252)

In short, we never have any single impression which corresponds to the term 'self'; all we ever experience is a variety of sense-perceptions and sentiments. And from this Hume concludes that the term 'self', insofar as it refers to anything in our experience at all, refers simply to a certain collection of impressions we have. The self, he says, is 'nothing but a bundle or collection of different perceptions, which succeed each other with an inconceivable rapidity, and are in a perceptual flux and movement' (ibid.). Hume would seem to say even this much because he does not want to have to say that the term 'self' is utterly meaningless, and refers to nothing at all (as he would seem committed to saying by his view that a term is meaningful only if it refers ultimately to some particular impression or set of impressions). We ordinarily suppose that perceptions are something we have; and Hume himself asserts that they are in the mind. But now it turns out that these perceptions are what we are; and that the mind *just is* 'a bundle or collection of perceptions.'

This, at least, is what Hume's doctrine about the origin and content of our ideas compels him to say, when he confines himself to conclusions which experience will support. Yet he does not simply stop here. He recognizes that in fact our ideas of objects and the self involve more than merely the notion of a group of quite distinct qualities which are constantly in flux, and which exist only intermittently in consciousness; just as he recognizes that our idea of causality involves more than simply the notion of the constant conjunction of events of certain types. Our idea of causality also involves the notion of a *necessary connection* of the types of events in question. And our ideas of objects and the self, as ideas of *substances* and not just qualities, also involve the notions of *continuity* and *identity* or unity. This raises a problem for Hume, given his thesis about the origin and content of our ideas, since he is not prepared to insist that our ideas of objects and the self are devoid of significant content insofar as they involve these further elements. But the problem this raises is one he thinks he can handle; and the way in which he tries to handle it is similar to the way in which he tries to handle the notion of necessary connection in the case of the idea of causality.

In the case of the idea of causality, he argues that we do have an impression corresponding to the idea of necessary connection; but that it is not anything objectively perceived. It rather is purported to be something subjective – a feeling or impression produced by a kind of disposition to think of one event when another occurs which is established in the imagination by the experience of the constant conjunction of events of these types. And Hume argues that the same sort of thing happens in connection with our ideas of objects and the self. The notions of continuity and identity, which are elements of these ideas, do not correspond to anything objectively perceived; but they *do* correspond to certain subjective impressions – certain *feelings* which are established in the imagination. There are held to be two other principles of the association of ideas; namely, 'Resemblance' and 'Contiguity'. When some of our sense-perceptions resemble each other, or when some of them occur together, and this happens repeatedly, Hume holds that the mind has a tendency to associate them together, and to consider them as unified. And it tends to project this unity beyond the period in which we actually perceive the impressions in question to be connected, and to regard them as having an enduring continuity and identity. It is only in our imagination that they do so; but they do have it there owing to the mind's disposition to associate them in this way. And this gives rise to certain subjective feelings when we perceive an object, which are the impressions to which the notions of continuity and identity correspond.

In this way, Hume feels that he has shown that our ideas of objects and the self are not utterly meaningless insofar as they involve these notions, while at the same time remaining true to his empiricist thesis that ideas are nothing but copies of impressions of one sort or another. But here again, as in the case of causality, the impressions he comes up with turn out to be subjective in origin. The continuity and identity of objects and the self, no less than the necessary connection of causes and effects, turn out to be something like fictions of the imagination, which are projected upon our perceptions. They are contributions of the mind to experience, rather than notions derived directly from sense-perception itself. (It is not very far from this view of the matter to Kant's.)

But it should be kept in mind that Hume is not denying absolutely that there is any more to objects or to the mind themselves than the bundles of perceptions upon which fictions of identity and continuity are projected, any more than he denies absolutely that there are things existing independently of the mind, which cause us to have the perceptions we do, and which *are* necessarily connected. He does not deny these things; rather, he holds that we can know nothing of them, one way or the other. He is only talking about the positive ideas we do have of causality, objects, and the mind or self, and the account that is to be given of the origin and content of these ideas.

There is little more that can be said about Hume's position with regard to objects generally, and also with regard to the body, and its relation to the mind. Though he speaks both of objects generally and of the body as though it is conceivable that they have an existence independent of our perceptions (or at least that something corresponding to our perceptions of them exists independently of our perceptions of them), we can have no knowledge or experience of this. Our ideas of them are confined to sets of sense-perceptions, which exist only in our minds, and on which we impose such notions as continuity, identity, and necessary connection, as the result of the operation of a number of tendencies at work in the mind, in accordance with which it arranges and associates its ideas.

Insofar as objects are conceived in terms of the kinds of qualities we commonly associate with them, Hume thus takes Berkeley's characterization of them to be correct; even though he is quite prepared to speak of them as everyone else does where everyday life is concerned. And the same holds true with respect to our bodies. Either my body is to be understood as a certain set of sense-perceptions I have, which is related to other sets of my sense-perceptions as they are to each other, and which is related to my feelings and desires and thoughts as one set of impressions to another (though in a way which Hume finds quite incomprehensible); or my body is to be understood as something existing independently of that set of sense-perceptions I have of it, in which case its nature and very existence are beyond the limits of my knowledge, and its relation to my mind is completely unintelligible.

One may wonder why Hume is willing to allow it to be meaningful even to speak of things (objects, the body, the material world generally) existing independently of our perceptions and ideas, given that he holds that we can never in principle have any experience of them as such, and given that he holds terms to be meaningless which do not refer either to sense-impressions themselves or to ideas which are copies of them. Berkeley had concluded, on the basis of the same assumptions, that it *is* completely meaningless to do so; why doesn't Hume? The answer would seem to be that, while he holds it to be impossible to say anything meaningful about such things; while, therefore, our words do not really convey anything when we talk about them; and while we have no idea of them with any significant content, this still does not warrant the conclusion that there *is* nothing other than what we directly perceive. And so, since the *possibility* of something else cannot be ruled out, it remains possible to speak of *there being* something else, provided that we do not forget that we cannot *know* that there is, and that we cannot say anything significant about it even if there is.

But while this may not pose any real problem for Hume's own analysis, a real problem *would* seem to arise in connection with his constant reference to the mind and its operations. His remarks about the 'self' are directly applicable to the mind; the mind is something which we never directly perceive as such. It would seem to follow, therefore, that we have no real idea of it, except as a bundle of perceptions into which a kind of unity and continuity are projected. Yet he says: 'It cannot be doubted that the mind is endowed with several powers and faculties, [and] that these powers and faculties are distinct from each other' (22). Further, in his discussion of how it is that we come to have the ideas of causality, objects, and the self, he speaks of various notions (necessary connection, continuity, identity) which are formed *in the imagination*, and which are projected *by the mind* onto the various impressions *the mind perceives*. It is *the mind* which operates in accordance with the three principles of the association of ideas he identifies (in Section III).

It would not seem to make sense, however, to say all of these things, and the many similar things Hume says along these lines, and at the same time to hold that the mind simply *is* nothing more than a bundle of perceptions. A bundle of perceptions simply could not *do* all of these things. It may very well be that, as he claims, the mind or self is nothing of which one ever has any sense-perception. But his own account requires constant reference to the *activity* of something which is not itself a sense-perception or bundle of sense-perceptions. The concept of the mind may not be a copy of an impression; but it is a concept that seems indispensable in the description of the status of our impressions and the ways in which they are produced and arranged.

On Hume's analysis of the origin and content of our ideas, the idea of the mind should be either meaningless or fictitious; but his own theory of knowledge and perception becomes incoherent unless at least one exception to this analysis is made, and the legitimacy of speaking of the activities and operations of the mind as he does is allowed. It may be that the analysis he gives of the idea of the self is valid insofar as the 'self' in question is that particular personality which I call 'me', and which I distinguish from *you*. But this same analysis cannot be applied to the idea of the 'self' insofar as this term refers to that entity which is the pure perceiving subject, and which acts upon the impressions it perceives in the various ways Hume describes. The existence of this entity is not discovered through any sense-perception; but it is logically presupposed by the sort of analysis of perception and knowledge Hume gives. This is one point at which Kant took a radical modification of Hume's position to be necessary.

Another radical modification of his position would seem to be required in connection with his account of our ideas of causation, objects, and the self. It pertains to his explanation of the elements of necessary connection, continuity, and identity or unity in these ideas. Hume is led by his recognition that these form an essential part of our ideas of causation, objects, and the self, and by his quite correct observation that none of these notions is a copy of any sense-perception, on the one hand, and by his empiricist doctrine that all ideas are copies of impressions, on the other, to argue that these notions correspond to certain feelings or inner impressions produced in the imagination by the association of our ideas in accordance with certain propensities or tendencies of our minds. But in fact, these notions are not copies of anything like our other inner impressions or sentiments, such as love, desire, pleasure and pain.

Hume speaks of 'impressions' in connection with the propensities of the mind to regard collections of qualities as unified substances, and to regard constantly conjoined objects as necessarily connected, because he *must* in order to save his thesis that all of our ideas are copies of impressions. It is not necessary to reject his contention that the necessary connections, continuity, and identity or unity we attribute to things are in fact contributions of the mind to our experience, however, to object to his analysis of these ideas in this way. One can grant his basic point – that these are not categories deriving directly from sense-perceptions, but rather categories which the mind projects upon them in accordance with its own laws or principles – and yet argue that these categories or notions are not copies of impressions of *any* sort, but rather *ideas of mental dispositions*.

After all, even if the operation of our minds in accordance with these dispositions *does* produce some sort of perceptible inner feelings of the sort Hume suggests, our ideas of causation, continuity, and identity or unity correspond not to the feelings produced but to the dispositions themselves which produce them. This is certainly true in his own discussion, in which he is not simply describing certain feelings, but rather is identifying the various types of dispositions in question. He is reluctant to admit it; but even if the ideas under consideration are subjectivized, as he argues they must be, and are traced to the operations of our minds rather than the phenomena we perceive, they cannot coherently be considered copies of impressions. They may be ideas we come to have only in the course of experience and reflection upon our impressions; but they are not ideas *of* any of these impressions themselves. Rather, they are ideas of the mental dispositions which we discover through the analysis of the associations of our ideas with each other. And if this is right, then, as Kant saw, there are important exceptions to the empiricist account of the origin and content of our ideas.

The God-hypothesis

Hume's *Dialogues Concerning Natural Religion* is one of the most important works in the entire literature of the philosophy of religion. In fact, it is probably fair to say that it marks a turning point in the history of philosophical theology; for the devastating attack he mounts in this book against the possibility of establishing anything with respect to the nature and existence of God, and indeed the case he makes against the reasonableness of continuing to cling to the idea of the existence of an omnipotent, omniscient, supremely good deity, leaves one with little choice other than 'to believe or not to believe,' where 'believing' requires something like a Kierkegaardian 'leap of faith.' The philosophy of religion makes for strange bedfellows; and surely it would be hard to think of a stranger pair of bedfellows than Hume and Kierkegaard. But however radically different they may be both in general philosophical outlook and in the positions at which they arrive at the end of the line (Kierkegaard the ardent Christian, Hume the resolute unbeliever), they in effect agree that rational or 'natural' theology is an utter failure where the establishment of anything like the existence of the God of Christianity is concerned, and that religious faith therefore not only generally is but essentially must be a fundamentally non-rational affair.

Philosophers and theologians after Hume did not invariably feel driven to accept this forced choice of unbelief or a leap of faith, some seeking other grounds than those Hume undermined for supposing that some sort of religion or theology is sound, and some attempting to revise the notions of God and the soul in such a way that the language if not the substance of traditional religion and theology can be saved. But few ever again tried to save or establish religious principles by employing the kinds of arguments he subjects to critical scrutiny in the *Dialogues*. One should not be misled by the fact that Hume has all of the characters in the *Dialogues* subscribe to some sort of religious faith, and has the narrator, Cleanthes's pupil Pamphilus, conclude that he thinks Cleanthes's views are the soundest of any of those voiced. The work is, after all, cast in literary form; and this enables Hume to avoid having to lay his cards directly on the table. Moreover, he seems to have felt no need to belabor the obvious. One who draws what is unmistakably a picture of a horse does not have to proclaim that he has drawn a horse in order to make it evident that it is a horse he has drawn; the picture speaks for itself. And so it is with the *Dialogues* – in which, it should further be observed, Hume artfully has not only Philo (who is clearly the philosopher most closely resembling Hume himself) but also both Demea and Cleanthes weigh in with critiques of various arguments being considered, each criticizing the other's; while, on the other hand, Philo pays polite lip-service to the beliefs of both of them. One must sort all of this out in order to see what Hume is saying.

As a general rule, in reading the *Dialogues*, one may consider Hume to be speaking whenever an argument supporting the existence and nature of God as traditionally conceived is under attack, and whenever a defense of a modified line with respect to either point is being criticized; while he is on the whole merely laying out the arguments to be criticized when he has one of the characters advance them. If there is an exception to this rule, it is to be found in the extremely vague and very weak affirmation he has Philo make on several occasions, to the effect that it is more likely than not 'that the cause or causes of order in the universe probably bear some remote analogy to human intelligence' (227). If this is the most that can be said on the basis of either reasoning or experience where the nature and existence of God are concerned, however, then as Philo points out, the difference between the upshot of natural theology and atheistic naturalism is so slight as to be scarcely worth arguing (218). Hume may retain the terms 'God' and 'religion' in this connection; but this is little more than a concession to the temperament of his time.

The greater part of the *Dialogues* is devoted to an examination of arguments relating to the nature and existence of God which are derived from experience or observation rather than from pure reasoning or metaphysical speculation. This is undoubtedly because Hume felt that arguments of the latter sort can be disposed of in short order, whereas arguments appealing to experience by their very nature call for more extended discussion. In any event, the consequence is that, much of the time, we find the skeptical Philo and the devout Demea making common cause against Cleanthes, who tries again and again to derive support from experience for the theistic propositions he wishes to assert (and believes to constitute the core of both true religion and Christian doctrine). It is only late in the *Dialogues* that Demea discovers what sort of ally he has had, and has to face criticisms leveled at his alternatives to Cleanthes's position by both Cleanthes and Philo, who then make common cause against him. In what follows, I shall trace the course Hume takes in the *Dialogues* as he proceeds with this demolition of the edifice of 'natural' theology.

At the beginning of Part I, Demea's pious insistence upon the desirability of humbling human reason to prepare the way for the inculcation of religious faith, rather than seeking to establish the latter on the basis of the employment of the former, is seen to have a certain affinity with the general tenets of Hume's skepticism, which Philo expresses, and which set the framework for most of what he goes on to say:

> Let us become thoroughly sensible of the weakness, blindness, and narrow limits of human reason: Let us duly consider its uncertainty and needless contrarieties, even in subjects of common life and practice: Let the errors and deceits of our very senses be set before us; the insuperable difficulties, which attend first principles in all systems; the contradictions which adhere to the very ideas of matter, cause and effect, extension, space, time, motion; and in a word, quantity of all kinds, the object of the only science [i.e., mathematics] that can fairly pretend to any certainty or evidence. When these topics are displayed in their full light. . . , who can retain such confidence in this frail faculty of reason as to pay any regard to its determinations in points so sublime, so abstruse, so remote from common life and experience [as those of theological and cosmological speculation]? (131)

It seems to Cleanthes that Philo thereby proposes 'to erect religious faith on philosophical scepticism' (132) – although Philo's actual strategy is to employ skeptical considerations to show that religious faith is utterly without any means of visible support. The position Philo *explicitly* takes, however, is neither Pro nor Con, but rather that 'we have here got quite beyond the reach of our faculties,' so that the only reasonable thing to do is to suspend judgment and adopt an agnostic stance (at least as long as we have our philosophical hats on). Philosophy can only make the negative contribution of deflating the overblown pretensions of human reason (in the hands of metaphysicians and theologians) to be able to establish as knowledge what is affirmed in the faith of the believer.

Cleanthes, however, is not so easily dissuaded, maintaining that, just as these skeptical scruples do not and should not detain us from forming conclusions from experience with respect to the world around us, they need not be taken to preclude a comparable exercise of thought with respect to the Creator of this world. If we are entitled to place some confidence in our reasonings about the world of ordinary affairs (even though, strictly speaking, the skeptical principles of Philo and Hume apply to them no less than elsewhere), then we are also entitled to do so in our reasonings about God – provided that we stick to the evidence and what may reasonably be inferred from it.

Thus Cleanthes readily concurs with Philo's empiricist principle, 'Wherever evidence discovers itself, you adhere to it' (136). And he contends that there is 'evidence' which supports 'the religious hypothesis' of God's existence, and enables us to draw inferences concerning the nature of God (138). The three characters agree, at the outset of Part II, that what is in question is the latter rather than the former; but they turn out to be more concerned to address themselves to the former than they here suggest themselves to be – and for good reason. For that question is too crucial, and the answer too problematical, to take an affirmative answer to it for granted (as Hume is very well aware).

Demea takes the position, very much to his own eventual disadvantage, that 'from the infirmities of human understanding,' the nature of God is 'altogether incomprehensible and unknown to us'; and that therefore while God surely is supremely perfect, we can only 'adore in silence his infinite perfections,' which we can never discern, and ought not even try to pry into. It later turns out that Demea nonetheless holds that our powers of reasoning *are* great enough to prove the *existence* of God; and so he has a higher estimation of them than he here seems to have – closer to that of Cleanthes than to that of Philo in this respect. But he is only too happy to agree with Philo that, precisely on grounds of piety, 'we ought never to imagine, that we can comprehend the attributes of this divine Being, or to suppose that his perfections have an analogy or likeness to the perfections of a human creature' (142). Cleanthes, on the other hand, contends that there is an argument from experience (or *a posteriori*), by which one can 'prove at once the existence of a Deity and his similarity to human mind and intelligence' (143). This is the argument *from design* and *by analogy*; and it is with this argument, in one form or another, that most of the book is concerned. As Cleanthes first formulates it, it runs roughly like this:

(1) The world exists.
(2) Inspection reveals the world 'to be nothing but one great machine,' the parts of which 'are adjusted to each other with an [astonishing] accuracy.'
(3) Nothing occurs without a cause of its occurrence.
(4) Order cannot occur without an Orderer or Author.

So (5) An Author responsible for the arrangement of the world exists.

(6) This 'curious adapting of means to ends . . . resembles exactly . . . the productions of human contrivance; of human design, thought, wisdom, and intelligence.'
(7) From similar effects one can infer similar causes.

So (8) 'The Author of nature is somewhat similar to the mind of man.'

So (9) There exists a being who is Author of nature, and who is somewhat similar to the mind of man. (Namely, God.)

Philo is quick to point out that (7) is a crucial premise; and while he is willing to grant it for the sake of the argument, he makes an important point concerning its use:

The exact similarity of the cases gives us a perfect assurance of a similar event. . . . But wherever you depart, in the least, from the similarity of the cases, you diminish proportionably the evidence; and may at last bring it to a very weak *analogy*, which is confessedly liable to error and uncertainty. (144)

As he goes on to observe, there is no 'entire and perfect' resemblance between the world and products of human contrivance; and so (6) must be rejected, and the argument therefore does not go through, at least as it stands. Moreover, the argument makes use of a metaphysical principle, (3), which can be established neither *a priori* nor *a posteriori*, and so cannot legitimately be used to carry the argument along. Thus Philo reformulates Cleanthes's argument for him as follows:

(1) The world exists.

(2) There is order and arrangement in the world.

(3) 'The adjustment of means to ends is alike in the universe, as in a machine of human contrivance.'

(4) 'Experience proves that there is an original principle of order in mind, not in matter,' which is involved wherever we consider the genesis of the order and arrangement to be found in an artifact.

(5) From similar effects one can infer similar causes.

So (6) The order the world exhibits has a cause with the character of mind, and is not to be found in the matter of the world itself.

So (7) There exists a being somewhat similar to the mind of man responsible for the order in the world.

Even in its revised form, however, this argument still is subject to the first sort of difficulty: the world is in fact so dissimilar to 'houses, ships, furniture, [and] machines' that 'the great disproportion bars all comparison and inference.' And there is a further difficulty, which Philo also brings forward: 'Thought, design, intelligence,' he observes, 'is no more than one of the springs and principles of the universe'; and it is illegitimate without any further ado simply 'to take the operations of one part of nature upon another for the foundation of our judgment concerning the origin of the whole.' Indeed, it would seem very dubious to 'select so minute, so weak, so bounded a principle as the reason and design of animals is found to be upon this planet' for the lofty role of the source of all order. 'What peculiar privilege has this little agitation of the brain which we call thought, that we must thus make it the model of the whole universe?' This, he suggests, would appear to be nothing but an 'illusion' springing from 'our partiality in our own favor,' which 'sound philosophy ought carefully to guard against' (148).

Nor is this all. There is a further and more general problem for any argument of the sort Cleanthes seeks to employ, as Philo goes on to observe. 'When two *species* of objects have always been observed to be conjoined together, I can *infer*, by custom, the existence of one wherever I *see* the existence of the other. And this I call an argument from experience' (149). But nothing at all like this is possible in the present case. All we have ever seen is things coming into existence out of other things, through the transformation of the latter. We have never experienced anything like 'the origin of worlds' and the origination of 'an orderly universe' in the first place. And this is so great and profound a disanalogy between the two cases that it would seem utterly to preclude any reasoning appealing to 'similar effects,' which must *be* clearly similar before similar causes are inferred.

Against this line· of attack, Cleanthes is unable to make any effective defence. He tries to deflect its force by constructing examples in which a putatively comparable degree of disanalogy would not be taken to rule out any such inference; but his efforts are so lame as to be embarrassing. Philo is not made to knock them down, perhaps because Hume did not want Cleanthes to be deprived of all respectability this early on, or perhaps because he preferred simply to allow the inadequacy of this or any other such attempted response to speak for itself.

In any event, we are next presented with a different line of criticism of this general way of conceiving of God's nature, which Hume puts into the mouth of Demea. The general point of this argument is that one cannot coherently maintain *both* that God's nature is to be conceived analogously to the mind of man (as Cleanthes proposes and tries to establish it to be), *and* that God is perfect and not subject to human limitations. This argument, which is of interest in relation not only to Cleanthes's position but also to the way in which most people tend to think of God, runs as follows:

(1) 'The ideas of internal sentiment, added to those of the external senses, compose the whole furniture of human understanding.'

(2) 'All the sentiments of the human mind . . . have a plain reference to the state and situation of man.'

(3) God is not to be conceived as being in the state and situation of man.

So (4) God is not to be conceived as being of such a nature that sentiments or ideas of either sort are attributable to him.

(5) Our ideas derived from the external senses are often 'false and illusive,' or at least are not proof against falsehood and illusion.

210

(6) God is not to be conceived as exposed to the liability of falling into error and illusion.

So (7) God is not to be conceived as being of such a nature that ideas of this sort are attributable to him.

(8) 'Our thought is fluctuating, uncertain, fleeting, successive, and compounded' in its *manner.*

(9) Such traits are manifestations of a very imperfect nature.

(10) God is not to be attributed imperfections of any sort.

So (11) God is not to be conceived in such a way that any such traits are attributed to him.

So (12) God is not to be conceived in terms of any of the things which characterize the very nature of human thought.

(13) 'It would . . . be an abuse of terms to apply . . . the name of thought or reason' or *mind* where it is inappropriate to speak of any of these things.

So (14) It is an abuse of terms to speak of 'thought' or 'reason' or 'mind' in connection with God's nature; or at the very least, if one does so use them, they cannot be supposed to have anything like the same meaning they do when we use them in connection with our own intelligence and experience. (156)

This argument, it should be observed, leaves one with a number of choices. None, however, will be very agreeable to someone like Cleanthes. If one continues to insist upon the analogousness of God's nature to that of the human mind, one can do so only at the cost of abandoning the idea of God's perfection. If, on the other hand, one either drops the use of such 'mental' language altogether or stipulates that when applied to God it does not mean anything like what it means when applied to us, then the idea of God's perfection is saved, but only at the cost of rendering his nature quite incomprehensible. And to this Demea subsequently adds, in Part IV, that the idea of God's 'immutability and simplicity' also is incompatible with the conception of his nature as analogous to that of the human mind; for the latter is characterized by change and complexity.

To this objection Philo adds another consideration, which further serves to undermine the motivation of the sort of argument Cleanthes has set out to advance. This consideration is that the very hypothesis of a divine Architect of the world and its order is unjustifiable because it accomplishes nothing, explaining nothing that cannot be accounted for equally well without it. Cleanthes supposes that the order of nature is explained only if it is traced to something outside of nature altogether: namely, a plan in a divine mind. A plan, however, is an ordered set of ideas. If *order* is what requires to be explained, then it requires to be explained as it is purported to obtain among these ideas, in this plan itself, no less than in the world, among and in things. If, on the other hand, it makes sense to say of the former (the ideas making up the plan) that they 'fell into order, of themselves, and by their own nature,' then one is obliged to show 'why it is not just as good sense to say, that the parts of the material world fall into order, of themselves, and by their own nature' (162). Neither reason nor experience provides one with grounds upon which to distinguish the two cases, and which warrant treating them differently. And if one therefore can stop just as readily with order in the world as with a postulated higher-level order in a divine plan, it makes more sense to stop with the former, rather than starting a regress to which there is no non-arbitrary termination. To this line of reasoning Cleanthes has no reply; he is reduced to mere reaffirmation of what now clearly is a groundless faith rather than anything he can purport to have demonstrated and to know.

The worst, however, remains to be said. Hume has Philo demonstrate to Cleanthes that the sort of argument the latter seeks to advance admits of a kind of *reductio ad absurdum*, at least in relation to the intentions of someone like Cleanthes who intends it to support his quite traditional theistic position. For what Philo goes on to do, in Parts V-VII, is to show that even if his earlier objections to drawing inferences from the character of the world as we apprehend it to the existence and nature of a supposed creator of the world are set aside, the evidence either supports the hypothesis of a very different sort of creator than Cleanthes has in mind, or at least fails to assign any greater likelihood to his conception of the world's creator than to any number of preposterous alternatives to it.

It must be allowed, Philo contends, that in any such reasonings one must adhere to the principle that 'the cause ought *only* to be proportioned to the effect' (166). One cannot abandon this principle without opening the door to utterly groundless speculation, in which no constraints are placed upon the conception of the creator one forms. But if one accepts this principle, one is entitled to predicate neither perfection nor infinity of the deity, since experience does not show the world to be either perfect or infinite. The same sort of consideration precludes the attribution of simplicity, immutability, and even unity to the world's source. All Philo is prepared to concede is that 'a man who follows your hypothesis is able, perhaps, to assert, or conjecture, that the universe, some-time, arose from something like design' (168–9).

For Cleanthes, 'That's enough.' It is by no means enough for Demea, however, who observes that 'It must be a slight fabric, indeed . . . , which can be erected on so tottering a foundation' (170). And as Philo goes on to point out, the data do not suffice to 'establish any system of cosmogony' (177) in preference to any other, rendering it no more probable that Cleanthes's God is the origin of the world than that its 'cause . . . is generation or vegeta-tion' (176). For, he contends, the world is at least as much like 'a plant or an animal, which springs from vegetation or generation,' as it is like 'any artificial machine, which arises from reason and design' (177). The argument from design and by analogy opens a Pandora's box, which Philo maintains were better left closed. Reason here oversteps its bounds:

> in such questions as the present, a hundred contradictory views may preserve a kind of imperfect analogy; and invention has here full scope to exert itself. Without any great effort of thought, I believe that I could, in an instant, propose other systems of cosmogony, which would have some faint appearance of truth; though it is a thousand, a million to one, if either yours or any one of mine be the true system. (182)

His conclusion, and Hume's, is that 'a total suspense of judgment is here our only reasonable recourse' (186–7). Hume avails himself of this opportunity, however, to suggest in passing what would appear to be his own actual picture of the world, which he seems to think has considerable plausibility, but which he refrains from advocating because he recognizes that there is no way in which he could demonstrate its validity. He has Philo say:

> Is there a system, an order, an economy of things, by which matter can preserve that perpetual agitation, which seems essential to it, and yet maintain a constancy in the forms, which it produces? There certainly is such an economy: For this is actually the case with the present world. The continual motion of matter, therefore, in less than infinite transpositions, must produce this economy or order; and by its very nature, that

213

order, when once established, supports itself, for many ages,
if not to eternity. . . . (183)

It is in vain, therefore, to insist upon the uses of the parts in
animals or vegetables, and their curious adjustment to each
other. I would fain know how an animal could subsist, unless
its parts were so adjusted? . . . Must not [the world likewise]
dissolve as well as the animal, and pass through new positions
and situations; till in a great, but finite succession, it fall at
last into the present or some such order? (185)

Philo, and Hume, content themselves with saying merely that
this 'new hypothesis of cosmogony . . . is not absolutely absurd
and improbable' (183). But they clearly regard it with much greater
favor than any of the 'religious systems,' which Philo goes on to
observe 'are subject to great and insuperable difficulties' (186).
Having floated this hypothesis thus circumspectly, however, Hume
turns from it to a different sort of question altogether, in Part IX:
the tenability of arguing for God's existence *a priori* rather than *a
posteriori*. It is this sort of argument which Demea favors, contending that here and here alone we find an 'infallible demonstration.'
His version of this argument is as follows (188–9):

(1) 'Whatever exists must have a cause or reason of its
existence.'

(2) 'That succession of causes, which constitutes the
universe,' whether it be finite or infinite, in fact exists.

So (3) There must be some cause or reason of the existence of
the universe.

(4) This cause, or whatever the ultimate cause of the universe
is, cannot be anything itself existing merely
contingently, since it too would then have to have a cause
or reason of its existence, and so by (1) would not be
the ultimate cause which the world's existence
presupposes.

So (5) The cause or reason of the existence of the universe must
be located in a 'Being, who carries the reason of *his*
existence *in himself*, and who cannot be supposed *not* to
exist without an express contradiction.'

So (6) 'There is such a Being.' Namely, God.

And (7) A Being carrying the reason of his existence in himself is
thereby 'necessarily existent.'

So (8) God not only exists, but by his very nature exists
   necessarily.

Hume grants Cleanthes the honor of demolishing this argument
– or rather, this pair of arguments, one of which proceeds from
the existence of the world to the existence of God (the cosmological
argument), and the other of which involves drawing upon the very
concept of God to establish that he cannot be conceived not to
exist (the ontological argument). These arguments have in common
the supposition that it is meaningful to speak of God, unlike the
world and finite things, as 'necessarily existent.' And it is on this
supposition that Cleanthes fastens. His counter argument is this:

(1) 'Nothing that is distinctly conceivable implies a
    contradiction.'
(2) 'Whatever we conceive as existent, we can also conceive
    as nonexistent.'
So (3) 'There is no being . . . whose nonexistence implies a
    contradiction.'
(4) 'Nothing is demonstrable, unless the contrary implies a
    contradiction.'
So (5) 'There is no being, whose existence is demonstrable.'

This is an argument intended to establish the impossibility of
proving the existence of *anything*; and its soundness is taken to
rule out the idea of proving the existence of God in any way, but
especially by way of an appeal to the inclusion of the predicate
'necessarily existent' in the conception of God. For the force of it
is that 'The words . . . *necessary existence* have no meaning, or,
which is the same thing, none that is consistent' (190). The crucial
premise is (1); and in support of it, Hume offers what is less an
argument than a kind of appeal to experience and challenge, having
Cleanthes assert that 'It will [always] be possible for us, at any
time, to conceive the non-existence of what we formerly conceived
to exist' (180). A *square circle* would be an example of something
of which it is *not* possible for us distinctly to conceive, and therefore which is not distinctly conceivable, and therefore to the (non-)
existence of which a kind of proof is relevant – but this is because
it involves the predication of incompatible qualities to one and the
same thing. But nothing of this sort occurs in the case of the idea
of a 'nonexistent Deity,' because 'existence' and 'nonexistence' *are
not predicates at all*, and so the question of incompatible predicates
does not even arise.

215

The issue here is not that of whether 'existence' is a *perfection*. It is more a fundamental one: namely, whether it is to be understood as a kind of a property or quality, which it makes any sense to predicate *of* things, as it must in order for it even to be a candidate for inclusion on a list of perfections (along with, e.g., omnipotence and omniscience). The ontological argument, Hume contends through Cleanthes, rests upon a mistake – as does the version of the cosmological argument Demea presents: the mistake of supposing that 'existence' is a predicate, and 'necessary existence' a special variant of it, which may coherently be included along with other predicates in the conception of God's nature, and traded upon in establishing his reality.

This is not Hume's only weapon, however, in dealing with the sort of metaphysical reasoning concerning God's existence which Demea is made to exemplify. Thus, should one not be persuaded of the soundness of the preceding point, Cleanthes makes several others, which do not actually refute Demea, but make a fairly strong case against the view that Demea's argument establishes his conclusion. First, Cleanthes suggests that if each and every thing that exists is granted to have a cause in the form of some other previously existent contingent thing, and if it further is allowed that the chain of causes reaches back in time without ever coming to an end, it is rather unreasonable to maintain that one still has left the existence of something contingent unaccounted for, and that an additional cause of the whole chain must also be posited. Demea's first premise is satisfied well enough if there is no particular thing whose existence remains unaccounted for.

Second, if it is thought to make sense to maintain that it is possible for *something* (namely, God) to exist without a cause outside of itself, then it makes equally good sense to conceive of this as possible in the case of the universe itself, therefore eliminating the necessity of positing a transcendent deity as its cause. Any mysterious quality which would (according to Demea and his kind) make the nonexistence of a Deity impossible, can with equal plausibility be assigned to the universe, thereby rendering its supposition useless for Demea's purposes (190).

With this, it would appear that Hume feels he has shown the ontological and cosmological arguments to be untenable, and the argument from design and by analogy to fail in its intended aim. We can neither so prove the existence of God, nor (even on the hypothesis of the existence of some such being) establish anything significant with respect to his nature by such arguments. Yet there is a very different sort of appeal which advocates of religion may make; and before concluding, Hume turns his attention to it.

The unfortunate Demea, deprived of his metaphysical props, is made to resort to this line of desperate, last-ditch defense, urging that the truth of religion may be grasped through a contemplation of man's general 'imbecility and misery,' which impels us 'to seek protection from that Being, on whom he and all nature is dependent' (193). The issue has now shifted considerably; for it is *feeling* rather than either reasoning or observation which is here put forward as the basis of the case for the God-hypothesis and religion. 'Who can doubt of what all men declare from their own immediate feeling and experience?' Demea asks. But what he has in mind is 'The miseries of life, the unhappiness of man, the general corruption of our nature, the unsatisfactory enjoyment of pleasures, riches, honors,' rather than the truth of religion directly. These circumstances are supposed to prompt us to turn to religion – and Philo readily allows that they very often do just that. Indeed, Philo says he is persuaded 'that the best and indeed the only method of bringing every one to a due sense of religion is by just representations of the misery and wickedness of men' (193). He thus joins with Demea in a chorus of lament for the wretched condition of mankind, which constitutes one of the severest indictments of human life in the annals of philosophy, surpassed if at all only by Schopenhauer.

Cleanthes's protestation that things really aren't all that bad is brushed aside by Demea, with Philo's approval. But Philo is actually working at cross purposes with Demea, while Demea is unwittingly only strengthening the case *against* the God-hypothesis by carrying on as he does. For it is not only the case (as Philo at length points out to him) that the wretchedness of human life and the generally harsh character of life in this world lend *no support* to the religious views Demea and other believers espouse, even though they may *motivate* their embrace of them; it is further the case that *this* evidence creates a presumption *against* the very sort of deity Demea affirms. 'Epicurus' old questions are yet unanswered. Is he willing to prevent evil, but not able? Then is he impotent. Is he able but not willing? then is he malevolent. Is he both able and willing? whence then is evil?' (198).

Philo concedes that if one *knows in advance* that there is a God who is omnipotent, omniscient and supremely good, it is not utterly impossible that this should be compatible with the sorry character of human existence and life in the world. But he insists that, since we do *not* know this in advance, the evidence counts *against* rather than in favor of all or at least part of this hypothesis. Philo is made to suggest that the supposed goodness of God is the most vulnerable part of it, concluding that 'there is no view of human life, or of the condition of mankind, from which, without the greatest violence, we can infer the moral attributes, or learn that infinite benevolence, conjoined with infinite power and infinite wisdom, which we must discover by the eyes of faith alone' (202). The last phrase is surely meant by Hume to be taken ironically.

The stakes here are very high, as Hume through Cleanthes maintains. Thus Cleanthes, who is if nothing else a reasonable sort, and ill-disposed to leaps of faith in directions opposite to those in which his understanding points him, exclaims: 'If you can make out the present point, and prove mankind to be unhappy or corrupted, there is an end at once of all religion. For to what purpose establish the natural attributes of the Deity, while the moral ones are still doubtful and uncertain?' (199). He is made to go on, in Part XI, to try to save the day by modifying the conception of God in such a way as to preserve both the idea of his goodness and the possibility of deriving support for his existence from a consideration of life and the world. He does this by proposing that God be thought of, not as omnipotent, but rather as limited in his powers. 'Benevolence, regulated by wisdom, and limited by necessity, may produce just such a world as the present' (203). But as Hume has Philo point out, this maneuver really is of little avail; for the world still is not as we would expect it to be if we consider how such a scaled-down deity might be expected to have arranged it. And this is because it would seem to require only a few relatively minor alterations of the world's nature and human nature to improve things immensely; while, with respect to the basic causes of the ills besetting us, 'none of them appear to human reason, in the least degree, necessary or unavoidable' (205).

Philo lays claim to no knowledge here; his point is strictly negative. No modification of the conception of God along the lines Cleanthes proposes will suffice to create, in conjunction with a consideration of life and the world, anything like a presumption in favor of the hypothesis of the existence of a God possessing qualities rendering him worthy of our adoration, or even worth a second thought. The line Demea begins Part XI by taking, of the significance of the wretched character of life, thus turns out to be of no help to him at all. It is a weapon which backfires when apologists of religion seek to use it as an argument. And Hume is clearly contemptuous of those who avail themselves of it simply as a means of motivating others or themselves in a merely psychological way to make a leap of faith and so embrace revealed religion.

Having routed his opposition, Philo concludes by dwelling for a time upon both the dispensability and the generally harmful character of religion in human life. Hume considers it important to stress this point in order to counter the view that, notwithstanding the problematical character of its hypotheses, the promotion of religion is desirable because it plays a salutary and highly useful role in human affairs. He has Philo make some seemingly large concessions to his opponents; but they have more appearance than substance to them. Demea would be pleased to hear him assert that 'The existence of a Deity is plainly ascertained by human reason' (217); and Cleanthes is delighted with his allowance that 'the works of nature bear a great analogy to the productions of art' (217). But what Philo here agrees to refer to as 'a Deity' whose existence reason 'plainly ascertains' is merely *whatever* may be the source of the world as we know it – as he puts it near the end, 'the cause or causes of order in the universe.' One can hardly deny that there is *some* explanation of the order which obtains in the universe; and Hume has no objection if one wishes to attach the name 'God' to that explanation. But he is unwilling to allow that we have any reason to go very much further.

Thus the 'great analogy' Philo is prepared to recognize between works of nature and productions of art is *only* great enough to warrant the vague claim that the 'cause or causes' in question 'probably bear some remote analogy to human intelligence' (227); while on the other hand he insists that even the theist must allow that 'there is a great and immeasurable, because incomprehensible, difference' between them. And he further suggests that this analogy is not worth making much of, since there is 'a certain degree of analogy among all the operations of nature,' and everything from 'the rotting of a turnip' to 'the generation of an animal' to 'human thought' are 'energies that probably bear some remote analogy to each other' (218). If that is the sort of 'remote analogy' which is the most either the evidence or reason entitles us to suppose, then 'the whole of natural theology,' which labors so mightily to produce this pitifully meager result, were better abandoned, restoring religion – for better or for worse – entirely to the province of faith.

Hume has Philo say that this is all to the good; but he clearly is not himself disposed to 'fly to revealed truth with the greatest avidity,' as Philo suggests one who has rid himself of all hopes of being able to 'erect a complete system of theology by the mere help of philosophy' may be expected to do (227). This may be what Demea does, and what many people of his stripe – and also of Cleanthes's, once disillusioned – have done and continue to do. And something very much like it is done by many others (including Kant), who scorn 'revealed truth' in the form of the various established religions, preferring to 'demythologize' it and dress it up in more intellectually respectable clothing; yet who nonetheless are only too anxious and happy to 'deny knowledge in order to make room for faith,' in the words Kant uses to express his own intentions. But Hume's intellectual conscience impelled him in the very opposite direction. He considered it the course of both wisdom and honesty to fly *from* what is purported to be 'revealed truth' with the greatest repugnance, as well as to renounce the enterprise of philosophical theology once and for all, in practice and in principle.

It was not until cautiously written books like Hume's had done their work and had their slow effect, however, that it became possible for like-minded philosophers to take this position openly without scandal. Abhorring scandal, Hume would not even allow his *Dialogues* to be published during his lifetime. He left this work as a genteel time-bomb for the next generation. But that is what it was; and it still retains its power of devastation. Hume may not have dealt philosophical theology a death-blow; but he deprived it of its most congenial territories, forcing it henceforth to live almost entirely in various harsh regions and climes of the spirit, where few can be induced to believe it wise or worthwhile to try to make themselves at home. After Hume the longstanding intimacy between philosophy and religion became increasingly strained. There has been no lack of attempts to save the marriage, and they continue here and there. But it is largely ended, thanks in no small measure to him. And I think nothing would have pleased him more.

CHAPTER VII

KANT

Immanuel Kant is commonly held to have been the greatest philosopher in the history of modern philosophy, if not the entire history of philosophy. Even those who dispute this only do so to the extent of arguing that there have been a few others who have been his equals. His influence has been enormous, both in Europe and in the English-speaking world; and his philosophical system stands as one of the great achievements in our intellectual history. Yet virtually all of the works on which his reputation rests were written only after he had reached the age of 50. His *Critique of Pure Reason* was published when he was 56; his *Critique of Practical Reason* when he was 64; his *Critique of Judgement* when he was 66; his *Metaphysics of Morals* when he was 73; and his *Anthropology* when he was 74. It is rare that one finds someone in any field of intellectual endeavour who is capable of such great intellectual originality and productivity at all, let alone so late in life.

Kant's early life was as unobtrusive as one could imagine. He was born in 1724 in the Prussian city of Königsberg (which is now in the Soviet Union, and is called Kaliningrad), and lived virtually all of his life there. His parents were poor and uneducated, and were staunch Pietists – Pietism being a kind of German fundamentalism. Somehow he managed to attend the local high school, and then the University of Königsberg – both quite unusual in Germany in those days (and even today, for that matter) for the son of a harness-maker. After receiving his degree from the university, the only employment he could find for some years was as a private tutor to several wealthy families in the area. He finally was able to obtain a position as lecturer at the University of Königsberg, at the age of 31. He did not become a professor there until much later, at the age of 46. He remained at Königsberg until his retirement because of ill-health in 1799; and he died five years later, in 1804.

Kant was a popular lecturer at Königsberg, and lectured on a

221

great many subjects, including anthropology, theoretical physics, geography and mathematics, in addition to logic, metaphysics, and moral philosophy. But until he published his *Critique of Pure Reason*, he was virtually unknown outside of Königsberg. By the time of his death, however, he was the dominant figure on the philosophical scene throughout Europe; and a great deal of Western philosophy since that time can be viewed as an attempt to come to terms with him, either by challenging his contentions on various issues, or by developing aspects of his philosophy in various ways. Since Kant, metaphysics has never been the same as it was before; and his influence upon subsequent discussions of epistemology, ethics and aesthetics has been enormous. Continental philosophy in the nineteenth century, beginning with Fichte and Hegel, is incomprehensible without a knowledge of Kant; and the same may be said of much that has gone on in Anglo-American philosophy in this century under the general name of analytic philosophy. Even phenomenologists like Husserl, and existentialists like Heidegger and Sartre, have been profoundly influenced by him. In short, he may fairly be said to be the pivotal figure in the history of modern philosophy. Without a knowledge of the other philosophers considered here, one's knowledge of the history of modern philosophy would be incomplete. But without a knowledge of Kant, one can scarcely even be said to *have* a knowledge of the history of modern philosophy.

Program and method

Metaphysics traditionally was conceived as an endeavor through which knowledge of the fundamental natures of things – the world, the soul, God – is sought through the use of pure reason. Such knowledge was sought through the use of pure reason because it has long been recognized that empirical knowledge based on the testimony of the senses both lacks the certainty taken to be one of the criteria of knowledge in the strictest sense of the term, and is conditioned by our senses in such a way that it cannot plausibly be said to acquaint us with the fundamental natures of things themselves. The rationalists did not question the ability of pure reason operating independently of the senses to give us knowledge of this sort; and Kant himself, until quite late in life, did not question this either. Locke had suggested the need for an analysis of the limits of human understanding, and had argued that these limits were much narrower than Descartes had thought; but his arguments had not been sufficient to convince Leibniz and many subsequent Continental philosophers, including the early Kant himself. It was Hume whose attack upon metaphysics made Kant realize that at the very least there was a problem here; and that there are in fact powerful objections to the attempts of metaphysicians to achieve the kind of knowledge they sought. In his Introduction to his *Prolegomena to Any Future Metaphysics* (1783), he states what he takes Hume's position to be with respect to metaphysics:

> Hume started chiefly from a single but important concept in metaphysics, namely, that of the connection of cause and effect. . . . He challenged reason, which pretends to have given birth to this concept of herself, to answer him by what right she thinks anything could be so constituted that if that thing be posited, something else also must necessarily be posited; for this is the meaning of the concept of cause. He demonstrated irrefutably that it was perfectly impossible for reason to think *a priori* and by means of concepts such a combination, for it implies necessity. . . .
>
> But Hume suffered the usual misfortune of metaphysicians, of not being understood. . . . The question was not whether the concept of cause was right, useful, and even indispensable for our knowledge of nature, for this Hume had never doubted; but whether the concept could be thought by reason *a priori*, and consequently whether it possessed an inner truth, independent of all experience, implying perhaps a more extended use not restricted merely to objects of experience. This was Hume's problem.

Hume perhaps would not have been altogether happy with this characterization of his position and 'problem'; but what matters here is that this is how Kant construed them, or found it useful to recast them. He then describes his response as follows:

> I openly confess my recollection of David Hume was the very thing which many years ago first interrupted my dogmatic slumber and gave my investigations in the field of speculative philosophy a quite new direction. I was far from following him in the conclusions at which he arrived. . . . [But] if we start from a well-founded, but undeveloped, thought which another has bequeathed to us, we may well hope by continued

reflection to advance further than the acute man to whom we owe the first spark of light.

I therefore first tried whether Hume's objection could not be put into a general form, and soon found that the concept of the connection of cause and effect was by no means the only concept by which the understanding thinks the connection of things *a priori*, but rather that metaphysics consists altogether of such concepts. I sought to ascertain their number; and when I had satisfactorily succeeded in this by starting from a single principle, I proceeded to the deduction of these concepts, which I was now certain were not derived from experience, as Hume had attempted to derive them, but sprang from the pure understanding. . . . [A]s soon as I had succeeded in solving Hume's problem, not merely in a particular case, but with respect to the whole faculty of pure reason, I could proceed safely, though slowly, to determine the whole sphere of pure reason completely from universal principles, in its boundaries as well as in its contents. This was required for metaphysics in order to construct its system according to a safe plan.

This is Kant's strategy in the first half of his *Critique of Pure Reason*. His last sentence suggests that his conclusion is radically different from Hume's; and that metaphysics is not something so inherently meaningless that all metaphysical writings should be 'committed to the flames,' as containing nothing but sophistry and illusion. Yet his actual conclusion is rather close to Hume's; for, like Hume, he in fact concludes that all speculation about the natures of things in themselves (including the soul and God), beyond the phenomena of perceptual experience, is devoid of all meaning, and cannot even in principle attain the status of knowledge. When he speaks of metaphysics now – thanks to his *Critique* – being able to 'construct its system according to a safe plan,' he has in mind a very much chastened metaphysics, which no longer aspires to knowledge of the ultimate natures of things through the use of pure speculative reason, but rather contents itself with the determination of the necessary features of all objects of possible experience, and of the structures of mind which themselves impart to all objects of possible experience the features they of necessity have.

This involves a rather fundamental change in the conception of metaphysics. Metaphysics, for Kant, comes to be characterized as that body of knowledge which is both synthetic and *a priori*, rather than that body of knowledge which pertains to the fundamental natures of things, and the soul and God. Now, to be sure, metaphysical knowledge traditionally had been at least implicitly regarded as both synthetic and *a priori* – synthetic in the sense that it involved an actual addition to our knowledge, rather than a mere analysis of the meanings of various concepts; and *a priori* in the sense that it proceeded independently of perceptual experience, rather than by gathering empirical data and generalizing from them. But metaphysicians traditionally conceived of their enterprise in terms of the objects whose natures they aspired to come to know in this way; and these objects were things in themselves (the world), the soul, and (if there is one) God. For Kant, however, all of these things are neither objects of possible experience, nor entities the natures or even the existence of which can be established by synthetic *a priori* reasoning. Since they are not objects of possible experience, no empirical or *a posteriori* knowledge of them is possible either. And since mere analytic propositions yield no knowledge of what actually exists, this means that *no* speculative knowledge either of their natures or of their existence is possible. For all knowledge is held to be of one or another of these types.

If there is to be any metaphysical knowledge at all, therefore, Kant holds that metaphysics cannot be characterized in terms of the traditional objects of metaphysical inquiry. Rather, it can only be characterized either in terms of the distinctive sort of knowledge we can and do have which is neither merely analytic nor empirical – namely, synthetic *a priori* knowledge (the *kind* of knowledge, at least, to which metaphysics traditionally had aspired) – or in terms of the rather different objects of which this sort of knowledge *is* possible: namely, the necessary structures of all possible objects *of experience*, and the basic features of the mind which account for them. For Kant, metaphysics can yield knowledge only of the essential structures of the phenomena we experience, and of the structures of the mind they presuppose, but not of the existence and natures of objects which are beyond the realm of possible experience.

But this does not mean that, for Kant, *there are no* things in themselves, or that it is impossible or impermissible even to speak of them. And he neither denies nor is skeptical about the existence of God and the freedom and immortality of the soul. With regard to the first point, he argues that the *notion* of things in themselves is an indispensable one:

though we cannot *know* these objects as things in themselves, we must yet be in a position at least to *think* them as things in themselves; otherwise we should be landed in the absurd conclusion that there can be appearance without anything that appears. (27)

In fact, he goes so far as to say that we 'must leave the thing in itself as indeed real *per se*, but as not known to us' (24). And with regard to the second point, he says, in perhaps the most famous line in the *Critique*, 'I have . . . found it necessary to deny *knowledge*, in order to make room for *faith*' (29). This makes it seem that Kant's whole epistemological and metaphysical enterprise was motivated by a desire to 'make room for faith' *rather than* to discover the truth in these matters. What he really means to say, however, is that his conclusions, far from ruling out the possibility of religion, leave room for it, though they require it to take the form of faith.

Yet this is misleading too, in the opposite way; for it suggests that Kant holds that the only possible foundation of belief in God and the freedom and immortality of the soul is either revelation or something like a Kierkegaardian 'leap of faith'; and this is far from Kant's actual view. The only type of religion he accepts is (as he puts it in the title of another of his works) 'Religion Within the Limits of Reason Alone' – only not *speculative*, but *practical* reason. He holds that reason in its *practical* (rather than purely speculative) employment provides strong rational grounds for 'faith' in these matters:

> When all progress in the field of the supersensible has thus been denied to speculative reason, it is still open to us to enquire whether, in the practical knowledge of reason, data may not be found sufficient to determine reason's transcendent concept of the unconditioned, and so enable us, in accordance with the *wish* of [traditional] metaphysics, and by means of knowledge that is possible *a priori*, though only from a practical point of view, to pass beyond the limits of all possible experience. Speculative reason has . . . at least made room for such an extension. (24–5)

I will not discuss the way in which he attempts this 'extension.' I would only point out, first, that he is by no means led to a position of skepticism in religious matters by his criticisms of previous metaphysics – and in particular, by his criticisms of all attempts to give speculative proofs of the existence of God and the indestructibility of the soul; and second, that his attempted 'extension' rests heavily on his distinction between appearances or phenomena and things in themselves. As he himself contends, if this distinction is rejected, or if the possibility of things in themselves is denied, the very possibility of any such extension – and of the 'faith' he claims to make room for – would be eliminated, if his account of the laws to which all phenomena are subject is correct.

The importance of this issue for Kant may be seen in his remarks about what he takes to be the significance of his entire philosophical enterprise in the first *Critique*. He asks: 'What sort of treasure is this that we propose to bequeath to posterity?' And he answers:

> On a cursory view of the present work it may seem that its results are merely *negative*, warning us that we must never venture with speculative reason beyond the limits of experience.

Here he sounds like Hume; but then he continues:

> So far, therefore, as our Critique limits speculative reason, it is indeed negative; but since it thereby removes an obstacle which stands in the way of the employment of practical reason [by distinguishing between the phenomena we experience and things in themselves, and arguing that speculative reason is limited to an analysis of the former] . . . , it has in reality a *positive* and very important use. At least this is so, [as soon as] we are convinced that there is an absolutely necessary *practical* employment of reason – the *moral* – in which it inevitably goes beyond the limits of sensibility. (26)

And a few pages later, he concludes that, thanks to his *Critique*,

> Not only will reason be enabled to follow the secure path of a science . . . ; our enquiring youth will also be in a position to spend their time more profitably than in the ordinary dogmatism by which they are so early and so greatly encouraged to indulge in easy speculation about things of which they understand nothing, and into which neither they nor anything else will ever have any insight. . . . But above all, there is the inestimable benefit, that all objections to morality and religion will be forever silenced, and this in the Socratic fashion, namely, by the clearest proof of the ignorance of the objectors. (30)

But once again, this last result depends upon the validity of

Kant's distinction between empirical phenomena (of which we do have experience, but which afford no proof or even evidence of the existence of God and the immortality of the soul), and things in themselves (of which we have no experience and can have no speculative knowledge, but which Kant feels can still be *thought*, and must be supposed). I will have more to say about this subsequently.

Since it is with scope and limits of *speculative* reason, as opposed to *practical* reasoning, that Kant is concerned in his first *Critique*, it is in fact a 'critique of pure speculative reason.' Kant characterizes his aim in it as follows: 'The subject of the present enquiry is . . . , how much we can hope to achieve by reason, when all the material and assistance of experience are taken away' (10–11). To this question, the rationalists would have answered: a knowledge of the fundamental natures of things and the soul and the existence and nature of God. The empiricists, on the other hand, would have answered: exactly nothing.

Kant, however, rejects both of these answers. He concludes that we cannot know any of the things the rationalists thought we could; but we can know a good deal more than the empiricists thought we could. He rejects the contention (or assumption) of the rationalists that the structure of ultimate reality must correspond to the determinations of human reason. Yet he maintains a radically modified version of this view – namely, that the structure of empirical reality or 'nature' must reflect the categories of the human mind, and therefore can be known with complete certainty. He agrees with the empiricists concerning the origins of our knowledge to the extent of granting that 'all our knowledge begins with experience;' but he rejects the empiricist thesis that 'it all arises out of experience' (41) – in other words, that all of our ideas are merely copies of particular impressions. For it is his contention that some of our ideas are contributed to experience by the mind itself; and that these ideas or concepts are so basic that experience would be impossible without them.

I will be discussing these points in due course. For now I simply want to say a word about Kant's method, suggested by this last point. The method he employs for the most part is neither that of the mere analysis of concepts and the straightforward logical deduction of their consequences; nor that of inductive generalization on the basis of the collection of empirical evidence; nor that of analysing concepts into their simple components and searching for impressions to which they correspond, and either assigning meanings to them accordingly or judging them meaningless. Rather, his method is one which has come to be known as the *transcendental* method. It consists in ascertaining various matters of experience which he takes to be undeniable, and then asking: what do they necessarily presuppose? What must be the case, in order for them to obtain? What, in his terms, is 'the ground of their possibility'?

For example: Kant takes it simply to be a fact that we possess mathematical knowledge, and that the judgments of mathematics are neither merely analytic nor empirical generalizations, but rather both synthetic and *a priori*. They are necessarily and universally valid, and so cannot be mere empirical generalizations; and they significantly extend our knowledge, and so cannot be merely analytic. The same is true, he maintains, of certain fundamental propositions in natural science: for example, the law of the conservation of matter (now we would say, of matter and energy) and the law of the conservation of motion, and the proposition that 'Everything which happens has its cause' (50). In his view, Hume was simply wrong to claim that propositions of this sort are mere empirical generalizations, on the one hand, and projections of mere figments of the imagination, on the other. He holds that they are both synthetic and *a priori*, and are necessarily and universally valid for all objects of possible experience. And his procedure, given that this is so, is to ask: What are the necessary presuppositions of the knowledge of this sort which we do have? 'What we must do,' he says, 'is to discover . . . the ground of the possibility of *a priori* synthetic judgments, to obtain insight into the conditions which make each kind of such judgments possible . . .' (51–2). Again: we 'have . . . to answer the questions: How is pure mathematics possible? How is pure science of nature possible? Since these sciences actually exist, it is quite proper to ask *how* they are possible; for *that* they must *be* possible is proved by the fact that they exist' (56). Kant proceeds in the same way where experience generally is concerned. Experience, viewed not simply as an unstructured stream of consciousness, but rather as a unified structure of empirical knowledge, is possible, since it is a given fact. The question therefore arises: *how* is it possible? How can the organization of the stream of consciousness into a unified structure of empirical knowledge be explained? What does this organization necessarily presuppose?

Kant's answer to these questions – which he regards as the only possible answer – is that the mind itself is not merely passive but active. It structures our experience in such a way that the synthetic *a priori* judgments of mathematics and natural science necessarily and universally apply within the realm of possible experience, and that our experience exhibits a unified structure. His discussion in the first half of the *Critique* is devoted to spelling out precisely what the nature of the mind must be, in order for these things to be possible. The results he achieves form his metaphysical system, to the extent that he has one; and this system is, in his view, the only possible metaphysical system which does not overstep the limits of human reason. And if it could be shown that his transcendental method is unsound or unreliable, then for him as for Hume, no metaphysics would be possible at all.

Mind and experience

'Though all our knowledge begins with experience,' Kant says, 'it does not follow that it all arises out of experience' (41). Rather than dogmatically asserting that, since we are not born with certain ideas or propositions already in our minds, all of our ideas and knowledge *must* be derived from experience, Kant asks: Do we in fact have certain ideas, and know certain things, which *cannot* be said to derive from experience? He maintains that we do; and that they should not be considered meaningless or devoid of significant content simply because they do *not* derive directly from experience. On the contrary, he argues that they are indispensable to human thought, and that without them we could have no meaningful experience at all. Mere experience can give rise to no propositions which are necessarily and universally valid. But some propositions *are* necessarily and universally valid, and occupy a position of great importance in human thought: for example, the propositions of mathematics, and the proposition that 'Everything which happens has its cause.' Therefore, Kant concludes, these propositions are not derived from mere experience, and so must be traced to some other source; even though experience may be necessary to occasion our coming to have a knowledge of them. He rejects Hume's analysis of our idea of causal connection on the grounds that it simply fails to do justice to the idea we do in fact have of it:

> the very concept of cause so manifestly contains the concept of a necessary connection with an effect and of the strict universality of the rule, that the concept would be altogether lost if we attempted to derive it, as Hume has done, from a

repeated association of that which happens with that which precedes, and from a custom of connecting representations, a custom originating in this repeated association, and constituting therefore a merely subjective necessity. (44)

Kant argues that the same holds true of certain of our concepts, as well as of certain of our judgments. He cites our concepts of *space* and of *substance* as examples. As the empiricists pointed out, neither our idea of pure space nor our idea of substance is a copy of any sense-impression we ever have. But Kant insists that we *do* have these ideas, and that they are quite essential: the first for mathematical knowledge, and the second for science and ordinary experience. And so he suggests that these ideas must have a different source – in the mind itself. He writes:

If we remove from our empirical concept of a body, one by one, every feature of it which is merely empirical . . . , there still remains the space which the body (now entirely vanished) occupied, and this cannot be removed. Again, if we remove from our empirical concept of any object, corporeal or incorporeal, all properties which experience has taught us, we yet cannot take away that property through which the object is thought as substance or as inhering in a substance. . . . Owing, therefore, to the necessity with which this concept of substance forces itself upon us, we have no option save to admit that it has its seat in our faculty of *a priori* knowledge. (45)

Kant's general line of argument here is that synthetic *a priori* judgments and pure concepts of this sort are possible, since we do make and have them. But they do not have their source in any impressions we receive through our senses. Therefore they must have some other source. This other source must be the mind itself. But they are not merely figments of the imagination, since they apply necessarily and universally to all possible objects of experience; although we have no right to extend their application beyond objects of possible experience (that is, beyond empirical phenomena or the appearances of which we have direct experience) to things in themselves. Therefore, while they have no transcendental validity, they have an objective validity within the realm of possible human experience, and not merely a subjective status of the sort Hume attributed to them.

Accordingly, Kant concludes his Introduction by suggesting that

'There are two stems of human knowledge, namely, *sensibility* and *understanding*. . . . Through the former, objects are given to us; through the latter, they are thought' (61). He holds that the former supplies us with the impressions or 'intuitions' which form the material of our experience, and that the latter supplies the categories according to which this material is structured. But he further contends that what he calls 'sensibility' is not purely passive, and that it as well as the understanding makes a significant contribution to our experience. All appearances have certain basic *forms*, which enable us to relate them to each other in various ways. Kant says: 'That in the appearance which corresponds to sensation I term its *matter*: but that which so determines the manifold of appearance that it allows of being ordered in certain relations, I term the *form* of appearance' (60). He holds that there are two such forms: those of *space* and *time*. The *forms* of appearance, to which all sensations are subject, cannot themselves *be* particular sensations or appearances. And they must be in a sense *prior to* all particular appearances or sensations, since they constitute what might be called the framework within which all particular appearances or sensations occur.

These forms, Kant argues, must therefore be traced to the nature of the mind itself. The mind is such that all sensations which come before it must be ordered in accordance with the forms of space and time, which it itself imposes upon them. How else, he asks, can the universal ordering of our sensations in terms of space and time be explained? Furthermore: how can there be such a thing as geometry, which 'determines the properties of space synthetically, and yet *a priori*'? Kant explains the fact of the ordering of all objects of 'outer sense' in space, and the existence of geometry as a set of synthetic yet universally and necessarily valid propositions, and our idea of pure space, in one fell swoop: space is not a property of things in themselves, but rather one 'form of intuition, [belonging] to the subjective constitution of our mind' (68), as 'the form of outer *sense* in general' (71). None of these things could be explained if space were regarded *either* as a property of things in themselves *or* as an empirical concept derived from perceptual experience. Indeed, Kant maintains that it is not even open to us to construe it in either of these other ways. For the concept of pure space cannot be derived from perceptual experience at all. And, on the other hand, since we never experience things in themselves (but rather only appearances), we cannot know any of their properties, let alone that space is one of them, and has the features described by geometry. He argues in the same manner where time is concerned, contending that it is to be regarded as the form of '*inner* sense' in general.

Kant therefore takes it to be a rule admitting of no exceptions that 'all things, as outer appearances, are side by side in space' (72); and another, that 'all things as appearances, that is, as objects of sensible intuition, are in time' (78). These rules are held to be necessarily and universally valid for all possible appearances since it is only under the forms of space and time that possible appearances *are* possible appearances. This is what he means when he says that these rules are 'objectively valid,' even though subjectively conditioned. They are subjectively conditioned, because they are nothing but forms of human sensibility, and not properties of things in themselves. But they are objectively valid, because all possible appearances must conform to them. This is what Kant means when he speaks of the 'empirical reality' of space and time.

It is of the utmost importance, however, to distinguish between *objective* validity and *transcendental* validity. The two rules Kant mentions are said to be *objectively* valid, but not *transcendentally* valid; that is, they do not apply to things in themselves. This is what he means when he speaks of the 'transcendental *ideality*' of space and time. 'Both,' he says, 'are in the same position; in neither case can their reality *as representations* be questioned, and in both cases they belong only to appearance' (80).

Having reached this point, Kant feels that he has given a partial answer to his initial question, of how the synthetic *a priori* judgments of pure mathematics and pure science of nature are possible. 'Time and space,' he says, are

> two sources of knowledge, from which bodies of *a priori* synthetic knowledge can be derived. . . . [They] are the pure forms of all sensible intuition, and so are what make *a priori* synthetic propositions possible. But these *a priori* sources of knowledge, being merely conditions of our sensibility, just by this very fact determine their own limits, namely, that they apply to objects only in so far as objects are viewed as appearances, and do not present things as they are in themselves. This is the sole field of their validity; should we pass beyond it, no objective use can be made of them. (80)

Kant should *not* be taken to be saying here that therefore space and time are only *illusions*. The concept of an 'illusion' applies only *within* the context of empirical knowledge; and it is only by reference to some experiences which satisfy our empirical criteria of reality that others may be said to be illusory. For the same reason, he would reject the interpretation that the concepts of space and time are only figments of our imagination. For the notion of a figment of the imagination is meaningful only in relation to other experiences which are *not* figments of the imagination. So the kinds of considerations which lead us to regard some of our experiences as illusory and imaginary are quite different from the considerations which lead Kant to maintain the inapplicability of our concepts of space and time to things in themselves. They have no transcendental validity; but they do have empirical validity, and so can hardly be said to be illusions or figments of the imagination. They apply to all human experience, and therefore to 'nature' or 'the world' viewed as the sum total of all possible objects of human experience; and in this sense, they have every bit as much 'reality' as either mathematics or empirical science could possibly require. It is only the legitimacy of extending the application of these concepts to things in themselves that Kant denies. One might want to say that if things in themselves cannot be said to have spatial and temporal properties, we cannot imagine what they would be like. To this, however, he would simply reply: Quite right. Kant summarizes his position with respect to 'the fundamental constitution of sensible knowledge in general' in the following way:

> All our intuition is nothing but the representation of appearance; the things which we intuit are not in themselves what we intuit them as being, nor their relations so constituted in themselves as they appear to us; and if the subject, or even only the subjective constitution of the senses in general, be removed, the whole constitution and all the relations of objects in space and time, nay, space and time themselves, would vanish. As appearances, they cannot exist in themselves, but only in us. What objects may be in themselves, and apart from all this receptivity of our sensibility, remains completely unknown to us. We know nothing but our mode of perceiving them – a mode which is peculiar to us, and not necessarily shared in by every being, though certainly by every human being. (82–3)

This is the first part of what Kant himself characterized as a Copernican revolution in philosophy. Prior to the original Copernican revolution, it was thought that the earth was at the center of the solar system, and that the sun revolved around it. Copernicus's revolution consisted in turning this around, maintaining that in fact the sun was at the center of the solar system, and that the earth revolved around it. Similarly, prior to Kant the accepted view was that the objects of human knowledge and experience have certain basic forms of ordering and arrangement, which the mind receives from them. Kant attempted to effect a kind of Copernican revolution by arguing that this should be turned around; and that in point of fact the basic forms of ordering and arrangement of these objects are derived from the nature of the human mind (that is, the forms of our sensibility) itself.

Having discussed the first of these in the part of the *Critique* entitled 'Transcendental Aesthetic,' Kant turns to the second in the part entitled 'Transcendental Analytic.' This is the second part of his Copernican revolution, in which he argues that we experience things as substances, causes and effects, and so forth, because the understanding structures our experiences in this way. This may seem a little anticlimactic, following as it does his more spectacular argument that space and time are simply forms of human sensibility, and not properties of things in themselves. But it is just as important a part of his analysis of human knowledge as the other is; and it has profound implications for many of the issues we have been considering.

Book I of the 'Transcendental Analytic' has two parts. The first part consists of what Kant calls the 'Analytic of Concepts'; while the second deals with what he calls the 'Deduction' of these concepts. By 'analytic of concepts,' he says, he means the 'dissection of the faculty of understanding itself, in order to investigate the possibility of concepts *a priori* by looking for them in the understanding alone, as their birthplace, and by analyzing the pure use of this faculty' (103). In what he rather misleadingly calls the 'Deduction' of these concepts, on the other hand, he attempts to provide an 'explanation of the manner in which concepts can thus relate *a priori* to objects' (121).

As I have already suggested, it is Kant's contention that we are in fact in possession of a number of concepts which are indispensable for all of our empirical knowledge, and in fact for experience in general as we know it, but which are not and cannot be derived directly from the various sensations which form the material of our perceptions. They also are not derived directly from the two fundamental forms of sensibility, space and time. Kant concludes that they must therefore derive from the second of the two 'stems of human knowledge' he mentions; namely, the *understanding*. We do have these concepts; but these concepts are neither empirical nor innate. So he asks: what features must be attributed to the understanding, in order to explain the fact that we *have* these concepts? And his answer is that the understanding must by its very nature have certain dispositions, in accordance with which our experience is organized in certain ways, and which thereby ultimately give rise to the concepts in question. Thus he says that his aim in the 'Analytic' will be to

> follow up the pure concepts to their first seeds and dispositions in the human understanding, in which they lie prepared, till at last, on the occasion of experience, they are developed, and by the same understanding are exhibited in their purity, freed from the empirical conditions attaching to them. (103)

Hume had been feeling his way toward a view of this sort; but his empiricist thesis about the origin and content of our ideas and the meaningfulness of our concepts had prevented him from working it out and explicitly adopting it. Kant seized upon the hints to be found in Hume along these lines; and because he was not held back by any ultimate commitment to Hume's empiricist thesis, he was able to work out the view suggested by these hints explicitly and systematically. The result is his 'Transcendental Analytic.'

Knowledge, Kant observes, is impossible except by means of concepts. Knowledge essentially involves the relation of impressions to each other; and the relation of impressions to each other is possible only through acts of *synthesis*. He takes this to be the function of *imagination* in a very broad sense of this term, in which it is understood to refer to the capacity of relating perceptual images to each other. But knowledge involves more than acts of synthesis of this sort. It further involves making *judgments*; and this involves applying *concepts* to these syntheses and relating them to each other. Some of our concepts – in fact, many of them – have a very considerable empirical component; but others do not. The latter, which pertain to the basic forms of possible judgments, Kant terms *categories*. For each function of thought in making judgments, there is a corresponding category; and so he takes as his guide to the discovery of these basic categories of the under-standing the various possible types of judgment we make.

These functions, he says, 'specify the understanding completely, and yield an exhaustive analysis of its powers' (113). And because all empirical knowledge must take the form of one or another of these judgments, he argues that the categories corresponding to them apply *a priori* to all possible objects of experience. Nothing can be an object of possible experience for us unless it conforms to these categories, because the understanding simply cannot deal with anything which does not conform to them. In order for appearances to be understood at all, they must be structured in terms of the categories of the understanding. 'By them alone,' Kant says, 'can [we] *understand* anything in the manifold of intuition, that is, think an object of intuition' (114). Our experience exhibits a considerable degree of unity and structure; and it is his contention that the unity and structure it has can be explained only in terms of the activity of the understanding, which organizes appearances in accordance with categories corresponding to its own inherent dispositions.

These categories (which include those of substance and causality) must correspond to basic dispositions of the understanding, Kant argues, since they cannot be derived from any particular impressions we have. As in the particular cases of the concepts of space and time, he holds that 'the categories as concepts of understanding . . . relate to their objects without having borrowed from experience anything that can serve in the representation of these objects' (121). But since they represent 'subjective conditions of thought,' the question again arises of how they 'can have *objective validity*, that is, can furnish conditions of the possibility of all knowledge of objects' (124). For Kant contends that they do. This is the question he attempts to answer in his 'Deduction' of these concepts. Objects of possible experience, he maintains, 'must . . . conform to the conditions which the understanding requires for the synthetic unity of thought,' even though their failure to do so would still be consistent with the mere fact of 'appearances presenting objects to our intuition' (124). His argument is as follows:

> All experience . . . contains, in addition to the intuition of the senses through which something is given, a *concept* of an object as being thereby given, that is to say, as appearing. *Concepts of objects* in general thus underlie all empirical knowledge as its *a priori* conditions. The objective validity of the categories as *a priori* concepts rests, therefore, on the fact that, so far as the form of thought is concerned, through them alone does experience [of objects] become possible. They relate of necessity and *a priori* to objects of experience, for the

reason that only by means of them can any *object* whatsoever
of experience be *thought*. (126)

Or, more concisely, Kant says that the categories 'are concepts
of an object in general, by means of which the intuition of an
object is regarded as determined in respect of one of the logical
functions of judgment' (128). His point is that while the immediate
apprehension of mere appearances presupposes only the forms of
space and time, any *thought* of any *object* at all – and therefore
all judgments, and therefore all knowledge – is possible only within
the framework of the categories. 'Only by means of these fundamental concepts,' Kant says, 'can appearances belong to knowledge' (147). And so he concludes his chapter on the 'Transcendental Deduction' of these concepts as follows:

> Pure concepts of understanding are thus *a priori* possible, and,
> in relation to experience, are indeed necessary; and this for
> the reason that our knowledge has to deal solely with
> appearances, the possibility of which lies in ourselves, and the
> connection and unity of which . . . are to be met with only in
> ourselves. (150)

This analysis has two remarkable and very important implications. First, it implies that the various basic categories Kant distinguishes (including those of substance and causality), like the
concepts of space and time, have objective validity and empirical
reality, but no transcendental validity. That is, while all objects of
possible experience must conform to them, these concepts cannot
be applied beyond the realm of objects of possible experience, to
things in themselves. This may come as no surprise, after Kant has
said the same thing of the concepts of space and time; but it is still
a very significant conclusion that things in themselves cannot be
thought of as substances, or as causally connected with each other
(and so on, where the other categories are concerned). It is his
position that we can legitimately assert no propositions about
things in themselves which make use of any of the categories; and
this means that we cannot say anything of a positive nature about
them at all.

The second point is simply the other side of the coin; though at
first glance, it sounds much more astonishing. It follows from what
has been said, according to Kant, that 'all empirical laws are only
special determinations of the pure laws of understanding, under
which, and according to the norm of which, they first become

possible. Through them appearances take on an orderly character' (140). And it further follows from this, he observes, that 'the order and regularity in the appearances, which we entitle *nature*, we ourselves introduce. We could never find them in appearances, had not we ourselves, or the nature of our mind, originally set them there' (147). In other words, as he puts it, 'the understanding . . . is itself the lawgiver of nature' (148).

This is the conclusion Kant draws from his Copernican revolution. It involves a radical departure from the view that God is the lawgiver of nature, and that the laws of nature we discover are in things prior to and independently of all human experience. The question of *why* the human mind has the structure it does, however, is not answered by Kant. This is a question he would regard as incapable of being answered by speculative reason. And it does leave the door open to those who might wish to suppose that God is *indirectly* the lawgiver of nature, through being the creator of the human understanding with its various categories. But for Kant, these are matters with which it is beyond the capacity of speculative reason to deal.

More important, for Kant, is the fact that while on his analysis we can have no metaphysical knowledge whatsoever of things in themselves, the fact that the understanding is the lawgiver of nature and that nature must conform to its categories means that a good deal of synthetic *a priori* knowledge with respect to it is possible. And if there is a large body of synthetic *a priori* propositions which we can know to apply to all objects of possible experience, then while this may be much less than the rationalists had hoped for, it is also much more than Hume had thought to be possible.

The world of experience

All judgments, according to Kant, are either analytic or synthetic; and there are certain principles to which all of them (as judgments of the understanding) must conform, if they are to be valid. These principles are in a sense ultimate, on his view, in that they constitute standards to which all such judgments must by their very nature conform, and in that 'they are not themselves grounded in higher and more universal modes of knowledge' (188). If the standard of *their* validity were thought to be correspondence with the fundamental nature of things in themselves, we could never know them to be valid; for we have no way of determining whether things in themselves conform to these principles. But Kant does not claim that there is any such correspondence. He claims only that these principles determine the validity of all judgments of the human understanding; and that they reflect, not the fundamental structure of things in themselves, but rather the fundamental structure of the human understanding itself. These principles are fundamental principles of human thought, and so are valid for all human thought; but nothing can be inferred from them about things in themselves.

Since judgments are of the two different sorts mentioned (analytic and synthetic), Kant holds that it is necessary to distinguish two such principles; for the fundamental criteria of validity in the two cases are not the same. (Otherwise they would not be different sorts of judgments.) The highest principle of all *analytic* judgments – and, for that matter, of 'all our judgments in general . . . is that they be *not self-contradictory*' (189). Kant says: 'The proposition that *no predicate contradictory of a thing can belong to it*, is entitled the principle of contradiction, and is a universal, though merely negative, criterion of all truth' (190). But this principle is the *sufficient* condition of truth only of *analytic* judgments. It *is* the sufficient condition of truth of analytic judgments, because the negation of an analytic judgment is self-contradictory. But it is not the sufficient condition of the truth of synthetic judgments, because a synthetic judgment and its negation can both be free of self-contradiction, and so this test does not show whether such a judgment is true.

The highest principle of all synthetic judgments, therefore must be some principle other than the principle of contradiction; for according to Kant, 'beyond the sphere of analytic knowledge [this principle] has, as a sufficient criterion of truth, no authority and no field of application' (190). Synthetic judgments relate to objects of actual or possible experience. Against the rationalists, Kant holds that 'concepts of every kind' would 'be without objective validity, senseless and meaningless, if their necessary application to the objects of experience were not established' (193). And from this he infers what the highest principle of all synthetic judgments must be: namely, that 'every object stands under the necessary conditions of synthetic unity of the manifold in intuition in a possible experience' (194).

A synthetic *a priori* judgment is valid, in other words, if and only if it is not self-contradictory, and also states some necessary and universal 'condition of the *possibility of experience in general*' (194). If such judgments satisfy this criterion, they are valid; and unless they can be shown to satisfy this criterion, neither the principle of contradiction nor any other principle can show them to be valid. Kant thinks that there are some which *can* be shown to satisfy it. If none could be, he would be forced to concur with Hume's conclusion about the impossibility of any metaphysics whatsoever. It should be kept in mind, however, that even if he is right, it does not follow that we can have any speculative knowledge whatsoever about things in themselves.

One of the principles which Kant holds can be shown to satisfy this condition is what he calls 'the principle of the *analogies of experience*' – namely, that 'Experience is possible only through the representation of a necessary connection of perceptions' (208). His argument is that experience by its very nature involves the connection of particular perceptions with each other – and further, that it involves their connection in accordance with certain *rules*, rather than in a purely random manner. If they were *not* connected in accordance with these rules, then while we might still be conscious of a stream of impressions, there would be no such things as *experience*, of which it is appropriate to speak only to the extent that our impressions are ordered in a regular and unified manner.

Now since all appearances are subject to the form of *time*, and since there are three 'modes of time' – namely, 'duration, succession, and co-existence' – Kant suggests that 'there will, therefore, be three rules of all relations of appearances in time' (209). Each rule, or 'analogy of experience,' states one way in which 'a unity of experience may arise from perception' (211) – one way, that is, in which particular appearances may be related in a regular fashion with others. These rules do not state *which particular* appearances are related to which other particular appearances. Rather, they are purely formal, and state only the *ways* in which particular appearances *must be* related to others, in order to *be a part of* experience as an ordered and unified whole *at all*. Further: Kant reminds us that these rules say nothing about the natures of things in themselves; 'these analogies have significance and validity,' he says, 'only as principles of the empirical, not of the transcendental employment of understanding' (211). It is for this reason that he calls them 'analogies'; for 'by these principles,' he says, 'we are justified in combining appearances only according to what is no more than an *analogy* with the logical and universal unity of concepts' (212) – a unity of concepts which has its foundation in the structure of the human mind, and not in the structure of the things in themselves which are supposedly the ultimate source of the content of the appearances.

I will restrict myself to a brief consideration of only the first two of the three 'Analogies' Kant mentions. The First Analogy is what Kant calls the 'Principle of Permanence of Substance' – namely, that 'In all change of appearances substance is permanent; its quantum in nature is neither increased nor diminished' (212). In this connection, he contends that the notion of substance as an enduring substratum of the flux of appearance is unavoidable, and in fact is 'a necessary condition under which alone appearances are determinable as things or objects in a possible experience' (217). This might seem like a rather conventional point, even though it goes beyond what Berkeley and Hume would allow. But in his analysis of what this substratum *is*, Kant departs radically from those who had made use of the notion of 'substance' before him.

He begins by observing that change can neither be perceived nor conceived except in relation to something permanent. Something permanent, therefore, is presupposed by our apprehension of the manifold of appearance, which is always changing. And this something permanent cannot be any of these appearances themselves, since *they* do not change, but rather simply occur and then give way to others. This something permanent must instead be the *substratum* of all appearances; and, as philosophers traditionally have held, 'the substratum of all that is real, that is, of all that belongs to the existence of things [experienced], is *substance*; and all that belongs to existence can be thought only as a determination of substance' (213).

But the concept of substance, as a category of the human understanding, cannot be applied to things in themselves. This permanent substratum which the possibility of experience presupposes, therefore, cannot be conceived as a thing in itself. Rather, it must be something which does not lie altogether outside of possible human experience. Now, all appearances are ordered *in time*. Time, as the form of all possible empirical intuition, does not itself change; rather, it is the permanent framework within which all appearances, and therefore all change, is perceived. So time itself, regarded as the all-embracing form of human sensibility, alone can be that in our experience to which the concept of substance corresponds. It is thus to time alone that the concept of substance may nontranscendentally (and therefore legitimately) be applied. And so Kant concludes:

Permanence, as the abiding correlate of all existence of appearances, of all change and of all concomitance, expresses time in general. . . . All existence and all change in time have thus to be viewed as simply a mode of the existence of that which remains and persists [namely, time in general]. (214)

Thus while Kant holds that 'Permanence is . . . a necessary condition under which alone appearances are determinable as things or objects in a possible experience' (217), and while he further holds that 'the permanent, in relation to which alone all time-relations of appearances can be determined, is *substance* in the field of appearances' (213), he also contends that the form of time in general is all that the fact of change in the manifold of intuition presupposes, and that the concept of substance has no legitimate application to anything else. And where *particular* substances are concerned, the notion of 'substance' refers only to a time-relation of particular appearances in the sensible manifold to each other. So, with Spinoza, Kant can refer to particular substances as simply so many different 'modes' of the one substance, or as 'only so many ways . . . in which the permanent exists' (213), while at the same time rejecting Spinoza's contention that this has any transcendental application.

This First Analogy, or the 'Principle of the Permanence of Substance,' is derived by Kant from time considered as *duration*. His Second Analogy is the Principle of Causality – the principle that 'All alterations take place in conformity with the law of the connection of cause and effect'; and he derives it from time considered as *succession*. This is another principle which he holds to express a necessary condition of possible experience: 'Experience itself – in other words, empirical knowledge of appearances – is . . . possible only in so far as we subject the succession of appearances, and therefore all alteration, to the law of causality' (219). He recognizes that sometimes the order of our perceptions might just as well have been reversed. 'But,' he says, 'in an appearance which constitutes a *happening* . . . , B can be apprehended only as following upon A . . . ; the order in which the perceptions succeed one another in apprehension is in this instance determined.' Again: 'In the perception of an *event* there is always a rule that makes the order in which the perceptions (in the apprehension of this appearance) follow upon one another in a *necessary* order' (221).

In other words, whenever we experience a succession of perceptions which is not haphazard, but rather constitutes a *happening* or an *event*, we regard the perceptions involved as being *necessarily connected*; otherwise the succession of perceptions would not be a happening or an event. The *unity* of *the* happening or *the* event presupposes that the perceptions succeed one another, as Kant says, '*in conformity with a rule*' (222). It is something *objective*, and not merely subjective, or it is no *event* at all. And, he observes,

> I render my subjective synthesis of apprehension objective only by reference to a rule in accordance with which the appearances in their succession, that is, as they happen, are determined by the preceding state. The experience of an *event* (i.e., of anything as *happening*), is itself possible only on this assumption. (223)

Kant is quite willing to grant to Hume that, by reasoning *a priori*, we can never determine what the cause of any particular effect may be, or what the effect of any particular cause may be. 'The sequence in time,' he says, 'is the sole empirical criterion of an effect in its relation to the causality of the cause which preceded it' (228). Further, he grants that neither experience nor reason is capable of showing us how anything occurring at one moment can bring about something else occurring at another moment. 'How anything can be altered,' he remarks, 'and how it should be possible that upon one state in a given moment an opposite state may follow in the next moment – of this we have not, *a priori*, the least conception' (230). But this, for Kant, is not the end of the matter. As was observed earlier, he is by no means satisfied with Hume's account of the status of our idea of a necessary connection between one observed state of affairs and another; namely, that it reflects the influence of custom upon the imagination. That might account for our subjective expectation that the one will be followed by the other; but it cannot account for the fact that the necessary connection associated with the very idea of causality is essentially something *objective*, characterizing the relation of the objects of our experience to each other, and is not simply something *subjective*, characterizing the association of our ideas of these objects in our imagination. Deny the objective character of the necessary connection, Kant in effect says, and the concept of causality is lost.

But at the same time, he is no more willing than Hume to allow that we have any knowledge of necessary connections among things in themselves. His problem thus is to show how the principle of causality can have objective (rather than merely subjective) validity, even though it cannot be applied to things in themselves. And he attempts to do this by pointing out that it is with the connections of objects of possible experience with each other that we are dealing, rather than those of things in themselves; and that all that is required to show that the principle of causality has objective validity is to show that objects of possible experience are necessarily connected with each other, and so are necessarily subject to this principle.

Now I have already observed that Kant grants that we cannot determine *a priori* which particular objects of experience or states of affairs will be connected with each other. 'But,' Kant says,

> apart from all question of what the *content* of the alteration
> . . . may be, the *form* of every alteration, the condition under
> which, as a coming to be of another state, it can alone take
> place, and so the succession of the states themselves . . . , can
> still be considered *a priori* according to the law of causality
> and the conditions of time. (230)

> If . . . it is a necessary law of our sensibility, and therefore
> a *formal condition* of all perceptions, that the preceding time
> necessarily determines the succeeding . . . , it is also an
> indispensable law of *empirical representation* of the time-
> series that the appearances of past time determine all existences
> in the succeeding time . . . according to a rule. (225)

And according to Kant, the 'rule by which we determine something according to succession in time, is, that the condition under which an event invariably and necessarily follows is to be found in what preceded the event' (226). So he concludes: 'The principle of the causal relation in the sequence of appearances is therefore . . . valid of all objects of experience (under the conditions of succession), as being itself the ground of the possibility of such experience' (227).

In other words: all perceptions, and all objects of experience, are ordered in a sequence of temporal succession. All alterations, whatever their content, are ordered states of affairs in the time sequence. It is necessarily true that any state of affairs or object of experience will have been preceded by others, and will be followed by others. No state of affairs or object of experience occurs without being connected with others in the time sequence. And since the preceding time in the time succession is necessarily connected with the following time, each appearance in the time sequence is necessarily connected with appearances occurring earlier in the time sequence; although it cannot be determined *a priori* with which ones it is necessarily connected. But since necessary connection is just what the notion of causality involves, this is to say that every possible object of experience has its cause in something preceding it in the time sequence. This can be known *a priori*; although it is necessary to resort to experience, attending to which types of phenomena are constantly conjoined with which others, in order to discover just what may be said to be the cause of what.

In this way, Kant feels he has shown the principle of causality not to have mere subjective standing, as a product of the imagination, but rather to have objective validity, in the sense that it necessarily applies to all possible objects of experience. In doing so, he feels that he has done what Hume did not: namely, to show that it is the objects of experience themselves that may be said to be necessarily connected with each other (as we are inclined to think), and not simply our ideas of them. But it should be observed that Kant's analysis departs from our ordinary understanding of causality, not only in denying the applicability of the notion of necessary connection to things in themselves, but also in leaving out the idea of one object actually *acting upon* another, and bringing about a change in it. He speaks of 'the series of causes and effects, the former of which inevitably *lead to* the exercise of the latter' (233); and he claims to have shown them to be necessarily connected 'according to a rule – a rule of succession in the time-sequence.' But this no more conveys the idea of the *action* of the one upon the other than Hume's 'constant conjunction' does; it merely suggests that this conjunction of one experienced state of affairs with another is not only constant but *necessary*. If his analysis is correct, this *is* an advance over Hume's conclusion. And it may be the strongest reconstruction of the concept of causality that is possible. But it is less than a complete vindication of the traditional and ordinary construal of this concept, even if the matter of its inapplicability to things in themselves is set aside.

I now shall turn briefly to Kant's famous attempted 'Refutation of Idealism.' He remarks, in his Preface to the Second Edition of the *Critique*, that it is 'a scandal to philosophy and to human reason in general that the existence of things outside us ... must be accepted merely on *faith*, and that if anyone thinks good to doubt their existence, we are unable to counter his doubt by any satisfactory proof' (34n). In this 'Refutation' he attempts to provide the proof which has been lacking. It might seem strange – since he is constantly insisting that appearances must be distinguished from things in themselves, and that nothing whatever can be demonstrated speculatively about the latter – that he should even attempt such a proof. But what is even stranger is the fact that he thinks the proof he offers actually refutes idealism. The most his 'proof' actually establishes is that inner sense presupposes outer sense. But since the objects of outer sense are still only appearances, and since – as he himself has argued – the 'something permanent' which experience presupposes is in fact only a form of human sensibility, nothing he says here rules out the possibility of idealism altogether.

'Idealism', according to Kant, 'is the theory which declares the existence of objects in space outside us either to be merely doubtful and indemonstrable, or to be false and impossible.' And he contends that 'The required proof [refuting idealism] must, therefore, show that we have *experience*, and not merely imagination of outer things; and this, it would seem, cannot be achieved save by proof that even our inner experience, which for Descartes is indubitable, is possible only on the assumption of outer experience' (244). He proceeds to argue, in a very forceful way, that 'The existence of outer things is required for the possibility of a determinate consciousness of the self. . . . Inner experience in general is possible only through outer experience in general' (247). His argument is as follows:

> I am conscious of my own existence as determined in time. All determination in time presupposes something *permanent* in perception. But this [something] permanent cannot be an intuition in me. For all grounds of determination of my existence which are to be met with in me are representations; and as representations themselves require [something] permanent distinct from them, in relation to which their change, and so my existence in the time wherein they change, may be determined. Thus perception of this permanent is possible only through a *thing* outside me . . . ; and consequently the determination of my existence in time is possible only through the existence of actual things which I perceive outside me. (245)

In the first place, however, what Kant asserts in this last sentence does not follow from what precedes it. He moves from speaking of 'something permanent,' which is presupposed by the perception of change, to speaking of 'a *thing* outside me,' to speaking of 'actual things . . . outside me.' But as he himself showed in his discussion of the 'First Analogy of Experience,' the necessary

conceptual correlate of change is 'substance,' conceived as a permanent substratum of appearances, and not 'a thing,' let alone 'actual
things.' And as he himself there argued, what this 'permanent
substratum' is is *time in general*, which is not the sort of thing
idealists mean to be denying – particularly since, for Kant, 'time
in general' is neither a thing in itself nor a property of things in
themselves, but rather a form of human sensibility. While time, as
a form of human sensibility, is *not* 'an intuition . . . to be met with
in me,' as Kant says the 'something permanent' he is talking about
cannot be, it is hardly something which exists independently of the
human mind, on his own analysis.

Of course, it *is* something to be distinguished from 'my own
existence,' if this is understood in the sense of my explicit self-
consciousness. So, for that matter, are the objects of outer sense
Kant speaks of, in relation to which my consciousness of myself is
formed. I, as an empirical ego, centred in a body, standing here,
exist in time; and all sorts of things exist outside me – you, this
book, the moon, and so forth. My explicit consciousness of myself,
as this particular person, has been formed through an interaction
with a great many such 'outer objects.' And as long as I regard
myself in this way, it would be silly of me to deny or even doubt
the existence of 'actual things . . . outside me,' and of the spatio-
temporal order in which both I and these things exist.

Does it follow from any of this, however, that idealism is refuted?
It does only if idealism is taken simply to be the view that objects
do not exist in space. This may be what some idealists have held.
But if one holds, on the one hand, that objects of possible experience are spatially ordered, and on the other, that these objects of
possible experiences are simply appearances, and that space in
general is simply a form of human sensibility (as Kant does), does
it follow that anything exists independently of *the mind*, if the
mind is construed not simply as my explicit self-consciousness, but
rather as that subject to which all these appearances appear, and
which structures them in accordance with the forms of sensibility
and the categories of the understanding? Kant himself is not an
idealist, because he contends that there must be things in themselves
which underlie these appearances, and which are distinct from the
mind in this broader sense. But in order really to refute idealism,
he would have to be able to prove that *this* is the case; and this is
something it is doubtful he can do. At any rate, he does not do it
here.

Soul, God, and things in themselves

I shall conclude my discussion of Kant by turning to his analysis of what can and cannot be said and known about the mind or soul and about God, and then finally, to the issue of things in themselves. His position on the question of the status of the mind or soul is very complex, and deserves a much more detailed discussion than it can be given in a few pages. All I will be able to do is to sketch the outlines of his position, and to indicate some of the distinctions he makes in the course of his analysis.

Perhaps the best place to begin is with his assertion, in his so-called 'Refutation of Idealism,' that 'I am conscious of my own existence as determined in time' (245). This might seem to express agreement with philosophers like Descartes and Berkeley, and disagreement with Hume. In fact, however, it does not. For the self of which Kant is speaking here – the self of which I am conscious – is not to be identified with the mind as he conceives it; nor is it anything like a pure thinking substance. Rather, it is something which, as he argues in the 'Refutation of Idealism,' is 'empirically determined' through and through, and derives whatever content it has from the perceptions of outer sense to which it relates itself. My explicit consciousness of myself, Kant contends, is completely determined by the objects of outer sense I perceive. It is nothing but a function of my perceptions of outer sense, and is no entity in itself apart from them. Take away all perceptions of outer sense, and you would cease to be conscious of yourself; your self consciousness would simply disappear. Hume was quite right, in arguing that when you look into what you call your 'self,' if you take away the various perceptions of which you are conscious, no impression remains to which the term 'self' corresponds. So while it may be appropriate to speak of being 'conscious of one's own existence as determined in time,' it does not follow that there is any object called the 'self' of which one is directly conscious, separate and distinct from the various objects of outer sense in one's experience.

But Kant does not conclude from this, as Hume does, that therefore the mind simply *is* just a 'bundle of perceptions.' This is already clear from his remarks in the second section of the 'Transcendental Deduction' of the pure concepts of the understanding. In that section, he contends that 'No fixed and abiding self can present itself in [the] flux of . . . appearances' (136). But he also argues that a 'unitary consciousness' is necessarily presupposed by the fact that all of my experiences are *my* experiences, and form a unity. If there were no unitary consciousness, he argues, the various appearances which *are* synthesized into a single unity could not *be* so synthesized:

> It is only because I ascribe all perceptions to *one* consciousness . . . that I can say of all perceptions that *I* am conscious of them. . . . The abiding and unchanging 'I' . . . forms the correlate of all our representations in so far as it is to be at all possible that we should become conscious of them. (145–6)

Now this unitary consciousness, or 'abiding and unchanging "I",' is not something of which I am directly aware, as an object of perceptual experience. But it is something Kant takes to be necessarily presupposed by the fact that all of my particular perceptions form a unified whole of which I am conscious. And by becoming aware of this fact, I achieve a kind of indirect self-consciousness – an awareness of myself as a unitary consciousness. It is not an empirical self-consciousness, because it does not involve a perception of any object of experience called the 'self'. Rather, it is pure, or non-empirical – something necessarily presupposed by experience, which reason discovers to be a necessary presupposition of experience. It would be meaningless to speak of it in the absence of experience, and it arises as an actual apperception or self-consciousness only as the result of experience. But it is not identical with my perceptions themselves; and without it, Hume's 'bundle of perceptions' would not *be* a *bundle* at all. In order for our experience to have the unity, forms and organization it does, it is necessary to make reference not simply to impressions or appearances, but also to a unitary consciousness which orders them in accordance with the forms of space and time, arranges them in accordance with the categories, and synthesizes them into a unified whole. To this extent, Kant goes considerably beyond Hume's account.

But given that it is necessary to make reference to a unitary consciousness or thinking subject, can anything be concluded about the sort of thing it is? Can it be regarded as a kind of object or substance, and can any substantial properties be attributed to it? It is to this question that Kant turns in the section of the *Critique* entitled the 'Paralogisms of Pure Reason.' In this section, he is concerned with the possibility of a 'rational psychology' – that is, with the possibility of a discipline which seeks to determine the nature and properties of the thinking subject viewed as a kind of entity by the use of pure reason alone, starting simply from the concept of a thinking subject. 'We have here,' he says, 'what professes to be a [pure] science built upon the single proposition "*I think*".' But as his use of the term 'Paralogisms' to refer to the propositions of rational psychology indicates, Kant wants to deny that it is really a science (yielding genuine knowledge) at all. For a paralogism is a formally fallacious argument, leading to a formally invalid conclusion. And he maintains that all of the conclusions of rational psychology are the results of paralogisms, in which, as he puts it,

> I conclude from the transcendental concept of the subject, which contains nothing manifold, the *absolute* unity of this subject itself, of which, however, even in doing so, I possess no *concept* whatever. (328)

The thinking subject, so far as we have any justification for speaking of it at all, is simply a unified consciousness; and a unified consciousness, while implied by the use of all concepts and the perception of all objects of experience, is itself neither a concept nor an object of possible experience. But what happens in rational psychology is that it is treated analogously to an object of possible experience, as a special kind of object (the 'soul'), and the categories applying to objects of possible experience are then applied to it. This yields the following basic propositions: First, that 'the soul is *substance*'; second, that 'as regards its quality it is *simple*'; third, that 'as regards the different times in which it exists, it is numerically *identical*'; and fourth, that 'it is in relation to possible objects in space' (330). And Kant suggests that all of the other concepts traditionally applied to the soul in rational theology are derived from combining these in various ways; for example, 'immateriality,' 'personality,' 'spirituality,' 'immortality,' and 'embodiment' (331).

Now the validity of applying these derivative concepts to the thinking subject is obviously dependent upon the validity of applying to it the more basic concepts of 'substance,' 'simplicity,' 'identity' through time, and 'relation' to possible objects in space. And Kant denies that *any* of these concepts can be validly applied to it. The crucial one is the concept of 'substance'; for if that concept cannot be applied to it, then none of the others can either. On this point, he says:

That the 'I', the 'I' that thinks, can be regarded always as *subject*, and as something which does not belong to thought as a mere predicate, must be granted . . . ; but [this] does not mean that I, as *object*, am for myself a *self-subsistent being* or *substance*. The latter statement goes very far beyond the former, and demands for its proof data which are not to be met with in thought. (369)

The concept of substance cannot be applied to the thinking subject because it is a category of the understanding, the only legitimate application of which, Kant contends, is 'to intuitions which cannot in me be other than sensible' (369); and our unitary consciousness itself is not the object of any sensible intuition. And with this he concludes his 'analysis . . . of the consciousness of myself as object' (370). He summarizes his critique of rational psychology as follows:

Rational psychology owes its origin simply to misunderstanding. The unity of consciousness, which underlies the categories, is here mistaken for an intuition of the subject *as object*, and the category of substance is then applied to it. But this unity is only unity *in thought*, by which alone no object is given, and to which, therefore, the category of substance, which always presupposes a given *intuition*, cannot be applied. Consequently, this subject cannot be known. (377)

Yet it does not follow, for Kant, that there *is no* thing in itself which corresponds to our unified consciousness. Speculative reason is powerless to prove that there *is* any such thing; but it is also powerless to prove there is *not*. Further: while my consciousness cannot legitimately be viewed as a *spiritual* substance, it cannot legitimately be viewed as a *material* substance either. So neither a spiritualistic nor a materialistic explanation and analysis of my existence and nature as a conscious subject is possible; 'and the conclusion,' Kant says, 'is that in no way whatsoever can we know anything of the constitution of the soul' (376). He does think that there are certain *moral* considerations which require us to conclude that the soul *is* a thing in itself, and that it is both free and immortal; but that is another matter, and goes beyond the limits of pure speculative reason.

Rational psychology involves one instance of what Kant terms the 'dialectical employment of reason,' which 'carries us altogether beyond the empirical employment of categories and puts us off with a merely deceptive extension of pure understanding' (298). In this way, it gives rise to what Kant calls '*transcendental illusions*,' of which the conclusions of rational psychology are examples. Other examples are to be found in the other two branches of traditional metaphysics, dealing with the other two objects of traditional metaphysical inquiry: namely, the world and God. Rational cosmology is the attempt to establish conclusions about the world in general by means of speculative reason; and rational theology is the attempt to establish conclusions in a similar way about the existence and nature of God. But Kant argues that in both of these cases, as in the case of rational psychology, reason oversteps its limits, and in fact is incapable of establishing any such conclusions.

Rational cosmology gives rise, not to paralogisms, but to what Kant calls 'antinomies of pure reason.' The trouble with it is not that it reaches its conclusions by arguments that are formally invalid, but rather that, by valid arguments, it yields conclusions which are logically incompatible with each other. For example: by one line of reasoning, it yields the conclusion that 'the world has a beginning in time, and is also limited as regards space'; and, by another line of reasoning, it yields the conclusion that 'the world has no beginning, and no limits in space' (396). Again: by one line of reasoning, it yields the conclusion that 'every composite substance in the world is made up of simple parts, and nothing anywhere exists save the simple or what is composed of the simple'; but, by another line of reasoning, it yields the conclusion that 'no composite thing in the world is made up of simple parts, and there nowhere exists in the world anything simple' (402). And Kant contends that the fact that the use of speculative reason in this context results in these antinomies shows that it is incapable of establishing anything one way or another along these lines.

Rational theology seeks to establish certain conclusions, not about the world in general or the soul, but about God. And in the section of the *Critique* entitled 'The Ideal of Pure Reason,' Kant attempts both to explain how we come to have the idea of God, or the 'ideal of pure reason,' and also to show that none of the possible attempts to prove the existence of a being corresponding to this idea by pure speculative reason succeeds. The goal of reason, he holds, is to give a complete analysis and to effect a complete integration of all of the objects of experience. In doing so, it is guided by an ideal to which reason itself gives rise, of a 'supreme and complete material condition of the possibility of all that exists

– the condition to which all thought of objects, so far as their content is concerned, has to be traced back' (491). Kant allows that 'Reason, in achieving its purpose, that, namely, of representing the necessary complete determination of things, does not presuppose the existence of a *being* that corresponds to this ideal' (491). But he suggests that it is a *natural illusion* of reason to suppose that there *is* a being which corresponds to this indispensable idea. And 'the concept of such a being,' he says, 'is the concept of *God*, taken in the transcendental sense' (493) – that is, in the sense of a being who transcends all objects of possible experience, and who is the source of their very possibility. But, he contends,

> in any such use of the transcendental idea, we [are] overstepping the limits of its purpose and validity. . . . Such a thing is a mere fiction in which we combine and realize the manifold of our idea . . . as an individual being. But we have no right to do this, nor even to assume the possibility of such an hypothesis. (493)

Recognizing that we have no right to do this without any further justification, rational theology attempts to provide *proofs* of the *existence* of a being answering to our idea. In this connection, Kant makes the following observations:

> There are only three possible ways of proving the existence of God by means of speculative reason. All the paths leading to this goal begin *either* from determinate experience and the specific constitution of the world of sense as thereby known, and ascend from it, in accordance with laws of causality, to the supreme cause outside the world; *or* they start from experience which is purely indeterminate, that is, from the experience of existence in general [and proceed in a similar way]; *or* finally they abstract from all experience, and argue completely *a priori*, from mere concepts, to the existence of a supreme cause. The first proof is the *physico-theological* [or the argument from design], the second the *cosmological*, the third the *ontological*. (499–500)

Concerning these proofs, Kant says: 'I propose to show that reason is as little able to make progress on the one path, the empirical, as on the other path, the transcendental, and that it stretches its wings in vain in thus attempting to soar above the world of sense by the mere power of speculation' (500). Against the physico-theological and the cosmological arguments, he makes two different points. First, he argues that each of them ultimately has to make use of the ontological argument, in order to reach the conclusion that a being answering to the ideal of pure reason exists; and that therefore they are not really independent arguments at all. And second, he argues that each of them makes use of the principle of causality in an illegitimate way. With regard to the first point he writes:

> The cosmological proof uses [the] experience [of the existence of something] only for a single step in the argument, namely, to conclude the existence of a necessary being. What properties this being may have, the empirical premiss cannot tell us. Reason therefore abandons experience altogether, and endeavours to discover from mere concepts what properties an absolutely necessary being must have. (510)

But this is just what the ontological argument does. By itself, therefore, even if it should be granted that the existence of anything contingent implies the necessary existence of something else, Kant contends that this argument 'is unable to demonstrate this necessity as belonging to any determinate thing' (510). The world itself, for all we know *a priori*, might have this characteristic of necessary existence, as Hume pointed out; and so this argument by itself cannot establish the desired conclusion.

The physio-theological argument likewise is obliged to have recourse to this argument (if the desired conclusion is to be reached), by way of having to fall back on the cosmological argument. If the use of the principle of causality beyond the realm of appearances is allowed, Kant observes, 'The physico-theological argument can indeed lead us to the point of admiring the greatness, wisdom, power, etc., of the Author of the world, but can take us no further' (532). In particular, he contends, it does not enable us to conclude that the Author of the world is a being who exists necessarily. 'Accordingly,' he says, this proof, 'failing in its undertaking, has in face of this difficulty [to fall] back upon the cosmological proof' (524). And then, like the cosmological proof, it has to resort to the ontological proof, in order to reach the conclusion that the supposedly necessarily existing Author of the world answers to the ideal of pure reason.

As for the ontological proof itself, Kant argues that it fails for quite different reasons. It fails, because it involves treating 'existence' as a predicate. And ' "*being*" ' (or existence), he maintains, 'is obviously not a real predicate; that is, it is not a concept of something which could be added to the concept of a thing. It is merely the *positing of* a thing . . . *as existing.* . . .' (504). He continues: 'When, therefore, I think of a being as the supreme reality, without any defect, the question still remains whether it exists or not' (505–6). In other words, the proposition 'God exists' is not necessarily true, because the proposition 'God does not exist' is not self-contradictory; and that proposition is not self-contradictory, because 'existence' cannot legitimately be predicated of 'God,' as constituting a part of the very concept of God. In fact, Kant goes so far as to say: 'There is [actually] a contradiction in introducing the concept of existence . . . into the concept of a thing which we profess to be thinking solely in reference to its possibility' (503). More generally, he remarks:

> In dealing with objects of pure thought, we have no means whatsoever of knowing their existence. . . . Our consciousness of all existence . . . belongs exclusively to the unity of experience; any alleged existence outside this field, while not indeed such as we can declare to be absolutely impossible, is of the nature of an assumption which we can never be in a position to justify. (506)

It still might be thought that, even though the existence of a being answering to the ideal of pure reason cannot be proven by any of these arguments, the cosmological and physico-theological arguments at least establish the necessary existence of *a* being who is the cause of the existence of the world and of the design it exhibits. But even this is a conclusion which Kant argues is invalid. For it is reached by applying the principle of causality in a way for which no justification can be given. This principle he insists, 'is valid only within the field of experience, and outside this field has no application, nay, is indeed meaningless.' (528)

> If we abstract from what it is as a principle that contains the condition of all possible experiences, and leaving aside all that is empirical, attempt to assert it of the contingent in general, there remains not the least justification for any synthetic proposition such as might show us how to pass from that which is before us to something quite different (called its cause). In this merely speculative employment any meaning . . . is taken away . . . from the concept of a cause. (527)

So Kant concludes that 'all attempts to employ reason in theology in any merely speculative manner are altogether fruitless and by their very nature null and void . . .' (528). But from this he does *not* infer either that God does not exist, or that no rational theology whatsoever is possible. With regard to the first point, he suggests that it follows from his critique of speculative reason that, while the existence of a transcendent God 'cannot indeed be proved, [it] also cannot be disproved, by merely speculative reason' (531). And, with regard to the second point, he holds that there are certain *moral* considerations which must lead us to suppose that such a God does in fact exist. But this, once again, goes beyond the scope of the first *Critique*. What he feels he *has* established here is that 'the only theology or reason which is [even] *possible* is that which is based upon moral laws' (528).

In conclusion, I would draw attention to a problem – raised by the very point Kant himself makes against the use of the principle of causality in rational theology – pertaining to his view of the relation of appearances to things in themselves. He says:

> everything intuited in space or time, and therefore all objects of any experience possible to us, are nothing but appearances, that is, mere representations, which, in the manner in which they are represented . . . , have no independent existence outside our thoughts. (439)

This means that we never can experience anything which might be considered a thing in itself, existing independently of our experience. Yet, as has been observed, Kant holds that there *are* things in themselves. But what is his justification for doing so? The justification he gives in the Introduction is that the very notion of an *appearance* or a *representation* necessarily implies that there is *something that appears* or *is represented*. But this is no real justification; for it can be replied simply that Kant should have chosen different terms, which do not have these conceptual implications (for example, like his own terms 'phenomena' and 'intuitions'), unless there are independent reasons for concluding that the phenomena we experience are in fact 'appearances' or 'representations' of something independent of our consciousness.

Now Kant does think there are independent reasons for this position; and he does give another justification for his supposition of things in themselves. But it is no more satisfactory; indeed, it would seem less so. His point in effect is that the phenomena we experience must have some sort of *cause*; and therefore there must be things in themselves, which are the *causes* of the phenomena we experience. To be sure, he allows,

The non-sensible cause of these representations is completely unknown to us, and cannot therefore be intuited by us as object. . . . We may, however, entitle the purely intelligible cause of appearances in general the transcendental object. . . . To this transcendental object we can ascribe the whole extent and connection of our possible perceptions, and can say that it is given in itself prior to all experience. (441)

But how can Kant say this, given his own contention that the principle of causality 'is valid only *within* the field of experience, and outside this field has no application, nay, is indeed meaningless' (528)? In the last analysis, he subscribes to a version of a causal theory of perception after all; but it would seem that he is not consistently entitled to do so. And if neither the principle of causality, nor the choice of terms like 'appearance' and 'representation' to characterize the phenomena we experience, can justify the supposition that there *are* things in themselves, existing independently of all possible experience, doubts must arise about just how meaningful the very notion of a thing in itself is. For if a thing in itself is something of which we can in principle never have any experience, and if it is in principle something to which we can apply neither the forms of space and time nor the categories of the understanding, and if it is something the very existence of which we have no justification for supposing, then it is questionable whether (as Berkeley would say) the idea of a thing in itself is at all different from the idea of *nothing*.

Kant insists time and again upon the importance to his arguments in the *Critique* of the distinction between appearances and things in themselves. And he is quite right to do so. But this means that if there *is* a real problem here, about the justification for supposing the existence of things in themselves, and in fact about the very meaningfulness of the notion, then his own analysis might have to be subjected to radical modification in order to retain any validity. Kant's successors – philosophers like Hegel and Nietzsche – felt that this *is* a problem for Kant, and that fundamental modifications of his position *are* accordingly necessary. That, however, is another story, long in the telling, and still in the making.

BIBLIOGRAPHY

A complete bibliography of the literature on the seven philosophers dealt with in this book would fill volumes. The short bibliography provided here is selective in a variety of respects. It indicates only some of the (main and more readily available) works and editions of the works of these philosophers themselves. It further includes only books and volumes of essays dealing with them, to the exclusion of most of the vast number of essays on them that have appeared in journals over the years. It is restricted chiefly to those that have been published or reissued during the past half-century – and moreover, to those that have been written in or translated into English. And it does not even include all of them. In particular, it is confined for the most part to works dealing with the aspects of the thought of the seven philosophers which are discussed in this book. The literature it does list, however, should suffice for the purposes of most English-speaking readers who might wish to do additional reading on these topics. Anyone with interests deep and serious enough to require more will know well enough how to go about proceeding further.

I also have not listed general histories of philosophy, or of classical modern philosophy. These are legion; and any good college or university library will contain a great many of them. Some may be consulted with more profit than others; but I will not presume to say which are the best. I would suggest, however, that one who feels in need of the sort of account of various philosophers one usually finds in such histories would often do best to consult the appropriate entries in the recently published *Encyclopedia of Philosophy* (New York: Macmillan and Free Press, 1967), most of which are fine essays by scholars who know their particular subjects very well.

The bibliography provided here is organized in a manner following the organization of this book itself, beginning with works by and about Descartes, and ending with works by and about Kant. I have thought it best not to designate volumes dealing with each philosopher which are (in my opinion) superior to the rest. I do wish, however, to draw the reader's attention to two series of volumes which are highly deserving of attention: the studies of various of these philosophers published by Routledge & Kegan Paul in their Arguments of the Philosphers series; and the 'Collections of Critical Essays' on each of them published by

Doubleday (Anchor), and recently reissued by the University of Notre Dame Press. Each has a strong claim to be one of the best series of its kind.

René Descartes (1596–1650)

Writings

Oeuvres, ed. Ch. Adam and P. Tannery. Paris: Cerf., 1897–1913. 11 vols.

Philosophical Works, ed. and tr. Elizabeth Haldane and G. R. T. Ross. Cambridge: Cambridge University Press, 1911. Reissued 1967. 2 vols.

The Philosophical Writings, tr. John Cottingham and Dugald Murdoch. Cambridge: Cambridge University Press, 1985. 2 vols.

Philosophical Letters, tr. and ed. Anthony Kenny. Oxford: Clarendon Press, 1970.

Commentary

Balz, Albert. *Descartes and the Modern Mind.* New Haven: Yale University Press, 1952.

Beck, Leslie J. *The Metaphysics of Descartes: A Study of the Meditations.* Oxford: Clarendon Press, 1965.

Beck, Leslie J. *The Method of Descartes: A Study of the Regulae.* Oxford: Clarendon Press, 1952.

Broadie, Frederick. *An Approach to Descartes' 'Meditations.'* London: Athlone Press, 1970.

Caton, Hiram. *The Origin of Subjectivity: An Essay on Descartes.* New Haven: Yale University Press, 1973.

Collins, James. *Descartes' Philosophy of Nature.* Oxford: Blackwell, 1971.

Curley, E. M. *Descartes Against the Skeptics.* Cambridge, Mass.: Harvard University Press, 1978.

Doney, Willis (ed.). *Descartes: A Collection of Critical Essays.* Garden City, New York: Doubleday (Anchor), 1967.

Frankfurt, Harry G. *Demons, Dreamers, and Madmen: The Defense of Reason in Descartes's 'Meditations.'* Indianapolis: Bobbs-Merrill, 1970.

Garber, Daniel. *Descartes' Metaphysical Physics.* Chicago: University of Chicago Press, 1992.

Gibson, A. Boyce. *The Philosophy of Descartes.* New York: Russell & Russell. (Reissue of 1932 edition.)

Grene, Marjorie. *Descartes.* Minneapolis: University of Minnesota Press, 1985.

Keeling, S. V. *Descartes.* London: Ernest Benn, 1934.

Bibliography

Kenny, Anthony. *Descartes: A Study of His Philosophy*. New York: Random House, 1968.

Schouls, Peter A. *The Imposition of Method: A Study of Descartes and Locke*. Oxford: Clarendon Press, 1980.

Schouls, Peter A. *Descartes and the Enlightenment*. Edinburgh: Edinburgh University Press, 1989.

Sebba, G. *The Dream of Descartes*. Carbondale, Ill.: Southern Illinois University Press, 1987.

Smith, Norman Kemp. *Studies in the Cartesian Philosophy*. New York: Russell & Russell, 1962. (Reissue of 1914 edition.)

Smith, Norman Kemp. *New Studies in the Philosophy of Descartes*. New York: Russell & Russell, 1963. (Reissue of 1952 edition.)

Spinoza, Benedictus. *The Principles of Descartes' Philosophy*, tr. Halbert H. Britan. LaSalle, Ill.: Open Court, 1978.

Taliaferro, Robert Catesby. *The Concept of Matter in Descartes and Leibniz*. Notre Dame, Indiana: University of Notre Dame Press, 1964.

Williams, Bernard A. O. *Descartes: The Project of Pure Enquiry*. Harmondsworth: Penguin, 1978.

Wilson, Margaret Dauler. *Descartes*. London: Routledge & Kegan Paul, 1978.

Gottfried Wilhelm Leibniz (1646–1716)

Writings

Sämtliche Schriften und Briefe. Darmstadt: Reichl, 1923–.

Philosophische Schriften, ed. C. I. Gerhardt. Berlin: Weidmann, 1876–90. 7 vols.

Discourse on Metaphysics and Correspondence with Arnauld, tr. George R. Montgomery. LaSalle, Ill.: Open Court, 1973.

Monadology and Other Philosophical Essays, tr. Paul Schrecker and Anne Martin Schrecker. Indianapolis: Bobbs-Merrill, 1965.

New Essays on Human Understanding, ed. Peter Remnant and Jonathan Bennett. Cambridge: Cambridge University Press, 1981.

Logical Papers: A Selection, tr. G. H. Parkinson. Oxford: Oxford University Press, 1966.

Philosophical Papers and Letters, ed. and tr. Leroy E. Loemker. Dordrecht: Reidel, 1970 (2nd ed.).

Philosophical Writings, ed. G. H. Parkinson, tr. Mary Morris, Towata, New Jersey: Rowman & Littlefield (Rev. ed. 1991.)

The Leibniz-Clarke Correspondence, ed. H. G. Alexander. Manchester: Manchester University Press, 1976.

Commentary

Broad, C. D. *Leibniz: An Introduction*, ed. C. Lewy. Cambridge: Cambridge University Press, 1975.

Brown, C. S. *Leibniz*. Minneapolis: University of Minnesota Press, 1984.

Carr, Herbert Wildon. *Leibniz*. Boston: Little, Brown, 1929.

Frankfurt, Harry G. (ed.) *Leibniz: A Collection of Critical Essays.* Garden City, New York: Doubleday (Anchor), 1972.

Hall, A. Rupert. *Philosophers at War: The Quarrel Between Newton and Leibniz*. Cambridge: Cambridge University Press, 1980.

Ishiguro, Hide, *Leibniz's Philosophy of Logic and Language*. Cambridge: Cambridge University Press, 1991. (Second edition.)

Loemker, Leroy, E. *Struggle for Synthesis: The Seventeenth Century Background of Leibniz's Synthesis of Order and Freedom*. Cambridge, Mass.: Harvard University Press, 1972.

Martin, Gottfried. *Leibniz: Logic and Metaphysics*, tr. K. J. Northcott and P. G. Lucas. Manchester: Manchester University Press, 1964.

Mates, B. *The Philosophy of Leibniz*. New York and Oxford: Oxford University Press, 1986.

Meyer, Rudolf W. *Leibniz and the Seventeenth Century Revolution*, tr. J. P. Stern, Cambridge: Bowes & Bowes, 1952.

Parkinson, G. H. R. *Logic and Reality in Leibniz's Metaphysics*. Oxford: Clarendon Press, 1965.

Rescher, Nicholas. *The Philosophy of Leibniz*. Towata, New Jersey: Rowman & Littlefield, 1979. (Reissue of 1967 edition.)

Ross, G. M. *Leibniz*. Oxford: Oxford University Press, 1984.

Russell, Bertrand. *A Critical Exposition of the Philosophy of Leibniz*. London: Allen & Unwin, 1900.

Taliaferro, Robert Catesby. *The Concept of Matter in Descartes and Leibniz*. Notre Dame, Indiana: University of Notre Dame Press, 1964.

Yost, R. M. *Leibniz and Philosophical Analysis*. New York and London: Garland, 1985.

Baruch/Benedictus de Spinoza (1632–1677)

Writings

Opera, ed. Carl Gebhardt. Heidelberg: Carl Winter, 1925. 4 vols.

Works of Spinoza, tr. R. H. M. Elwes. New York: Dover, 1951. 2 vols.

Earlier Philosophical Writings, ed. Frank A. Hayes. New York: Irvington, 1973.

The Ethics and Selected Letters, ed. and tr. Samuel Shirley. New York: Hackett, 1982.

The Collected Works of Spinoza, ed. Edwin Curley. Princeton: Princeton University Press, 1985.

Bibliography

Commentary

Allison, Henry. *Benedict de Spinoza*. New Haven: Yale University Press, 1987. (Rev. ed.)

Bennett, J. F. *A Study of Spinoza's Ethics*. Indianapolis: Hackett, 1984.

Collins, J. D. *Spinoza on Nature*. Carbondale, Ill.: Southern Illinois University Press, 1984.

Curley, E. M. *Spinoza's Metaphysics: An Essay in Interpretation*. Cambridge, Mass.: Harvard University Press, 1969.

Curley, E. M. *Behind the Geometrical Method*. Princeton: Princeton University Press, 1988.

Delahunty, R. J. *Spinoza*. London: Routledge & Kegan Paul, 1985.

Donagan, Alan. *Spinoza*. Chicago: University of Chicago Press, 1989.

Grene, Marjorie (ed.). *Spinoza: A Collection of Critical Essays*. Garden City, New York: Doubleday (Anchor), 1973.

Hallett, Harold Foster. *Benedict de Spinoza: The Elements of His Philosophy*. London: Athlone, 1957.

Hampshire, Stuart. *Spinoza*. Harmondsworth: Penguin, 1988. (Reissue of 1951 edition.)

Harris, Errol E. *Salvation from Despair: A Reappraisal of Spinoza's Philosophy*. The Hague: Martinus Nijhoff, 1973.

Joachim, H. H. *A Study of the Ethics of Spinoza*. New York: Russell & Russell, 1964. (Reissue of 1901 edition.)

Mark, Thomas Carson. *Spinoza's Theory of Truth*. New York: Columbia University Press, 1972.

McKeon, Richard P. *The Philosophy of Spinoza: The Unity of His Thought*. New York: Longmans, Green, 1928.

Naess, Arne. *Creation and Cognition in Spinoza's Theory of Affects*. Oslo: University of Oslo Press, 1967.

Naess, Arne. *Freedom, Emotion and Self-Subsistence: The Structure of a Central Part of Spinoza's Ethics*. Oslo: University of Oslo Press, 1975.

Norris, C. *Spinoza and the Origins of Modern Critical Theory*. Oxford: Blackwell, 1991.

Parkinson, G. H. R. *Spinoza's Theory of Knowledge*. Oxford: Clarendon Press, 1954.

Scruton, Roger. *Spinoza*. Oxford: Oxford University Press, 1986.

Wolfson, Harry A. *The Philosophy of Spinoza*. Cambridge, Mass.: Harvard University Press, 1983. (Reprinting.)

Yovel, Yirmiyahu. *Spinoza and Other Heretics*. 2 vols. Princeton: Princeton University Press, 1990.

John Locke (1632–1704)

Writings

Works. Oxford: Clarendon Press, 1975–.

An Essay Concerning Human Understanding, ed. Peter H. Nidditch. Oxford: Clarendon Press, 1979.

The Reasonableness of Christianity and A Discourse on Miracles, ed. I. T. Ramsey. Stanford: Stanford University Press, 1958.

Two Treatises of Government, ed. Peter Laslett. Cambridge: Cambridge University Press (3rd rev. ed. 1988.)

The Correspondence of John Locke, ed. E. S. DeBeer. Oxford: Oxford University Press, 1976–89, 8 vols.

Commentary

Aaron, Richard I. *John Locke.* 3rd ed. Oxford: Clarendon Press, 1971.

Armstrong, D. M., and Martin, C. B. (eds.). *Locke and Berkeley: A Collection of Critical Essays.* Garden City, New York: Doubleday (Anchor), 1968.

Bennett, Jonathan. *Locke Berkeley Hume: Central Themes.* Oxford: Clarendon Press, 1971.

Cranston, M. *John Locke.* London and Oxford: Oxford University Press, 1985.

Dunn, J. *Locke.* New York and Oxford: Oxford University Press, 1984.

Jenkins, J. J. *Understanding Locke.* New York: Columbia University Press, 1982.

Kraus, John L. *John Locke.* New York: Philosophical Library, 1968.

Mabbott, J. D. *John Locke.* London: Macmillan, 1973.

Mackie, J. L. *Problems from Locke.* Oxford: Clarendon Press, 1976.

O'Conner, D. J. *John Locke.* London: Penguin, 1952.

Schouls, Peter A. *The Imposition of Method: A Study of Descartes and Locke.* Oxford: Clarendon Press, 1980.

Woolhouse, R. S. *Locke's Philosophy of Science and Knowledge.* New York: Barnes & Noble, 1971.

Woolhouse, R. S. *Locke.* Minneapolis: University of Minnesota Press, 1983.

Yolton, John W. *Locke and the Compass of Human Understanding.* Cambridge: Cambridge University Press, 1970.

Yolton, John W. *John Locke: An Introduction.* Oxford: Blackwell, 1985.

Yolton, John W. *Locke and French Materialism.* Oxford: Oxford University Press, 1991.

Yolton, John W. *John Locke and the Way of Ideas.* Oxford: Oxford University Press, 1956.

Bibliography

George Berkeley (1685–1753)

Writings

The Works of George Berkeley, ed. A. A. Luce and T. E. Jessop. London: Thomas Nelson, 1948–57. 9 vols.

Philosophical Works. Towata, New Jersey: Rowman & Littlefield, 1980.

Principles, Dialogues and Philosophical Correspondence, ed. Colin M. Turbayne. Indianapolis: Bobbs-Merrill, 1965.

Commentary

Ardley, Gavin. *Berkeley's Renovation of Philosophy*. The Hague: Martinus Nijhoff, 1968.

Armstrong, D. M. and Martin, C. B. (eds). *Locke and Berkeley: A Collection of Critical Essays*. Garden City, New York: Doubleday (Anchor), 1968.

Bennett, Jonathan. *Locke Berkeley Hume: Central Themes*. Oxford: Clarendon Press, 1971.

Bracken, Harry M. *Berkeley*. New York: St. Martin's Press, 1975.

Broad, C. D. *Berkeley's Argument*. New York: Haskell, 1975.

Brook, Richard J. *Berkeley's Philosophy of Science*. The Hague: Martinus Nijhoff, 1973.

Dancy, J. *Berkeley*. Oxford: Blackwell, 1987.

Hicks, G. Dawes. *Berkeley*. New York: Russell & Russell, 1968. (Reissue of 1937 edition.)

Luce, Arthur. A. *Berkeley and Malebranche*. Oxford: Clarendon Press, 1934.

Luce, Arthur A. *Berkeley's Immaterialism*. New York: Russell & Russell, 1968. (Reissue of 1945 edition.)

Park, Désirée. *Complementary Notions: A Critical Study of Berkeley's Theory of Concepts*. The Hague: Martinus Nijhoff, 1972.

Pitcher, George. *Berkeley*. London: Routledge & Kegan Paul, 1977.

Ritchie, A. D. *George Berkeley: A Reappraisal*. Manchester: Manchester University Press, 1967.

Stack, George J. *Berkeley's Analysis of Perception*. The Hague: Mouton, 1970.

Tipson, I. C. *Berkeley: The Philosophy of Immaterialism*. London: Methuen, 1974.

Urmson, J. O. *Berkeley*. Oxford and New York: Oxford University Press, 1982.

Walmsley, P. *The Rhetoric of Berkeley's Philosophy*. Cambridge: Cambridge University Press, 1990.

Warnock, Geoffrey J. *Berkeley*. Baltimore: Penguin, 1969.

Wild, John. *George Berkeley: A Study of His Life and Philosophy*. New York: Russell & Russell, 1962. (Reissue of 1936 edition.)

Wisdom, John D. *The Unconscious Origin of Berkeley's Philosophy*. London: Hogarth Press, 1953.

David Hume (1711–1776)

Writings

The Philosophical Works, ed. Thomas H. Green and H. Hodge Gross. New York: Adler, 1964. 4 vols. (Reissue of 1882 edition.)

Dialogues Concerning Natural Religion, ed. Norman Kemp Smith. Indianapolis: Bobbs-Merrill, 1947.

An Inquiry Concerning Human Understanding, ed. Charles W. Hendel. Indianapolis: Bobbs-Merrill, 1965.

An Inquiry Concerning the Principles of Morals, ed. Charles W. Hendel. Indianapolis: Bobbs-Merrill, 1957.

Of the Standard of Taste and Other Essays, ed. John W. Lenz. Indianapolis: Bobbs-Merrill, 1965.

A Treatise of Human Nature, ed. L. A. Selby-Bigge and P. H. Nidditch. Oxford: Oxford University Press, 1978.

The Letters of David Hume, ed. J. Y. T. Grieg. Oxford: Oxford University Press, 1969. 2 vols.

Commentary

Anderson, Robert Fendel. *Hume's First Principles*. Lincoln, Nebraska: University of Nebraska Press, 1966.

Ardal, P. S. *Passion and Value in Hume's Treatise*. Edinburgh: Edinburgh University Press, 1966.

Ayer, A. J. *Hume*. New York: Hill & Wang, 1980.

Beauchamp, Tom L. and Rosenberg, Alexander. *Hume and the Problem of Causation*. New York: Oxford University Press, 1981.

Bennett, Jonathan. *Locke Berkeley Hume: Central Themes*. Oxford: Clarendon Press, 1971.

Botwinick, Aryeh. *Ethics, Politics and Epistemology: A Study in the Unity of Hume's Thought*. Lanham, Maryland: University Press of America, 1980.

Bricke, John. *Hume's Philosophy of Mind*. Princeton: Princeton University Press, 1980.

Chappell, V. C. (ed.). *Hume: A Collection of Critical Essays*. Garden City, New York: Doubleday (Anchor), 1966.

Danford, J. W. *David Hume and the Problem of Reason*. New Haven: Yale University Press, 1990.

Bibliography

Flew, Anthony. *Hume's Philosophy of Belief*. London: Routledge & Kegan Paul, 1961.

Fogelin, Robert J. *Hume's Skepticism in the Treatise of Human Nature*. London and New York: Routledge, 1985.

Harrison, Jonathan. *Hume's Moral Epistemology*. Oxford: Clarendon Press, 1976.

Hendel, Charles, W. *Studies in the Philosophy of David Hume*. Indianapolis: Bobbs-Merrill, 1963.

Laird, John. *Hume's Philosophy of Human Nature*. Hamden, Conn.: Archon, 1967. (Reissue of 1932 edition.)

Livingston, D. W. *Hume's Philosophy of Common Life*. Chicago: University of Chicago Press, 1984.

MacNabb, D. G. C. *David Hume: His Theory of Knowledge and Morality*. Oxford: Blackwell, 1966.

Noxon, James. *Hume's Philosophical Development*. Oxford: Oxford University Press, 1973.

Passmore, John. *Hume's Intentions*. New York: Basic Books, 1968. (Reissue of 1952 edition.)

Penelhum, T. *Hume*. London: Macmillan, 1975.

Penelhum, T. *David Hume*. Lafayette, Ind.: Purdue University Press, 1992.

Price, H. H. *Hume's Theory of the External World*. Oxford: Oxford University Press, 1940.

Salmon, C. V. *The Central Problem of David Hume's Philosophy*. New York and London: Garland, 1983.

Smith, Norman Kemp. *The Philosophy of David Hume*. London: Macmillan, 1941.

Stove, D. C. *Probability and Hume's Inductive Scepticism*. Oxford: Oxford University Press, 1973.

Stroud, Barry. *Hume*. London: Routledge & Kegan Paul, 1977.

Talmor, Ezra. *Descartes and Hume*. New York: Pergamon, 1980.

Wilbanks, Jan. *Hume's Theory of Imagination*. The Hague: Martinus Nijhoff, 1968.

Wright, J. P. *The Sceptical Realism of David Hume*. Minneapolis: The University of Minnesota Press, 1983.

Zabeeh, Farhang. *Hume: Precursor of Modern Empiricism*. The Hague: Martinus Nijhoff, 1960.

Immanuel Kant (1724–1804)

Writings

Werke, ed. Prussian Academy of Sciences. Academy text-edition, Berlin: De Gruyter, 1979, 9 vols.

Bibliography

Critique of Pure Reason, tr. Norman Kemp Smith. New York: St Martin's Press, 1969.

Critique of Practical Reason, tr. Lewis White Beck. Indianapolis: Bobbs-Merrill (3rd ed. 1992).

Critique of Judgment, tr. J. C. Meredith. Oxford: Oxford University Press, 1952.

Anthropology from a Pragmatic Point of View, tr. Lyle Dowdell, ed. and tr. rev. Hans. H. Rudnick. Cardondale, Ill.: Southern Illinois University Press, 1977.

Lectures on Philosophical Theology, tr. Allen W. Wood and Gertrude M. Clark, Ithaca, New York: Cornell University Press, 1978.

Foundations of the Metaphysics of Morals, tr. Lewis White Beck. Indianapolis: Bobbs-Merrill, 1959.

Prolegomena to Any Future Metaphysics, tr. Lewis White Beck. Indianapolis: Bobbs-Merrill, 1950.

Religion Within the Limits of Reason Alone, tr. Theodore M. Greene and Hoyt H. Hudson. New York: Harper & Row, 1960.

Philosophical Correspondence, ed. Arnulf Zweig. Chicago: University of Chicago Press, 1967.

Commentary

Al-Azm, Sadik, J. *The Origins of Kant's Arguments in the Antinomies*. Oxford: Oxford University Press, 1972.

Allison, Henry. *Kant's Transcendental Idealism*. New Haven: Yale University Press, 1986.

Allison, Henry. *Kant's Theory of Freedom*. Cambridge: Cambridge University Press, 1990.

Ameriks, Karl. *Kant's Theory of Mind: An Analysis of the Paralogisms of Pure Reason*. Oxford: Oxford University Press, 1982.

Beck, Lewis White. *Early German Philosophy: Kant and His Predecessors*. Cambridge, Mass.: Harvard University Press, 1969.

Beck, Lewis White. *Essays on Kant and Hume*. New Haven: Yale University Press, 1978.

Beck, Lewis White. *Studies in the Philosophy of Kant*. Indianapolis: Bobbs-Merrill, 1965.

Bennett, Jonathan. *Kant's Analytic*. Cambridge: Cambridge University Press, 1966.

Bennett, Jonathan. *Kant's Dialectic*. Cambridge: Cambridge University Press, 1974.

Bird, Graham. *Kant's Theory of Knowledge*. London: Routledge & Kegan Paul, 1962.

Bibliography

Brittan, Gordon, G. Jr. *Kant's Theory of Science*. Princeton: Princeton University Press, 1978.

Broad, C. D. *Kant: An Introduction*, ed. C. Lewy. Cambridge: Cambridge University Press, 1978.

Camois, B. *The Coherence of Kant's Doctrine of Freedom*. Chicago: University of Chicago Press, 1987.

Cassirer, Ernst. *Kant's Life and Thought*, tr. James Haden. New Haven: Yale University Press, 1981.

Cassirer, H. W. *Kant's First Critique*. New York: Humanities Press, 1978. (Reissue of 1954 edition.)

Ewing, A. C. *A Short Commentary on Kant's Critique of Pure Reason*. Chicago: University of Chicago Press, 1987. (Reissue of 1938 edition.)

Findlay, J. N. *Kant and the Transcendental Object: A Hermeneutic Study*. Oxford: Clarendon Press, 1981.

Friedman, Michael. *Kant and the Exact Sciences*. Cambridge, Mass.: Harvard University Press, 1992.

Gram, Moltke S. *Kant, Ontology, and the A Priori*. Evanston: Northwestern University Press, 1968.

Guyer, Paul. *Kant and the Claims of Taste*. Cambridge, Mass.: Harvard University Press, 1979.

Guyer, Paul. *Kant and the Claims of Knowledge*. Cambridge: Cambridge University Press, 1987.

Hartnack, Justus. *Kant's Theory of Knowledge*, tr. M. Holmes Hartshorne. New York: Harcourt, Brace & World, 1967.

Heidegger, Martin. *Kant and the Problem of Metaphysics*, tr. James S. Churchill. Bloomington, Ind.: Indiana University Press, 1962.

Howell, Robert. *Kant's Transcendental Deduction*. Dordrecht: Kluwer, 1992.

Kemp, John. *The Philosophy of Kant*. Oxford: Oxford University Press, 1968.

Kitcher, Patricia. *Kant's Transcendental Psychology*. New York and Oxford: Oxford University Press, 1990.

Körner, S. *Kant*. New Haven: Yale University Press, 1982.

Martin, Gottfried. *Kant's Metaphysics and Theory of Science*, tr. P. G. Lucas. Manchester: Manchester University Press, 1955.

Melnick, Arthur. *Kant's Analogies of Experience*. Chicago: University of Chicago Press, 1973.

Melnick, Arthur. *Space, Time, and Thought in Kant*. Dordrecht: Kluwer, 1989.

Paton, H. J. *Kant's Metaphysics of Experience*. London: Allen & Unwin, 1936. 2 vols.

Pippin, Robert. *Kant's Theory of Form*. New Haven: Yale University Press, 1982.

Powell, C. T. *Kant's Theory of Self-Consciousness*. Oxford: Oxford University Press, 1990.

Scruton, R. *Kant*. Oxford: Oxford University Press, 1982.

Smith, Norman Kemp. *A Commentary to Kant's 'Critique of Pure Reason'*. New York: Humanities Press, 1962.

Strawson, P. F. *The Bounds of Sense*. London: Methuen, 1966.

Walker, Ralph C. S. *Kant*. London: Routledge & Kegan Paul, 1978.

Walsh, W. H. *Kant's Criticism of Metaphysics*. Chicago: University of Chicago Press, 1976.

Waxman, W. *Kant's Model of the Mind*. New York: Oxford University Press, 1991.

Weldon, T. D. *Kant's Critique of Pure Reason*. Oxford: Clarendon Press, 1958. (Reissue of 1945 edition.)

Werkmeister, W. H. *Kant: The Architectonic and Development of His Philosophy*. LaSalle, Ill.: Open Court, 1980.

Wilkerton, T. E. *Kant's Critique of Pure Reason*. Oxford: Clarendon Press, 1976.

Wolff, Robert Paul. *Kant's Theory of Mental Activity*. Cambridge, Mass.: Harvard University Press, 1963.

Wolff, Robert Paul (ed.). *Kant: A Collection of Critical Essays*. Garden City, New York: Doubleday (Anchor), 1967.

Wood, Allen W. *Kant's Moral Religion*. Ithaca, New York: Cornell University Press, 1970.

Wood, Allen W. *Kant's Rational Theology*. Ithaca, New York: Cornell University Press, 1978.

Yovel, Yirmiahu. *Kant and the Philosophy of History*. Princeton: Princeton University Press, 1980.

INDEX

Index

274